Praise for *Get It in Writing*

"They say you don't know what you don't know. This book changes that. Be prepared to enjoy a confidence that isn't just a feeling—it's a right."

—**JEFFERSON FISHER**, bestselling author of *The Next Conversation*

"This book breaks down the complex process of pursuing a legal claim against an employer into clear, actionable steps. There's no gatekeeping here, and Stygar empowers workers with practical guidance on how to protect themselves, cover their bases, and stand up to corporate America."

—**PAIGE SPARKS**, plaintiff employment lawyer
and owner of Sparks Legal

"Everyone who works for a living should read this book! In *Get It in Writing*, Ryan Stygar pulls back the curtain on how workplaces really operate and what your boss hopes you don't know. This book is packed with clear explanations, real stories from the front lines, and practical scripts you can actually use. It's not about being litigious; it's about being informed."

—**ZACHARY RUBIN**, MD, author of *All About Allergies*

"Everyone deserves to know their rights in the workplace, and Attorney Ryan breaks everything down in a way that's easy to understand. A great guide to have by your side!"

—**LAURA WHALEY**, business owner, content creator, and public figure

"This book is a *lifesaver* for anyone needing to advocate for themselves in the workplace! Stygar may be an attorney and go-to expert in the field of employment law, but there's no confusing legalese here—*Get It in Writing* is an easy-to-understand guide for any worker."

—**ERIN McGOFF**, founder of AdviceWithErin and
author of *The Secret Language of Work*

"Working people in America are always in danger of finding themselves on the wrong side of a power imbalance that takes money out of their pockets and leaves them feeling disrespected on the job. Knowing your rights is the first step toward fighting back. *Get It in Writing* is a great primer for any worker who wants to deal with the boss as an equal."

—**HAMILTON NOLAN**, author of *The Hammer: Power, Inequality, and the Struggle for the Soul of Labor*

"*Get It in Writing* doesn't just explain your rights: It arms you with the exact language to use in emails, meetings, and HR conversations. It's the practical companion to salary transparency I've been waiting for!"

—**HANNAH WILLIAMS**, founder of Salary Transparent Street, *Forbes* 30 Under 30 honoree, and TIME100 Creator

"To anyone who fears retaliation if they speak up against unfair working conditions: You need this book. Stygar expertly explains your legal rights and recourse while introducing you to the everyday baristas, personal trainers, salespeople, and more who did fight back—and won."

—**CLAUDIA SALINAS**, criminal justice advocate and staff attorney at the Innocence Center

Get It in Writing

Get It in Writing

[THE ULTIMATE GUIDE
TO YOUR RIGHTS AT WORK]

RYAN STYGAR

Creator of @AttorneyRyan

PORTFOLIO • PENGUIN

Portfolio / Penguin
An imprint of Penguin Random House LLC
1745 Broadway, New York, NY 10019
penguinrandomhouse.com

BOOK DESIGN BY NICOLE LAROCHE

LIBRARY OF CONGRESS CATALOGING-IN-PUBLICATION DATA
Names: Stygar, Ryan, author.
Title: Get it in writing : the ultimate guide to your rights at work / Ryan Stygar.
Description: New York : Portfolio / Penguin, 2026. | Includes bibliographical references and index.
Identifiers: LCCN 2025048986 (print) | LCCN 2025048987 (ebook) |
ISBN 9798217044221 (hardcover) | ISBN 9798217044238 (ebook)
Subjects: LCSH: Employee rights—United States | Labor laws and legislation—United States |
Employees—Dismissal of—Law and legislation—United States |
Discrimination in employment—Law and legislation—United States |
Wages—United States | Family leave—United States |
Independent contractors—Legal status, laws, etc.—United States
Classification: LCC KF3455 .S79 2026 (print) | LCC KF3455 (ebook)
LC record available at https://lccn.loc.gov/2025048986
LC ebook record available at https://lccn.loc.gov/2025048987

Printed in the United States of America
1st Printing

The authorized representative in the EU for product safety and compliance is
Penguin Random House Ireland, Morrison Chambers, 32 Nassau Street,
Dublin D02 YH68, Ireland, https://eu-contact.penguin.ie.

I dedicate this book to you, the working-class person who gets up every day and tries to make an honest living. I know how hard you are working, and I share your dream for a brighter future. I hope this book helps make life a little easier for you in some way.

If you have ever had to work for a paycheck, this book is dedicated to you. I see you, I am proud of you, and I salute you.

CONTENTS

PART III

Protect Your Health

PART IV

Embrace Your Power

AUTHOR'S NOTE

This book is an educational guide. It is not legal advice for any specific situation. Nothing in this book is a replacement for a lawyer's services, and you should always consult a lawyer in your jurisdiction for legal advice.

Stories contained herein are based on real cases but have been dramatized for educational purposes. Such stories are for entertainment and illustration only. Stories based on cases have had identifying facts omitted or altered to preserve confidentiality. None are intended to depict real people, and any similarities to any case or person are purely coincidental. Further, such case stories cannot be used as a predictor of any case outcome. Case results depicted in this book are for illustrative and educational purposes; they are not a promise or guarantee. Past results do not guarantee future outcomes.

This book contains templates for communications; such templates are for illustrative and educational purposes only, and they are not a replacement for seeking an attorney's advice on a given situation. Nothing in this book is a promise of representation, nor is an attorney-client relationship formed by simply reading or purchasing this book.

Phew, I feel like I need a shower after writing that. Let's get into the book!

PREFACE

The year was 2010. I arrived at a parking lot in east San Diego County. Rows of ambulances lined each side of the asphalt. They looked spectacular from a distance, but as I got closer, the vans were clearly worn-out. The stench of leaking motor oil, diesel fumes, and disinfectant spray stung my nose.

I had applied to every ambulance company in Southern California. The interviews included oral questions on emergency medical procedures, followed by simulations to demonstrate my skills. Because I was young and fresh out of EMT school, the interviewers imposed extra scrutiny on my demonstrations. They grilled me with questions as I assessed various mannequins for injuries and treatment. I passed them all, but competition for jobs was fierce. This was my first and only full-time job offer after dozens of applications.

I walked into the dispatch office to report for my first day on duty. The building looked like an old motel with brown stucco walls. An air-conditioning unit hung haphazardly out of a dirty screen window. Beside it, a door was cracked open. Inside, a morning talk show crackled from the radio.

"Hello?" I called.

No response.

"Hello?" I asked again.

A balding head rose from behind a computer monitor. The man wore a wrinkled blue polo with tan cargo shorts. "Yeah?" he said, not hiding his annoyance.

"I'm Ryan Stygar, I'm the new hire starting today."

"Hmm." Wrinkled Polo replied. He looked up at a clock on the wall. "You're late," he said.

"My shift starts at 8:00," I answered.

Wrinkled Polo scoffed. Standing from his seat, he crumpled an empty McMuffin wrapper and tossed it into an overflowing trash can by his desk. "It's 7:45. If you want to be taken seriously, you should be here by 7:30. Not a good start, Snyder."

"It's Stygar, sir."

"Not a good start," he whistled.

He walked me to the training officer, a twenty-eight-year-old EMT wearing a sharp, clean uniform. Wrinkled Polo gave me a silent nod and pointed at the ambulance. "You'll be on Unit 98 today. Get your rig ready, starting with inventory checks," he said. "And be on time tomorrow."

When I had graduated from EMT school, I dreamed of heroic adventures. Saving lives, yanking people from the brink of death, protecting and serving my community. I hoped my first call would be something exciting. But when I got to my assigned ambulance, these dreams were quickly dashed.

The ambulance I got assigned to was—and I'm saying this gently—a rusty old shitbox. The thing reeked. But worst of all, it was missing essential supplies.

"We're out of gauze rolls," I told my trainer.

"Take it from another ambulance," he answered.

"Won't they need those?" I asked.

"Probably, but that's not our problem."

Our pagers beeped: *BLS Unit 98 . . . 64-yo F . . . Stomach Pains . . .*

"Lights and sirens?" I asked.

"Nope. BLS means basic life support," the trainer explained. "We don't go lights and sirens for a BLS call. Look up the address in our map book and tell me how to get there."

He drove while I navigated. Along the way, I asked about the manager who told me to arrive at work thirty minutes early.

"My schedule says 8:00, so can I fix my time card to say 7:30, since I'll be working?"

The trainer shook his head. "You're not gonna last if you're only here for the money," he laughed.

"It's just . . . if we're working, shouldn't we get paid for those thirty minutes?"

He let out a long sigh. Clearly, I was getting on his nerves.

"Listen, Stygar. This is an at-will state. Do you know what that means?"

"I don't think I do."

"It means if management doesn't like the color of your boots, you're out of here. And if you get fired before doing six months on the ambulance, then no fire academy is gonna even look at your application. You'll be blacklisted."

It hurt to admit it, but he had a point. I was already serving as a volunteer firefighter during my days off, but until I got six months of ambulance experience *plus* a letter of recommendation from my employer, then that was all I would ever be: a volunteer. The whole point of working on the ambulance was to get accepted into fire academy. From there, I could get hired as a full-time, paid firefighter.

But bills didn't pay themselves, and at ten dollars per hour and no benefits, every penny mattered.

"I'm sorry," I replied meekly. "I'm not trying to be greedy, I just . . . if we're working, I'd like to get paid. We don't make much, and I have to pay bills somehow. I'm not trying to be a problem."

"Well, you're already on their radar for the wrong reason. If you complain about not getting paid, then you're just gonna get shitcanned."

He pulled the ambulance up to a skilled nursing facility where our first patient was waiting for us. He parked and looked over at me. "You want my advice? Just keep your head down. I don't care if your check is wrong, just suck it up. There are a million people trying to get their EMT hours for fire academy. You're lucky to be here. Don't fuck it up, Stygar."

I nodded and vowed to drop it. Maybe he had a point. Thirty minutes per day was only five dollars. Of course, that meant losing just over one hundred dollars a month. But I didn't want to be an EMT forever. This was a stepping stone toward my big dream: getting a full-time, paid firefighter job. That's what I really wanted. Maybe coughing up some of my wages now was a small price to pay?

We entered the facility to greet our patient. I took her vitals, then asked about her pain level, diet, medications, et cetera.

During the assessment, I learned she had stomach pain because she had not had a bowel movement in over a week, and her abdomen was swollen and sore from the fecal backup. It was not immediately life-threatening, but she needed treatment to clear her bowels and prevent a serious infection. Calls like this, I soon found, were very common. Not quite the "heroic adventures" I had hoped for, but I was still happy to help a real patient in a real ambulance. We took her to the nearest emergency room for further treatment.

After dropping off our patient, I got busy sanitizing the stretcher while my trainer finished our report. A call came in on the radio.

BLS Unit 98 . . . report to HQ.

My trainer answered the call. "I copy, 98 en route," he said.

"What's that about?" I asked.

My trainer shrugged. He pointed to the driver's seat. "You drive. I'll finish the paperwork."

My belly stung as we drove back to HQ. It was still the first call of the first day; what could I have done that they already wanted me back at the office?

Wrinkled Polo was waiting for us when we arrived. He curled his finger in a *come here* motion.

"Welp, it was good knowing ya," my trainer said.

Inside the office, Wrinkled Polo took a seat at his desk. One of the EMT supervisors, a blond woman with a crisp uniform, acknowledged me with a nod. She indicated that I should take a seat on the other side of the desk, where a write-up was waiting for my signature.

"Not a good start today," Wrinkled Polo began. "We're an at-will company. That means you can be replaced any time, for any reason, even for no reason. We don't have to say why you're fired here, so if I don't like your attitude, like how you sassed me this morning, then you're gone."

Wrinkled Polo rattled off the charges against me. "You were late on your first day, and instead of apologizing, you started making excuses with an attitude. I know you're young, but you need to grow up fast. I'm not gonna fire you today, Snyder, but we're writing you up and putting this in your file."

It was humiliating. All the hard work to get my EMT training, all the job applications, all the interviews, all the rejections. Now I finally had a paying EMT job and I was about to lose it.

"I'm sorry," I muttered. "Really, I want to work, I didn't mean any disrespect."

Wrinkled Polo sighed. He appeared content that I had been sufficiently humbled. He flicked a pen across the table. "Sign it and get back on the rig."

I needed the job. I couldn't afford to get fired. I signed the write-up without reading it.

The EMT supervisor spoke for the first time. "One more thing, Snyder," she said. "If you want to be a firefighter, you need to act like one. If you're early, you're on time. If you're on time, you're late. And late is unacceptable. We won't have any more problems from you, will we?"

"No, ma'am," I answered.

That ambulance job was one of the most degrading work experiences I've had. We were treated like children at best and prisoners at worst. Write-ups were a weekly occurrence. Management ensured that every "infraction" was accompanied by a stern reminder that one bad word from them would blacklist us from every fire academy in the state. Threats of summary termination hung over our heads with every change in the supervisors' moods. They preached professionalism, but they paid us pitiful wages as we worked in dirty, decaying ambulances. They preached honesty but denied us even the basic right to be paid for all hours worked.

We did not get lunch breaks, but management deducted thirty minutes from our checks every day regardless. We were scheduled for ten-hour shifts, which almost always dragged on into twelve-, thirteen-, and fourteen-hour shifts, but we never got a penny of overtime—they paid ten dollars per hour no matter how much we worked in a week.

In my third month, I got the flu and called in sick. Wrinkled Polo accused me of "faking it" to conceal a hangover.

"I know what you kids do on your nights off," he scolded. "You want to party and not have any real consequences? You think a fire department will put up with that?"

"It's not a hangover," I pleaded meekly. "I am really sick, and I can't come in."

Wrinkled Polo huffed. "I'm pulling you off the schedule until you have a doctor's note confirming this is a true illness. If you were partying all night that's not my problem."

We had no health benefits. Losing a day of work meant losing a day of wages, plus unaffordable costs if we needed a doctor's note. Still, no one dared speak up. We worried that doing so would ruin our careers forever.

Like most Americans, we worried that we didn't have any control over our lives at work.

HOW DO YOU TAKE CONTROL OF YOUR LIFE AT WORK?

I worked a big mix of jobs before I went to law school. I'd been a lifeguard, an EMT, and a firefighter. But I also worked as a landscaper, a tutor, a coffee salesman, a recruiter, and even spent a summer building vacation cabins. My shortest gig was a three-week stint at a corporate gym, which was the only job I ever walked out on. Funny enough, I actually got a check from a class action lawsuit against that gym (apparently I wasn't the only employee who'd gotten fed up with them).

I've tried a lot of jobs, made a lot of mistakes, and learned a lot of lessons the hard way. I stayed quiet when I should have spoken up. I trusted the wrong people. I put the demands of my job ahead of the people who mattered most. These mistakes taught me some hard but valuable lessons:

HARD LESSON NUMBER 1: Your employer does not care about you. Sure, your boss may be nice, your coworkers may be friendly, but ultimately your employer is not interested in your personal or financial well-being. You were hired to do a job, for which they will pay as little as possible for as long as possible. Employers are watching their bottom line, and they are simply not interested in your hopes and dreams.

HARD LESSON NUMBER 2: Money buys happiness (sort of). In a study by the Wharton School of the University of Pennsylvania, researchers found that for most people, rising income strongly correlated to rising levels of happiness.* Researchers found the sharpest increases in happiness when subjects earned at least $75,000 per year. Another sharp spike occurred at $100,000 per year. After that, the money-happiness curve more or less leveled off. But the results are clear—money buys happiness (up to a certain point). Therefore, an employer who doesn't pay what you've earned isn't just taking your money, they are taking a piece of your potential happiness.

HARD LESSON NUMBER 3: Unless you take action, you will never be in full control of your life. The default position for most humans is *passivity.* Think of all the occasions in your life where you have defaulted to *passivity.* You scroll social media because the algorithm selects content for you. You stay at a job you dislike because changing careers is hard. You stick with a toxic friend group because you've known them since high school. The years go by, then one day you look back and realize you haven't gone anywhere. Passivity slowly and steadily chews up your dreams and spits them out.

These hard lessons, which I learned the hard way, motivated me to go to law school, open a workers' rights law firm, and post information about your rights on social media.

My years of experience representing workers against bad bosses inspired me to do something that would shift the balance of power in

*Mathew Killingsworth, "Experienced Well-Being Rises with Income, Even Above $75,000 per Year," *PNAS* 118, no. 4 (2021): e2016976118, doi.org/10.1073/pnas.2016976118.

favor of people like you. The mistakes I made in my firefighting career taught me to choose a life of *initiative*. I learned how to use the law to help myself become an active player in my life. This has liberated me. I want the same for you. That is why I wrote this book.

This is all rather meta for a book about your rights at work. But I know how scary it is to stand up for yourself at work—I've experienced it too. But when you learn your rights, you can get past that fear. Because you deserve to be treated with fairness and dignity, and you also deserve to have all your labor rights respected. Take it from someone who learned the hard way: When you know the rules, you can win the game.

INTRODUCTION

Everyone who works for a living needs this book. It is the ultimate guide to your rights at work. You will learn how to get what you're owed with practical, easy-to-understand advice directly from the most well-known workers' rights lawyer in America. (That's me!)

It's not your imagination; life for working people is getting harder and more expensive. While employers clamp down with return-to-office mandates, productivity trackers, and layoffs, employees struggle to keep up with daily expenses. Long, unpaid commutes waste the few nonworking hours you get each day. Pitiful "raises" that barely touch the inflation rate. Unaffordable childcare. Vacation requests denied, weekends spent pulling extra hours (off the clock, of course). You miss doctors' appointments, you ignore that weird pain in your abdomen, you miss graduations and birthdays and weddings. All these are sacrifices employees are *expected* to make for their employers. And what do we get in return? Too often, it's a surprise meeting with HR followed by a swift and unceremonious termination.

We deserve better than that. *You* deserve better than that. So we must return to the core question this book seeks to answer: How do we stand up for ourselves at work?

To answer this, we must first answer many other questions you probably have, such as:

Does *at will* really mean I have no rights?

What do I do if my boss is bullying me?

What if I'm too injured to keep working?

Am I getting paid what I'm owed?

What can I do about a creepy manager?

There is a common thread to these questions: Most people are afraid to deal with employment problems because their livelihood is at stake. But we can't let fear control us. This book will give you the answers they should have taught you in school.

I am here to help you claim what's rightfully yours—fair pay, fair treatment, and the time to enjoy your life outside work. Sure, our employers can be intimidating. They have money, power, and legal departments. But we can level the playing field. In this book, you will find the knowledge and experience I've acquired as a workers' rights lawyer. You'll read stories from real cases, along with a few tips and tricks for dealing with difficult situations at work.

Your job is a tool to support your life outside of work. It should not dominate your existence. If you are working a full-time job, you should earn enough money to meet your needs. You deserve time off for family and recreation—not because you "earned" it but because you are inherently entitled to it as a human being.

We will no longer let our careers dictate our lives. Millions of working people are winning back what is rightfully theirs. It's time for you to join them.

HOW TO USE THIS BOOK

This book serves two purposes: First, to teach you about your workplace rights. Second, to empower you to advocate for yourself at work.

This book can be read straight through, and it can also serve as a reference—a guide to turn to when you have a problem at work. In any case, I recommend starting with part I first. This section will dispel many of the myths (and straight-up lies) you might have heard throughout your career.

What myths and lies, you ask? Throughout my own career, plus in thousands of real employment cases, I came across four major lies that employers use to control us. We will expose the *facts* that bad employers don't want you to know. And we will do it in four parts:

PART I: KNOW YOUR RIGHTS

LIE NUMBER 1: Your employer holds all the cards.

THE TRUTH: When you know the rules of the game, you can win.

LESSON: *Your career is a lifelong game. Like any game, there are rules, and your ability to master those rules will affect the final outcome. In this section, I will teach you the most basic rules that control your career.*

PART II: PROTECT YOUR MONEY

LIE NUMBER 2: Loyalty and hard work will be rewarded.

THE TRUTH: The silent workhorse will toil until they collapse, then they will be unceremoniously replaced.

LESSON: *Your time is an irreplaceable resource. Your effort is precious. Both of these things deserve fair compensation for all hours worked. In this section, I will teach you the rules about what you should be paid, when, and how much.*

PART III: PROTECT YOUR HEALTH

LIE NUMBER 3: If you don't put your job first, you will get left behind.

THE TRUTH: You are replaceable at work; you are NOT replaceable at home.

LESSON: *The purpose of a job is to support your life outside of work. Putting life first is not "falling behind." Rather, it is the surest way to avoid the pain of regret when your career inevitably* *ends. Do not let emails, meetings, or "urgent" calls rob you of the memories that make life worth living. Even if you've made this mistake, it is not too late to turn things around. This section will teach you how to avoid that fate.*

PART IV: EMBRACE YOUR POWER

LIE NUMBER 4: You can't stand up to your boss!

THE TRUTH: The age of fear is over. We know our rights, and we're not afraid to use them.

LESSON: *Every time you fail to stand up for yourself, something inside you dies a little. But the opposite is also true. Whenever we push back against a bully, we grow stronger. Speak up, even if your voice shakes. Stand up, even if your knees wobble. Because each act of courage builds you up, while shrinking away tears you down.*

WHAT IF THE WORST-CASE SCENARIO HAPPENS?

Let's be clear about one thing: **I expect most people who read this book will never actually *sue* their employer.** The goal is not to look for a lawsuit in every situation. Rather, you will learn how to effectively use your legal rights to protect your time, money, and sanity at work. A positive side effect of these strategies is that *if* a case becomes necessary, then you will be prepared.

That said, let's not shy away from the elephant in the room. What happens if you *do* have to sue your employer? Usually this will be your final option when you are illegally fired, forced out, or seriously abused. I know it is scary, but you have more control over this worst-case scenario than you think.

I have represented thousands of workers in various employment cases. I have recovered millions in compensation for my clients. Every case is unique, but here are the common traits in cases where employees have won:

- **WINNERS KNEW THEIR RIGHTS.**

  They didn't know all the legal details, but they knew something illegal was probably going on when they saw it. They had a general idea of what they were supposed to be paid, how they were supposed to be treated, and how to distinguish common disrespect from actual illegal labor practices. Knowing their rights helped employees make a *paper trail* that built a strong case.

- **WINNERS KEPT A PAPER TRAIL.**

  This is the most crucial idea that I will repeat over and over in this book. **Get things in writing!** Every lawsuit is a battle of evidence. When you sue an employer for breaking the law, you, the accuser, will have the burden of proof. But unlike a criminal case, you don't have to prove your case "beyond a reasonable doubt." These are civil cases, and the standard of proof is much lower. You need only prove your case "by a preponderance of the evidence." In plain English, this means you have to prove it is "more likely than not" that your employer broke the law.

  That's where your paper trail comes in. Keeping track of important events at work, communicating with supervisors and HR via text and email, and saving important work documents are all ways employees have kept a paper trail that helped them win their cases.

- **WINNERS ASKED FOR HELP.**

  In many cases, the employer is not obligated to pay any damages unless you can show they knew or should have known about the violation of your rights. By asking for help (**IN WRITING!**), you can put the employer on official notice that something needs to be done. But there are *right* ways and *wrong* ways to do this. Knowing how to talk to human resources and managers about problems at work is a top-tier skill every working person should learn. This book contains several useful scripts and templates you can use to do things the right way.

- **WINNERS TALKED TO A LAWYER (LIKE ME!).**

  Many people are (understandably) nervous about speaking to an attorney. They're concerned about the cost, because it's well known that lawyers are expensive. But here are some things you should know about employment lawyers:

  - Most of us take cases on *contingency*. This means you pay no hourly fee. In exchange, we get a percentage of what we win for you. If we don't win, you don't owe us a dime. When I take a contingency case, I cover the litigation expenses; if we lose, I don't ask clients for reimbursement. Not all lawyers do this, but many of us do. Ask potential lawyers about their policy for covering the costs of suit.
  - Some lawyers will charge a consultation fee, others won't. It's up to you to find a lawyer who suits your needs. For those who charge a consult fee, get a clear understanding of what value they are offering for the fee.
  - SHOP AROUND! Your case is too important to hire the first attorney who takes your call. Consult with several offices to find the professional you trust most.

In sum, the most successful cases start with employees who know their rights, keep a paper trail, ask for help, and lawyer up.

Unsuccessful cases, on the other hand, look like the opposite of what we just outlined. I am excellent at what I do. *But I am not undefeated.* I've lost hard cases before. I do not regret those rare situations where I have lost. In a way, I am proud of them. I chose to stand up for my clients when no one else would, and I learned valuable lessons from those losses.

And I want *you* to learn from *other* people's failures (including my own). Here are some common traits I see in losing cases:

- **LITTLE TO NO EVIDENCE:** The employee did not create a paper trail. I cannot overstate how crucial this step is; text messages, emails, performance improvement plans, even your work schedule and pay stubs are all evidence for your paper trail.
- **NOT SPEAKING UP:** In many cases, the employer cannot be held liable unless they *knew* or *reasonably should have known* that something illegal was happening to you. Furthermore, the law places time limits on when you can file a lawsuit. This is called a *statute of limitations,* and once it passes, you lose the right to file a claim. The statute of limitations varies depending on the kind of case, but *generally* it is one to three years for most employment-related issues.*
- **TRUSTING THE WRONG PEOPLE:** Human resources (HR) is not your friend. Ultimately, their job is to protect the company, not you. When it's not clear where someone's loyalty lies, ask yourself, "Who signs this person's paycheck?" That's whose side they are really on. An employer can also use misplaced trust to trick you into acting against your own interests; talk to a lawyer before signing anything.

No matter how big or small the company is, no matter what your boss has told you about your rights, if you experience wrongful termination, retaliation, discrimination, wage theft, or sexual harassment, it is illegal. You *can* make a case for yourself with the help of this book (and a good lawyer). Each section gives you the tools to know your rights and enforce them in a way that will improve your quality of life.

Are you ready to embrace your power?

---

*Exceptions apply for certain sexual assault and sexual harassment claims.

PART I

Know Your Rights

[**LIE:** Your employer holds all the cards.

TRUTH: When you know the rules, you can win the game.]

BROKE OFF: MY WORST BOSS EVER

In 2013 I was assigned to a wildland firefighting crew in San Diego County. My reputation for hard work earned me a place at one of the busiest and most disciplined stations in the whole department.

I thought I was ready for anything a fire could throw at me.

What I was *not* ready for was being assigned to work under a sadistic bully.

My first shift lasted eighteen straight days with back-to-back wildfires. There was no time for orientation. There was no safe space to learn the ropes. I was among the flames within a few hours of my first day on the job.

Smoke stung my nostrils as we marched through scorched terrain to the front lines. Once-proud trees were reduced to ghostly black twigs sprouting up from the ash. I adjusted my brimmed yellow helmet. It was midmorning, but the temperature had already climbed past one hundred degrees. Columns of smoke dimmed the sun; its light cast an eerie orange hue on the blackened landscape.

My leg muscles burned as we hiked. Despite being one of the youngest and most physically fit firefighters on the strike team, I struggled to keep up. The reason was simple: I had been ordered by my company officer to wake up early for extra exercises before the long day of firefighting.

He was an engineer in his early thirties named Joe.* Over the course of eighteen days, I would come to know Joe very well—and it was not

---

*For those unfamiliar with fire department hierarchy, an engineer is an officer's rank just below captain. Engineers will sometimes command fire engines when a captain is not available.

pleasant. Joe had the unkindest eyes of any person I had met or have yet to meet. His jagged jaw slouched downward in a permanent frown. Joe was a deeply troubled man.

Unfortunately for me, hazing new firefighters was the only thing that brought him joy.

During exceptionally hot days, Joe believed that making his subordinates feel "broke off" was the best way to prepare for fires. *Broke off* was slang we used to describe a state of extreme exhaustion. Saying you felt broke off was considered a white flag—a signal that your body was dangerously exhausted and rest was urgently needed. It was typically reserved for describing how you felt after intense, prolonged periods of wilderness firefighting. In short, being broke off was a dangerous condition for any firefighter.

But Joe believed that making us feel broke off was, in his words, "the whole point of training." No matter what work lay ahead for the day, he forced me to engage in strenuous cardio and calisthenic exercises before going on the fire line. To any experienced leader, this should have been a red flag. What good was there in pushing your crew to exhaustion *before* they were even called to serve in an emergency? At best, it was foolish. At worst, it was dangerous.

One day, I worked up the courage to push back.

"Shouldn't we conserve our energy?" I asked. "We might be called to a fire for a long time without relief today."

"I don't like you, Stygar," Joe snapped. "You don't belong here. I want to make coming to work as painful as possible until you quit."

I am not exaggerating. That was his response. When I said that Joe was a deeply troubled man, I meant it. Joe eventually got his wish. My love of firefighting died a slow, painful death under his supervision. There was no brotherhood under Joe: no trust, no honor, no love for our community. There was only hazing and exhaustion. Nine months later, I handed in my resignation.

IT WAS NOT UNTIL *after* law school that I began to master the fundamentals of labor law. While learning these rules, I often thought back to my firefighting days: Had I been in a hostile work environment? Was Joe illegally harassing me then? If I had gotten seriously hurt from Joe's hazing, would I have lost my job?

And most important, could I have done something to stand up to Joe?

Sadly, I was not the only firefighter targeted by Joe. Shortly after I left, I got horrible news. Another firefighter died of heat exposure during a training exercise under Joe's supervision. The official fire department report painted a damning picture: Joe had hazed this firefighter just like he hazed me. I was lucky to get out.

I wish I had known my rights back then. Specifically, my rights around at-will employment, harassment, and retaliation. In part I, you will learn how to take control of your career so you don't have to wonder what you can do—you will *know* what to do!

[CHAPTER 1]

At-Will Employment and Wrongful Termination

FIRE AT WILL!

Let's go back a few pages to the opening story of this book. When I worked as an EMT, I was told on my very first day that my employment was at will. Wrinkled Polo's description—"You can be replaced any time, for any reason, even for no reason"—scared me.

I had no money, no power, and it seemed to me that my employer held all the cards. I know I'm not the only one to have felt this way; it's a common sentiment. But the fear is not proportionate to the threat. You have rights and you can enforce them; you just have to understand the rules first. That information is what I was missing, and it's something I want you to have.

Most people in the US are employed at will. But most people don't actually know what that means! This basic terminology is crucial for understanding your rights at work. Let's dive in.

AT-WILL EMPLOYMENT

So, what is at-will employment? At-will employment means that you can be fired for any legal reason, including no reason, with or without notice, and it is the standard in most US states. No cause is required;

you can be legally terminated from an at-will position even if the reason is objectively unfair.* At will is also the *default condition,* meaning that if you do not have a contract specifying otherwise, then you are probably an at-will employee.

At-will states may go with a different name depending on where you live. For example, your employer might use a phrase like *fire at will state,* or even (incorrectly) *right-to-work state.* Whatever the name, the at-will rule is the same. Every state in the United States is an at-will state—except Montana. Under the Montana Wrongful Discharge from Employment Act, employers generally must have "good cause" to terminate an employee (once the employee has finished an established probationary period).†

As a starting point, *most* terminations are legal. However, there are many exceptions to the at-will presumption. The key to every wrongful termination case—a concept we'll tackle later in this chapter—is proving your termination was one of those exceptions!

RIGHT-TO-WORK STATES

At-will and right-to-work states are not the same thing. *Right to work* is a phrase often mistakenly used by employers who mean to say *at will.* But right-to-work laws only mean that **employees cannot be required to join a labor union to qualify for a job**. Additionally, in some right-to-work states, employees cannot be required to pay dues to a union if they opt out of membership. As of the writing of this book, twenty-five states have right-to-work laws.

So, since every state (except Montana) is an at-will state, that means every right-to-work state is also an at-will state. But not every at-will state is a right-to-work state. Being a right-to-work state has nothing to do with why an employer might legally fire you. If your boss says some-

*Note that "unfair" is not necessarily illegal.

†Other exceptions apply, but this is not a book about Montana law, so the general rule is good enough for our purposes.

thing like "This is a right-to-work state, which means I don't need a reason to fire you," they are simply wrong.

WHY DO THE STATES HAVE DIFFERENT RULES?

Let's take a quick detour to clear something up, because knowing *why* the states have different rules will put you one step ahead of a slimy supervisor.

Many bad bosses will say something like "Your rights depend on what state you're in" to downplay your legally entitled labor protections. It is true that your rights will vary somewhat from state to state. However, and more important, it is also true that *federal* laws apply to all fifty states, including laws about labor protections. Federal law provides the basic rules that all states must follow. However, states are free to enact laws on a wider range of issues than the federal government. Generally, the Tenth Amendment of the Constitution allows states to make their own rules **so long as they do not conflict with federal law**. This is why each of the states have slightly different laws, even though federal law still applies equally to all states.

So, what happens when state laws and federal laws disagree?

Here is the basic rule that will guide you in most situations. When state and federal law are in conflict, federal law prevails; but if the state law provides *more* labor protections than federal law, then generally the state law prevails.

States can have different laws where federal law is silent. States may *add* protections on top of federal rules but cannot undermine those rules. For example, the federal minimum wage is $7.25 per hour as of the writing of this book. States may *not* make a law for a minimum wage lower than $7.25 per hour.* However, states are free to make their

*Astute readers may notice that their state has a "tipped minimum wage," which is lower than $7.25 per hour. Federal law allows tipped employees to be paid as low as $2.13 per hour so long as they earn at least $30 in tips per month *and* their tips (divided by total hours worked) come out to at least the federal minimum wage. We will discuss tipped vs. minimum wages in more detail in part II.

minimum wage higher if they choose to. If a state does not enact its own minimum wage, then the federal minimum wage applies.

EXCEPTIONS TO AT WILL

Let's get back to at will. The default presumption is that your termination is legal. But if an exception applies, then the termination is *not* legal.

What are the exceptions to the at-will presumption? At-will employment is no excuse to break the law. There are several situations in which it is illegal to terminate you even if you are an at-will employee. **Even if you signed a contract saying you can be fired for "any" reason, it is *still* illegal to fire you for illegal reasons.**

I'm not saying these laws will stop you from getting fired. Just like how a stop sign won't magically make cars stop. What I'm saying is that if you are fired for an *illegal* reason, you can have legal recourse and could be owed significant compensation once your case is proved. Typically, being fired for an illegal reason (a.k.a. an exception to the at-will presumption) falls under one of the following:

- You were terminated in violation of applicable state, federal, or local law.
- You were terminated because of a protected characteristic (such as your disability, gender, race, etc.).
- Your termination violated the terms of a contract between you and the employer. (In this case, you would have both a breach of contract claim and a wrongful termination claim.)
- You were terminated for making a whistleblower complaint.
- You were terminated after exercising a protected legal right.
- Your termination didn't violate a specific law, but it went against an established and substantial public policy.

Being fired for one of these reasons is called *wrongful termination*.

WHAT IS WRONGFUL TERMINATION?

Wrongful termination is a fancy way of saying that you have been fired for an illegal reason. Wrongful termination is illegal in all fifty states, including the forty-nine at-will states. In addition to the reasons for illegal termination above, here are some of the most common forms of wrongful termination I see:

- You requested medical leave under FMLA and then got removed from the schedule.
- You got fired for requesting reasonable accommodations for your disability.
- You got fired after refusing to go on a date with the boss.
- You were terminated for discussing your wages.
- You were "laid off" while on maternity leave under FMLA.*
- You were fired after reporting harassment, discrimination, or other unlawful conduct.
- You were fired because a new manager doesn't want someone of your race or gender or with your disability on their team.
- Your boss overheard you speaking of your same-sex partner and fired you for "not being a culture fit."
- You requested extra breaks to accommodate your pregnancy and got pulled from the schedule.
- Your boss asked you to "massage the numbers" on a government report. You refused, so you were fired for being "insubordinate."
- You were fired after reporting a safety concern to OSHA.†

---

*I have now referenced the federal Family and Medical Leave Act (FMLA) twice. It is a very important federal rule that protects your time off in a number of situations. You will find detailed information about your FMLA rights in part III. For now, just know that firing you in retaliation for taking FMLA is illegal.

†The Occupational Safety and Health Administration is a federal agency that enforces safe workplace standards. Recently, there have been efforts by the Trump administration to abolish OSHA, but as of this writing, the agency still exists and reporting safety violations to them is protected. Some states have their own state-based OSHA programs as well.

- You recently turned sixty-one years old. Your boss started dropping hints that you're "too slow," then laid you off.
- You were fired for cooperating in an investigation against your employer.
- You reported your boss for touching you inappropriately, and you got removed from the schedule.

From these examples, you can see there is a general formula to look for: You were fired *because* of a protected characteristic or for engaging in a legally protected activity.

Protected characteristics include your race, national origin, gender, disability, religion, LGBTQ+ identity, or age. Protected activities include (but are not limited to):

- Reporting sexual harassment
- Making a whistleblower complaint
- Filing a report of safety violations to OSHA
- Taking protected leave under the Family and Medical Leave Act
- Requesting accommodation for your disability
- Discussing pay and work conditions with coworkers*
- Cooperating in a US Department of Labor investigation against your employer
- Reporting acts of discrimination based on age, race, gender, national origin, religion, or other protected characteristics
- Taking time off to perform military service, such as National Guard drills†
- Requesting accommodations for pregnancy

*Protected by the National Labor Relations Act (NLRA), 29 U.S.C. § 151-169 (1935).

†Protected by the Uniformed Services Employment and Reemployment Rights Act (USERRA), 38 U.S.C. § 4301-4335.

CASE STUDY: WRONGFUL TERMINATION

Griselda was in tears when we began our call.

"I don't know what to do," she began. "I lost my baby. I lost my job. But a friend said you could help."

What Griselda went through was devastating. She'd been working as a cashier at a fast-food restaurant. When she became pregnant, her manager refused to let her keep water near her workstation. As the pregnancy progressed, Griselda asked for a stool to sit on while she worked.

That request was denied. Management claimed it was a "tripping hazard."

To make matters worse, Griselda began to suffer from severe back and abdominal pain. One day, she noticed she was bleeding in her pants.

A few hours later, she learned she had miscarried.

Griselda called out sick because she needed a few days to recover from the loss of her pregnancy. But in a move that is all too common in the US, her manager simply pulled her off the schedule. When she asked to come back to work, management said she had been fired for being "unreliable."

Outrageous.

It was clear that Griselda was fired because she had been pregnant, because she requested accommodations for her pregnancy, and because she needed time off to recover from a medical condition. Still, she was worried she had no case.

"They said I was fired because I'm unreliable? And that's legal, isn't it?"

"Yes, they can *say* that, but it doesn't make it true," I replied. "Firing an unreliable employee is legal, but it's *not* legal to fire someone just because they are pregnant."*

*We will discuss the specific protections for pregnancy and related medical conditions in part III. For now, just know that there is a law protecting Griselda, even though her employer lied about why she was fired.

I signed Griselda as a client on a contingency basis. We sued her prior employer for wrongful termination, discrimination, retaliation, and a number of other violations. I am happy to report that after a few months of litigation, we got Griselda a substantial money settlement.*

Why Did Griselda Win?

Laws against wrongful termination do not *prevent* wrongful termination. Just as a posted speed limit does not make speeding impossible. Rather, it gives you *recourse* if your employer breaks the law.

In this case, Griselda won even though her employer lied about the reason she was fired. Here were a few factors that helped us win:

- Griselda informed her manager via text message that she was pregnant, so it was impossible for them to deny they *knew* she was pregnant.†
- Griselda requested to have water and a stool at her workstation via text message. This was a request for accommodation under the Pregnant Workers Fairness Act, and it was a legally protected request.‡
- Griselda refused to sign any exit paperwork that could have waived her rights. She talked to a few lawyers first, and ultimately chose my office. (It was an honor to fight for her!)

Unfortunately, I see dozens of cases like Griselda's every year. But hers highlights an important issue—wrongful termination takes many forms. And it is still illegal even if the employer lies about why you were fired.

---

*In these cases, we almost never seek reinstatement as a remedy. Why would you want to work for someone who violated your rights? We usually seek money damages instead.

†Title VII of the Civil Rights Act, as amended by the Pregnancy Discrimination Act of 1978, prohibits termination based on childbirth and related medical conditions. The Pregnant Workers Fairness Act, also a federal law, prohibits retaliation for requesting pregnancy-related accommodations. Again, we will discuss this in more detail in part III.

‡The use of text messages created a paper trail of evidence, thus making Griselda's case much stronger.

But overcoming the lies bad bosses tell isn't always simple. Let's talk about it in more detail so you can protect yourself if it happens to you.

WHAT IF THE EMPLOYER LIES ABOUT THE REASON YOU GOT FIRED?

In Griselda's case, her employer lied about why she was fired. They said it was due to her being "unreliable," but really, they fired her because of her pregnancy, which is illegal.

One of the most common and important employment law questions I get is what to do if an employer *lies* about why you are being fired. Many people reasonably believe that if an employer lies about the reason you were fired (e.g., downsizing, layoffs, poor performance, lack of work, etc.), there is nothing you can do.

Fortunately, this is not correct.

If someone is arrested on suspicion of robbing a store, will the police simply let them loose if they say they didn't do it? Of course not! There will be an investigation and a process for determining the facts, and ultimately a jury will decide who is lying and who is telling the truth.

In an employment case, it is common for employers to lie about the reason you were fired. Some will simply say it was "downsizing" or "lack of work." Others may say, "It's at-will employment, so I don't have to give the reason." I've seen every excuse you can think of. (I've also seen a few reasons no one would ever think of. I once had a case where the defendants claimed my client was fired because she was a "witch." She was not a witch; she just had tattoos.)

But if the real reason for termination was illegal, then we can prove it and win our case.

I understand this is very different from what you may have been told in the past. So I want to be very clear. Just because your boss . . .

- Says you are fired "at will"
- Lies about why they fired you
- Refuses to give a reason for your termination

- Removes you from the work schedule against your will
- Calls it a "layoff"

. . . doesn't mean you don't have a case. Once we make an allegation of wrongful termination, supported by at least *some* proof (like Griselda's text messages), then the boss has a serious problem on their hands.

The employer would be unwise to simply scream "At will!" and do nothing.* The employer will need to put up a defense to show that what they did *was* legal. This becomes harder and harder for them the more evidence you have.

Remember, *every lawsuit is a battle of evidence and credibility.*

No employer will admit they broke the law. I have never had an employer say "I fired your client because they are Asian" or "Your client reported sexual harassment, so I fired them." Often, the employer will concoct a cover story—a *pretext* for the termination. Again, this does not automatically ruin your case. *It is a natural and expected reaction to an accusation.*

But what does *pretext* look like, and how can you fight it?

CASE STUDY: FILE PADDING

Maureen came to my office with a problem. For years, she was a top-three performer at her medical equipment sales job. She consistently had positive feedback from her managers.

Her good reputation and performance were well documented. That made what happened particularly troubling. The company hired a new sales manager, a boisterous and confident man in his late thirties named Nick. Nick was a walking caricature of modern sales-bro culture. His Instagram feed was filled with pictures of Leonardo DiCaprio's Jordan Belfort from *The Wolf of Wall Street*. He was a Birddogs-wearing, golf-playing, deal-making machine (according to him at least).

---

*Doing nothing risks a loss by default, which can have devastating legal and financial consequences for the accused.

Of course, confidence is a must for a good salesperson. But there was a problem with Nick: His vision for a "perfect sales team" did not include women, who he believed were weak, easily manipulated, and not "aggressive" enough to close big sales.

Nick's disdain for Maureen was obvious. Although she had been a top performer, Nick chose not to include her on big sales calls, despite her being involved in such calls under her prior manager. At meetings, Nick ignored Maureen. When she voiced her opinion, he talked over her.

When Maureen mentioned a meeting with a big potential client, Nick replied, "Just smile and look cute. Maybe if you flirt with them, you'll get an upsell."

Maureen was furious. Never in her career had she been treated with such disrespect. And she was not alone: Other women in the office reported similar run-ins with Nick the Dick, as they called him.

One morning, after a particularly frustrating team meeting in which Nick again talked over Maureen, she had had enough. Maureen sent an email to human resources with the subject *Gender Discrimination and Harassment*. She reported Nick's misogynistic behavior—that he was targeting her and other women at the office for disrespectful treatment. She also specifically called out his suggestion that she should flirt with clients to get their business.

Human resources investigated, but after three weeks claimed that Maureen was "misinterpreting" Nick's leadership style. The HR rep also suggested that Maureen should "grow thicker skin" if she wanted to succeed in sales. Disappointed, Maureen saved her complaint and HR's response to a folder on her personal computer in case she needed proof of their correspondence in the future.

She made the right call. What followed, unfortunately, was a *file padding* campaign by Nick specifically to push Maureen out under the pretext of poor performance.

Nick started writing monthly performance reports accusing Maureen of failing to follow through with new leads, insulting customers with poor manners, and generally failing to be a team player. Maureen's sales numbers were fine, so Nick concocted "anonymous" complaints from clients to place in her file.

Nick was a dick, but he wasn't a stupid dick.

After several months of padding Maureen's file with false complaints, Nick made his move: He recommended her for termination. After reviewing the complaints in her file, the sales director (Nick's boss) agreed that Maureen should be terminated. Nick, the sales director, and an HR rep called Maureen into a surprise Zoom meeting where she was terminated.

When Maureen asked if she was being fired because she reported Nick for sexist behavior, the sales director said, "California is a right-to-work state. We don't have to give a reason."*

It was shocking, humiliating, and terribly unfair. Maureen's sales were excellent, but just because she had spoken up about a sexist boss, she was fired. Maureen came to my office for help. We won a settlement for her because we proved the following issues:

1. Maureen made a good faith complaint of sexist behavior from Nick the Dick.
2. HR investigated but took no action to protect Maureen.
3. Maureen's poor performance reviews occurred *after* her legally protected complaint, and the barrage of "client complaints" was not supported by anyone except Nick the Dick (no clients who allegedly made the complaints ever came forward).
4. Finally, we proved that Maureen was retaliated against and eventually fired because she had complained about sexist behavior.

Although Maureen was employed at will, public policy protects employees when they make a good faith report of unlawful labor practices. In this case, Nick the Dick was creating a discriminatory environment for female employees, and Maureen had a legal right to be protected from retaliation for reporting the discrimination. When the company

---

*California is *not* a right-to-work state. The director was simply lying. Had this book been available at the time, Maureen would have been able to spot this lie.

fired her as punishment for reporting Nick the Dick, they broke the law, and it was an exception to the at-will employment rule.

Even if you are employed in an at-will state, that doesn't mean that you have no rights as an employee. Being fired for an illegal reason is *always* illegal, regardless of the pretext (or lack thereof) for termination.

But what if you're *not* fired? What if, instead of padding Maureen's file, Nick had simply harassed Maureen until she had no choice but to quit? That's where we're headed next.

[Summary]

- At-will employment means you can be fired for any *legal* reason, with or without notice, with or without cause.
- The at-will presumption means most terminations are legal, but there are many exceptions to this default rule.
- Right-to-work laws have no impact on terminations. Instead, they mean that union membership cannot be required for your job.
- The federal government makes laws that apply to all fifty states. States can make their own rules, but only if they do not conflict with the federal rules.
- Just because you are terminated "at will" does not mean the termination was legal—the true motivation for the termination must not have been illegal; otherwise, it is wrongful termination.
- At-will employment is the default rule for forty-nine states; Montana is the only exception. But in all fifty states, you can still sue for wrongful termination (and win) when the termination had an unlawful motive.

- If the employer refuses to say why you were fired, or if they make up an excuse, or *pretext*, for why you were fired, you can still have a wrongful termination claim.
- Some employers might try to pad your file when they know they are about to illegally fire you. You can fight back by creating a paper trail like Griselda and Maureen did.
- A paper trail is any written evidence about your job. Text messages, social media messages, emails, write-ups, pay stubs, and other documents all count.
- A good paper trail can save your career. If you are wrongfully terminated, it can be the difference between winning a life-changing settlement and walking away with nothing.

CHAPTER 2

Constructive Dismissal / Constructive Wrongful Termination

THE LAST STRAW

The case on my desk was unusual. The client said she had been forced out of her coffee shop job, and she wanted to know if she had a wrongful termination claim. There was just one catch—she had not actually been fired. Rather, she had felt she had no choice but to quit.

While investigating this peculiar situation, I interviewed a witness who had worked with my client. The witness described how the manager treated women.

“It’s always the same with him,” the witness told me. “If you reject him, you’re on his list. He knows better than to fire us, so he thinks he’s clever. He just starts bullying you until you quit.”

The witness worked at the coffee shop with my client. We will call her Arlene.

Arlene was a beautiful young woman. On top of that, she had a bubbly personality that made her instantly likable. Unfortunately, those attributes had also made her a target for unwanted attention from the coffee shop’s manager, John.

John had a crush on Arlene. He flirted with her constantly; he made repeated comments about how "perfect" she was; he called her "goddess" and "queen" during work. He pressured her into "work lunches" that in reality were just clumsy efforts at dates.

During one really bad shift, John hugged Arlene from behind—grazing her breasts and pressing his hips against her butt.

She'd had enough.

Arlene whipped around and told John to cool it.

He tried to laugh it off.

"I'm serious," she huffed. "This isn't funny, you're making me uncomfortable."

Arlene was brave to stand up to John, but it came at a price. John stopped scheduling Arlene on shifts with him, which effectively cut her hours to part time. He started rumors about Arlene, saying she was "arrogant because she's hot." Not satisfied, John started writing Arlene up for "poor attitude."

When Arlene complained to the owner, he responded, "Obviously you don't have to date John, but he's your boss, so you need to show respect. And I've gotten some concerning reports about arrogant behavior from you . . ."

That was the last straw. Arlene felt she had no choice but to quit.

She wasn't *fired*. But she had clearly been pushed out because she rejected John's advances. It was unacceptable. Fortunately, I am happy to report that the owner of this shop paid a hefty price for mistreating her.

The six-figure question for this case was: If Arlene quit, how could she win a settlement for wrongful termination?

The answer lies in a little-understood area of employment law called *constructive dismissal*.*

---

*Every state has slightly different rules and names for this, but for simplicity I will stick with the term *constructive dismissal* in this chapter. In addition to the constructive dismissal claims, Arlene also had a claim for sexual harassment. We will discuss sexual harassment claims in more detail later in part I.

WHAT IF YOU'RE FORCED TO QUIT?

As a general rule, you cannot sue your employer for wrongful termination if you quit on your own. You may have other claims, but it's hard to say you were wrongfully fired if you were not actually fired. This creates a pretty concerning incentive for abusive employers. What if, instead of *firing* you (and risking a lawsuit), they could just make you quit?

Unfortunately, this happens quite often. You've probably seen it happen yourself. An employee falls out of favor for one reason or another, so over the course of days, weeks, or even months, management targets them until they are so exhausted from the abuse that they quit.* At first glance, it looks like the scummy boss found a loophole.

Fortunately, we have a backup plan to deal with this. Constructive dismissal, also called *constructive discharge* or *constructive wrongful termination*, captures the gray area between being *fired* for illegal reasons and being *forced out* for illegal reasons. With a constructive dismissal claim, you can get compensated for damages as if you had been fired, even if you resigned.

To show constructive dismissal, you need to prove a few essential elements (this varies by state, but these are the most common general rules):

1. Your employer *knowingly* or *intentionally* created intolerable conditions;
2. The conditions were so intolerable that any *reasonable person* would feel they had no choice but to resign;
3. You made a good faith effort to preserve the employment relationship;

*This was precisely what Joe did to me when I was a young firefighter. He didn't want me *fired*; he wanted to make me miserable until I quit.

4. You reasonably felt you had no choice but to resign despite a sincere effort to continue working; and
5. You suffered actual and provable damages as a result.*

Let's dive a little deeper into what exactly are *intolerable conditions*. To understand that, we will also need to know what it means to view things as a *reasonable person*, and how to make a *good faith effort*.

WHAT MAKES WORK CONDITIONS *LEGALLY* "INTOLERABLE"?

Constructive dismissal occurs when the employer *creates* or *knows about* intolerable conditions but does nothing to fix them. Simply quitting and then claiming the conditions were intolerable won't be enough most the time. For example, in *Turner v. Anheuser-Busch, Inc.*, the California Supreme Court wrote: "An employee cannot simply 'quit and sue.'" The circumstances require an examination of the specific facts in each case because "the conditions giving rise to the resignation must be sufficiently extraordinary and egregious."† The hardest part of every constructive dismissal claim is proving the work conditions were *objectively* intolerable. Every case is unique, but here are some examples in which a job has historically been found to be intolerable:

- Severe and persistent wage theft
- Severe and persistent discrimination

---

*This standard comes from the California Supreme Court case *Turner v. Anheuser-Busch, Inc.*, 7 Cal. 4th 1238, 1251 (1994), which held that "to establish a constructive discharge, an employee must plead and prove . . . that the employer either intentionally created or knowingly permitted working conditions that were so intolerable or aggravated at the time of the employee's resignation that a reasonable employer would realize that a reasonable person in the employee's position would be compelled to resign." Each state is different, but this is the general basis you will find in most cases.

†7 Cal. 4th 1238, 1251 (2014). I'll remind readers that constructive discharge claims vary slightly from state to state. The California standard is typical, but you will want to consult a lawyer in your state about your specific claims.

- Assault/sexual harassment
- Urgent safety violations
- Pressured to do something illegal

With that in mind, not all unpleasant work conditions meet this standard. Even in California, which is generally very employee-friendly, courts have held that the following examples are not always "intolerable" by themselves:

- Getting rescheduled from day to night shifts against your wishes
- Getting yelled at by your boss in front of your coworkers
- Getting a pay cut or a demotion
- Getting transferred to a less desirable location
- Being talked down to, micromanaged, or treated like a child by your supervisor

If several of these things occur at once, or if they are exceptionally serious, or if they occur for a long period of time, then the situation might be "intolerable." But again, the courts have set a very high bar. It can't just be intolerable for *you*, it has to be intolerable to a "reasonable person."

WHAT IS *LEGALLY* CONSIDERED A "REASONABLE PERSON"?

In the movie *Idiocracy*, the US military conducts a top-secret experiment to put a human in hibernation for one year.* After a survey of all

*Unfortunately, but also hilariously, the experiment goes awry—keeping the test subject frozen in time for hundreds of years. He awakens to a horrifying future where idiots rule the world. Much like some of the workplaces I have sued for my clients.

US troops, the government finds the most perfectly average man in the force: Private Joe Bowers (played by Luke Wilson). He has exactly average intelligence, average skills, average height. He is the most ordinary, average, uninteresting person alive.

Much like the US military in *Idiocracy,* the courts use a fictional, average person like Private Joe Bowers to evaluate whether a "reasonable person" would agree you were forced out. This reasonable person would not be *you,* but rather a blank slate, an avatar totally unburdened by your unique talents, traumas, or triggers.

This can be frustrating for some employees. Let's use an example to show why:

Mark is an auto technician with prior military service. Due to his combat experience, he feels overwhelming anxiety when a vehicle engine gets too loud. Mark makes a written complaint about the conditions, telling his boss that they are intolerable due to his post-traumatic stress disorder (PTSD) and the triggering effect of the engine noise. The boss promises to make a change, but the engine noises persist. Mark says, "I can't work like this, it's intolerable. I have no choice but to quit."

It's a sad story, and I feel terrible for Mark. If he came to my office, I would advise him that he might have a claim for failure to accommodate his disability (more on that in part III). But the question on Mark's mind is whether he can sue for constructive dismissal.

The answer is probably no.

Mark is particularly sensitive to loud noises due to his combat experience. But we use the reasonable person standard to measure "intolerable work conditions." An average person of ordinary sensibility, unburdened by Mark's unique problems, would not find working in an auto shop intolerable due to engine noise.

Mark's case failed because it did not meet all of the elements of a constructive dismissal claim. The employer did not intentionally make the noise to abuse Mark; it was a coincidence of the job. Sure, they knew about the issue, and one could argue that they broke their promise to fix it, but that's not egregious enough to say Mark was *forced out.* Our *Idiocracy*-grade "reasonable person" would probably not feel forced to quit under similar circumstances.

WHAT, *LEGALLY*, IS A GOOD FAITH EFFORT?

You cannot simply quit, then turn around and sue for constructive dismissal. The law requires that you make a sincere, honest effort to make things right before you leave. I understand that sounds unfair. But this rule exists for a reason. It would be chaos if anyone could just quit for no reason, file a surprise lawsuit, and then try to shake down their employer for easy cash. That would totally discredit the honest employees who have real claims.

Before quitting, you should make a paper trail that shows you are trying to make things right. That is what a good faith effort is. Here are a few examples:

- Report a manger for harassment *in writing*, and follow up on those complaints with further requests for help if the harassment continues.
- Alert your manager *in writing* if your pay is incorrect, and give them a reasonable amount of time to correct the issue.
- If there is an unsafe condition, you should not simply quit unless it is a true emergency. Instead, report it *in writing* and explain why it is dangerous.

The above examples have a few major themes: (1) Report issues in writing—this way you can prove you made a good faith effort; (2) give the employer notice that there is a problem; and (3) give the employer a fair opportunity to fix the problem.

You do not have to tolerate the intolerable, but you can help your case by giving your employer *notice* and an *opportunity* to fix the issue. Documenting this process will help you prove you made a good faith effort for the purpose of a constructive dismissal claim, should that become necessary down the road.

WHAT TO DO NEXT

Remember: Constructive dismissal is a form of wrongful termination, but it is a very high bar to prove. Successful constructive dismissal claims only apply to very egregious, objectively offensive circumstances. If you are being forced out, your best move is to resign in such a way that you preserve a potential constructive dismissal claim. Keep a paper trail, and never sign any documents without consulting a lawyer.

These are sample resignation emails you might consider working with in a constructive dismissal situation. Note that they are quite short—saying *less* is more effective in situations like this.

Sample Email Template: Forced to Resign (Safety)

Dear Manager,

I am writing because I feel I have no choice but to quit. On [DATE] I reported an urgent safety concern to management. The safety issue was too urgent for a report to OSHA, and I feel I was at serious risk of death or injury if the issue was not addressed.

Since making that report, I have been targeted for severe and persistent harassment. I reported the harassment, and it has not stopped.

Despite my sincere desire to remain employed, I feel I have no alternative but to quit because of these serious safety concerns.

Sincerely,
Employee

Sample Email Template: Forced to Resign (Harassment)

Dear Manager,

I am writing because I feel I have no choice but to quit. On [DATE] I reported sexual harassment from [NAME] to management. The harassment included offensive comments and unwanted touching.

Since making that report, I have been targeted for severe and persistent harassment. I reported the harassment, and it has not stopped.

Despite my sincere desire to remain employed, it is clear that tolerating sexual harassment has become a condition of keeping this job. Because of this, I feel I have no alternative but to quit.

Sincerely,
Employee

[Summary]

- Constructive dismissal, also called constructive discharge or constructive wrongful termination, is when an employer knowingly creates or allows intolerable work conditions.
- Constructive dismissal claims capture the gray area between being *fired* and being forced to quit.
- To show you were forced to quit, you need to demonstrate *objectively* intolerable conditions that even a fictional, perfectly average person would not tolerate.
- You must show that you made a good faith effort to address the issue before quitting.
- Constructive wrongful termination requires a very high standard of proof. You cannot simply quit and sue. Making a paper trail, including a written complaint of the conditions, followed by a responsibly worded resignation letter, can help.

[CHAPTER 3]

Retaliation

YOU CAN'T HANDLE THE TRUTH

Maria Gatchalian looked at the courtroom clock again. It had been only a minute since she last checked, but it felt like a lifetime.

The jury had been deliberating her case for hours. There was nothing to do but wait. And wait. And wait. And hope the jury came to the right decision.

Maria had been a nurse for over thirty years. As a charge nurse in the neonatal intensive care unit (NICU), she had been a mentor, a leader, and a fierce advocate for her patients.

Until she was abruptly fired in June 2019.

The termination was part of a retaliation campaign against Maria for raising safety concerns with management. Among other things, she reported that a patient's father had brought a knife into her unit; management did nothing. She reported that a baby had not been fed properly; management did nothing. She reported improper catheter use on a baby in critical condition; again, management did nothing.

Finally, when Maria reported that a patient's confidential health information had been improperly disclosed, management put a target on her back.

For starters, the hospital dragged their feet in every investigation Maria called for. Most of the safety issues she reported were never addressed. In an effort to isolate Maria, the hospital excluded her from important communications, including key information she needed to do her job as a charge nurse.

Then they launched a sham investigation to create a pretext to fire her. Management took pictures of Maria asleep on a recliner with her bare feet touching a plastic crib. Maria was on break, but they wouldn't let facts interfere with their plans.

However, no one else was being fired for napping while on a break. The hospital's disproportionate response was retaliation for her making legally protected complaints related to patient safety. At trial, the hospital tried to make Maria look lazy and unreliable, and even got a few witnesses to attack her. Maria had to sit quietly as management took the stand and made hurtful statements about what a "bad nurse" she was.

When the trial concluded, all Maria could do was hope. Hope that the jury could see that she was only protecting her patients. Hope that they wouldn't believe the awful lies management had told about her.

Maria's fate was in the jury's hands.

The bailiff's voice broke the silence. "All rise," he boomed.

The jurors entered the courtroom. The foreperson handed the verdict form to the judge. A decision had been made.

Despite the hospital's attempt to smear Maria's reputation, the jury had not been fooled.

They awarded her $2.5 million for lost wages, $9 million for mental suffering, and a whopping $30 million in punitive damages to punish the hospital that fired her.*

In a later ruling, the judge noted, "There was sufficient evidence here for the jury to determine that Plaintiff's termination was pretextual and disproportionate, and that [the hospital] acted with fraud, malice, or oppression."†

That's some sweet, sweet justice baby.

---

*Most cases in this book come from my office. In an effort to present a broader picture, I have included a handful of high-profile cases that I have not personally worked on, but that illustrate the labor rights we are covering in the chapter. This is the first instance of such a case.

†Maria Gatchalian v. Kaiser Foundation Hospitals et al., rulings.law/rulings/judge-maurice-a-leiter/21stcv15300-2023-05-10.html.

RETALIATION IS A BULLY'S FAVORITE WEAPON

The number one reason people do not stand up for their rights at work is fear. Fear of termination, fear of a bad performance review, fear of being forced to resign in disgrace. We call these things *adverse employment actions*. Essentially, this means any action taken against you that materially and negatively affects your pay, career prospects, work conditions, or quality of life.

Retaliation is when an employer takes an adverse employment action against you as punishment for exercising a legal right or engaging in a protected activity. Maria's case followed this formula. She engaged in a legally protected activity by reporting patient health and safety violations. As punishment for doing so, the hospital hit her with a series of adverse employment actions. Ultimately, they fired her. This was retaliation *and* wrongful termination.

But not every instance of a boss lashing out at you is illegal. To be unlawful retaliation, the employer must be targeting you for a protected activity. Recall the list of protected activities from chapter 1. All of the examples I gave there were activities protected by a law specifically prohibiting retaliation for doing those things.

Here are a couple other examples of retaliation (with happy endings!):

- In 2011 a Haitian American employee filed a race and national origin discrimination complaint against her supervisor. She worked for the City of Boston, and she filed her complaint with the Massachusetts Commission Against Discrimination. In retaliation for her protected complaint, her boss stripped her of her management title, denied overtime pay, and padded her file with negative performance reviews. At trial, the jury awarded her $389,000 in lost wages, $500,000 for emotional distress damages, and $10 million in punitive damages.
- In 2010 an Amtrak employee reported possible fraud and passenger safety concerns. Almost immediately, he got slapped with his first-ever negative performance review. His position

was later eliminated, and he was ultimately fired. But he filed a whistleblower retaliation claim with OSHA. Amtrak was ordered to pay the employee $892,551 and reinstate him to his position.

WHAT IS *NOT* RETALIATION?

As a workers' rights lawyer, I pursue retaliation claims for employees all the time. But not all activities that you have a *right* to do are legally protected. As a general guideline, here are some examples that would *not* be protected from adverse employment actions by your boss:

- Reporting a manager for saying "fuck" in a company meeting
- Complaining about a lunch thief to HR
- Complaining that your manager is friendlier to his buddies than to the rest of the staff
- Getting fired for requesting a pay raise
- Arguing with a customer who was rude to you
- Reporting coworkers for taking long breaks*

The line between merely *unfair* retaliation and *illegal* retaliation is gray, but remember, if you have engaged in a *legally protected activity*, then retaliation is illegal. It is not illegal to curse at work or to be rude to employees. But you do have legal protections against harassment, as well as the legal right to report harassment.

WHISTLEBLOWER COMPLAINTS

You might have heard about whistleblowers in the news. But what makes someone a whistleblower?

A whistleblower is a person who reports illegal activity. Like Maria

*Mind your business. No one likes a snitch.

from earlier in this chapter. This matters because whistleblowers are protected from retaliation. As part of those protections, whistleblowers may be entitled to significant financial awards if the employer fires or retaliates against them.

But to get these protections (and to get paid if you experience retaliation), you must meet a few essential criteria:

1. You had a good faith belief that you witnessed illegal activity, and
2. You reported the illegal activity to someone with authority to take action, and
3. You experienced retaliation as a result of your whistleblower report.

The law will vary somewhat from state to state. But nine out of ten times, these points are what's really at issue when dealing with a whistleblower case.

What If You're Wrong About Suspected Illegal Activity?

You are *not* expected to be a legal expert. All you need is an honest, good faith belief that it was illegal. If you were mistaken, and what you saw was *wrong* but not necessarily *illegal*, then in some cases you could still be protected.

For example, imagine a construction worker submits an OSHA complaint for unsafe scaffolds at a jobsite. They are wobbly, and the worker has a reasonable, good faith belief that they are not up to code. During the investigation, OSHA finds that the employee was wrong; the scaffolds are up to code (they just wiggle a bit more than most workers would like).

So is the employer free to terminate the employee "at will"?

Probably not. OSHA's antiretaliation rules are designed to favor employees who make a report, even if they are wrong, just so long as they did so with some reasonable basis for believing the situation was illegal.

If I were a lawyer-fairy on this construction worker's shoulder, I'd give her this advice:

- Document the unsafe condition, take pictures, note who else witnessed the unsafe condition.
- Document why you feel the condition is unsafe; keep this in a journal somewhere.
- Make your report to management so they cannot deny that they knew of the problem. Do it in writing and keep a copy for yourself.
- At the same time, make a report to OSHA. Keep a copy of that report.
- *If* you are punished for making the report, talk to a lawyer *immediately*. File a retaliation report to OSHA within thirty days of the retaliatory behavior.*

What Is OSHA?

The Occupational Safety and Health Administration (OSHA) is a federal agency created by Congress in 1970. Its job is to regulate workplace safety. OSHA has the authority to investigate, fine, or even close down unsafe workplaces. OSHA cannot be everywhere at once, so they rely on reports from employees to catch abusive employers. That is why whistleblowers who make reports to OSHA are legally protected from retaliation.

REPORTING SUSPECTED ILLEGAL ACTIVITY

As a general rule, your best response to an unfair, retaliatory action from your boss is to make a written complaint so you have a paper trail. This protects you during an internal review, a future performance

*OSHA requires that retaliation reports be received within thirty days of the retaliation. Not all antiretaliation rules have such a tight window.

evaluation, or in the worst-case scenario, if you have to sue for wrongful termination. In the example below, you are an employee who witnessed harassment. As you will learn later in part I, bystanders are encouraged to report such harassment, and they are generally protected for good faith reports of harassment (even if done for someone else).

Sample Email Template: Reporting Unsafe Orders and Harassment

Dear Manager,

I am writing to report harassment I witnessed against my coworker, Carlos, by our supervisor, Alex. On Tuesday, May 18, I witnessed Alex calling Carlos a "pussy" for refusing to work on the roof without adequate fall protection. Alex said Carlos is "not a real man" and called him lazy.

This conduct is severe and pervasive, and I believe it is causing a hostile work environment. What will the company do to help?

Respectfully,
Employee

I understand many workers do not have emails. Fortunately, a **text message** counts as a written complaint! In this example, let's see how a line cook can blow the whistle on unsafe conditions at a restaurant.

Sample Whistleblower Text Message (Safety)

Hi boss, I need to report a serious safety concern. While entering the restaurant, I noticed a strong gas smell. I immediately evacuated with the rest of the staff. I don't think it's safe to go in there until the fire department checks it out.

These are just two examples, but in both, we have employees making complaints. The first complaint concerns harassment—an unlawful labor practice. The second complaint deals with an urgent safety issue. (As a former firefighter, I can attest that a gas leak is extremely dangerous!) Of course, we hope that the employer will do the right thing. But if something goes wrong, the employees have a paper trail establishing their protected whistleblower status.

Everything starts with a protected complaint. And remember, you do not need to be a legal expert: If you make the complaint in good faith (meaning you *reasonably* believed it was illegal), then the protection may still attach. Reasonableness is a key factor here. If you are bullied by a boss shortly after you made a complaint of discrimination, it is reasonable to presume you are being targeted for the discrimination complaint.

IS REPORTING WORTH THE RISK?

As you read these pages, you might be thinking, *I don't want to get fired, even if I might win a case later. It's just not worth the risk.*

Losing a job is a scary prospect, so let's talk about it.

Safety concerns are *always* worth the risk. Your life is irreplaceable. If you suspect your workplace is unsafe, report it in writing, and do not proceed until the unsafe condition is fixed.

Safety aside, you deserve to be treated with dignity and respect.

Finally, you work for money, not for a boss's approval. If they are not paying you correctly (or at all), then it is time to speak up.

Summary

- Adverse employment actions include things like demotions, pay cuts, write-ups, and termination.
- Retaliation is an adverse employment action that punishes you for exercising your rights or engaging in a legally protected activity.

- Whistleblower complaints are a protected activity. They consist of making a good faith report of suspected illegal activity to someone with authority to act.
- The best way to protect yourself from retaliation is to make a paper trail. Make reports in writing and keep copies for yourself.
- Save your complaints for issues of important legal or ethical significance. Safety is *always* worth reporting.

CHAPTER 4

Harassment and Hostile Work Environments

DR. ROID RAGE

Patricia was a nurse in a urology center. Her boss, who we will call Dr. Roid Rage, was a partner at the clinic. His hulking, six-foot-three frame towered over tiny Patricia. In addition to his size and strength, he was also an avid student of martial arts, with a blue belt in karate.

Unfortunately, Dr. Roid Rage was also a bully. But he tended to bully only women, not men. Sadly, Patricia was his favorite target.

Dr. Roid Rage was so emotionally dysregulated that, while screaming at Patricia, he threw punches within inches of her face. He never landed a hit—he just wanted to make sure she knew how "tough" he was. These threats made Patricia a nervous wreck. She suffered anxiety, stomachaches, and sleeplessness because of the abuse.

After one particularly aggressive outburst, Patricia had enough. She reported the harassment in writing to another doctor at the office. But the response she got was disappointing (to say the least).

While sitting at her desk, she was confronted by Dr. Roid Rage. He demanded to know why Patricia reported him. She told him it was because she suffered severe anxiety from him screaming at her.

Enraged, he gripped the back of her chair, leaned over her, and howled, "If you want to hear yelling, I'll show you yelling!" He pushed his face close to hers. "Now I'm yelling at you! Now you know what real yelling sounds like!"

It was the final straw. Shaken, but by no means broken, Patricia filed a claim with the Equal Employment Opportunity Commission (EEOC). Eighteen days later, she was fired in retaliation for the complaint, but Dr. Roid Rage claimed it was for "poor performance."

Patricia wasn't done fighting yet. She filed a lawsuit for retaliation, hostile work environment, assault, sexual harassment, and intentional infliction of emotional distress.

Patricia was able to prove harassment and discrimination because she had a good paper trail. Ultimately, she settled the case for $440,000.

The lessons we need to learn from this case are as follows:

- Know what harassment looks like so you can stand up for yourself.
- Report bullying, do it in writing, and don't give in if it continues.
- Pay attention to bullies who single out specific groups of people over others. In my experience, women get bullied more than men because they are (wrongfully) perceived as easier targets.

As we proceed with this chapter, remember the following:

- Bullies are insecure, which is why they try to dominate others.
- Bullies achieve short-term success, but at a high price.
- Bullies have more rivals, fewer friends, and less security.
- All bullies are vulnerable. We can use their vulnerability against them.

WHAT IS ILLEGAL HARASSMENT?

In this chapter, we'll discuss harassment and what to do if it happens to you at work. But first, let's answer a basic question: What *is* harassment, and when does it become illegal?

Harassment must be motivated by your protected characteristic to be illegal. Bullies become harassers when we expose an unlawful *reason* for their harassment. Laws such as the Age Discrimination in Employment Act of 1967, the Americans with Disabilities Act of 1990, and the Pregnancy Discrimination Act of 1978 provide additional antidiscrimination and antiharassment protections. Generally speaking, federal law includes protections for the following protected characteristics:

- Race*
- National origin
- Color
- Religion
- Sex, gender, gender identity, sexual orientation†
- Age (40+)
- Pregnancy
- Disability

Harassing an employee for any of these characteristics is against federal law. State laws may offer *more* protection, but not less (you may recall this from chapter 1). Bullying becomes illegal harassment when one of these protected characteristics is the motive for the behavior.

Illegal harassment can occur in a million different ways, but here are a few examples that come up the most often:

- Offensive jokes
- Name-calling
- Offensive imagery, memes, posters, or videos (such as porn)
- Invasive questions about your body, appearance, religious practice, or sex life

*There's an incorrect assumption that these laws to not apply to white people. While discrimination against white employees is rare, it is equally illegal and equally protected. Remember, *race* is the protected characteristic, not *certain* races.

†Readers in "red" states may be surprised to learn that sexual orientation is protected. In many states, this was not the case until 2020. The US Supreme Court held in *Bostock v. Clayton County, Georgia* that "sex" as defined in Title VII of the Civil Rights Act includes gender expression, sexual orientation, and gender identity.

- Unwanted touching, shoving, hitting, grabbing, or blocking your path
- Direct or implied threats (such as "Watch your step")
- Offensive hand gestures
- Favoring employees who lack the protected characteristic over those who have it

Of course, none of this is illegal if the conduct is welcomed. If you have a habit of sharing dirty stories or racial jokes with your boss, and you usually enjoy them, then it's very hard to suddenly say, "Okay, *now* I am offended." So as a general rule, it is best to avoid these behaviors at work.

I once had a case where my client, a Black woman, was paired with a manager who had the social skills of a drunk baboon. When she was first hired, the manager called a stand-up meeting to "get to know" her. This would have been fine, but the manager proceeded to ask a series of invasive, personal questions that stunned the office:

"Do you have any kids? Is the dad in the picture?"

"Do you know where your ancestors are from? No, like in Africa. Where are you really from?"

"Is the fried chicken thing real, or is that just a myth?"

My client was offended but wrote the whole thing off as an isolated instance of an ignorant boss just trying to be funny.

But then things got worse.

During meetings with my client, the manager liked to tell stories about other Black people he had known in his life. He was Latino, but talked about things he'd do with his Black friends while growing up "in the hood." He called them his "n—gas."

My client stopped him.

"We do not use that word in my home; I'd prefer not to hear it at work," she said.

Embarrassed, but learning nothing, the manager doubled down. "Hey, Black and brown, we're all cool, it's all cool. I'm your n—ga too."

What a jackass.

The constant remarks and jokes about Black people kept coming.

Never did the manager *attack* my client for her race, but the jokes and weird stories and racial slurs became so pervasive that it created a hostile work environment.

What made this illegal harassment, rather than just bullying? It was the motivation (her race), the actions (severe and pervasive comments about race), and the impact (it created a hostile work environment).

BULLYING IS NOT ILLEGAL *BY ITSELF*

The line between bullying and illegal harassment can be hard to spot. I get a lot of calls to my office from people who've been bullied at work.

"My boss keeps calling me stupid, do I have a case?"

"My manager always acts dismissive and rude."

"I have a coworker who stares me down at the office."

"Katie won't stop stealing my lunch, can I throw some ghost peppers in there to teach her a lesson?"*

All these are bullying behaviors. And let's be clear, none are acceptable at work. But what's morally *unacceptable* and what's legally *actionable* are very different things. None of these would trigger any legal protections on their own. Because bullying is not illegal, but harassment is.

What's the difference?

It's all about the *reason* you are being bullied. If the motivation for the bullying behavior is illegal (meaning it has an unlawful motive), then it is harassment.

Learning your rights will help you know when and how to stand up to a bully. But you do *not* have to be a legal expert. As you may recall from our discussion on retaliation in chapter 3, you can still be protected

*As much as this would be good karma, I do not recommend spiking anyone's food, even your own, with peppers. In 2019 a New York man put Epsom salt, magnesium sulfate, and laxatives into a coffee maker. The result was many sick people and criminal charges. Similarly, although the food thief is wrong, it is also illegal to knowingly set a trap to cause pain to the thief. This is the law's way of saying "two wrongs don't make a right."

even if you mistake bullying for illegal harassment. You must have had a good faith belief that what happened was illegal.

With that in mind, it is generally better to make a written complaint of harassment if you suspect it could be illegal. When in doubt, call it out.

WHAT IS A HOSTILE WORK ENVIRONMENT?

When I was defining illegal harassment, I mentioned that my client was facing a *hostile work environment* because of the weird racial "jokes" and slurs she faced from her manager. But what constitutes a hostile work environment? Harassment creates a hostile work environment when:

- It is unwelcome, unwanted, or nonconsensual,
- The harasser is motivated by a protected characteristic or protected activity,
- The harassment is so severe it has no place in civil society, and/or it is occurring so frequently that it is pervasive, *and*
- It negatively affects the victim's employment, leading to, for example, demotion, termination, failure to promote or hire, or lost wages.

In most cases, you have to prove all four of these elements to win a claim for a hostile work environment. But watch out for one more important detail. Federal antiharassment laws typically only apply to employers of at least fifteen workers. Public entities are usually covered at any size. In some states, antiretaliation laws will apply to smaller businesses.*

This matters because it's how you can prove you experienced harassment and a hostile work environment, and hold bad employers accountable. Often, if you follow the tips in this book, you can do this without the need for a lawsuit.

---

*In California and Oregon, for example, these laws apply to employers of five or more workers.

WHAT IF THEY SAY THEY'RE "JUST KIDDING"?

Malicious intent is *not* required for illegal harassment. Instead, you must show that you were targeted because of your protected characteristic. A boss being merely ignorant, a coworker making a crass joke, or a peer asking offensive questions while "just making conversation," can all become harassment under the right conditions. A perfect illustration comes from the TV series *The Office*. The show follows the antics of a bumbling, incompetent boss named Michael Scott (played by Steve Carell) who is the regional manager of a paper supply company called Dunder Mifflin. And to put it bluntly, he is a doofus.

In one episode, Michael—a white guy—recites a joke from Chris Rock's comedy special *Bigger & Blacker* about the difference between "n—gas vs. Black people."

From a Black comedian in a comedy special, the joke was edgy and controversial. From a white supervisor in an office setting, it was cringey and horrifying. It also created a hostile work environment for the employees, especially the character Stanley Hudson, a Black man (played by Leslie David Baker).

While Michael Scott's offensive behavior actually stems from a desperate desire to be liked, his motivation doesn't matter. His remarks cross the line into illegal harassment because they target a protected characteristic. If Stanley were my client, I would have sued Michael for creating a hostile work environment. And when we won, Stanley would have gotten paid!

WHEN IS THE COMPANY LIABLE?

If you win your lawsuit, then who pays for it? Employers are liable (or legally responsible) for a hostile work environment when they knew or *should* have known about the harassment and failed to take prompt and appropriate action to protect you. This matters, because your harasser may not have the money to compensate you when you win a case, but your employer (or their insurance carrier) probably will.

Harassment by Supervisors = Automatic Liability

Generally, employers are automatically liable for harassment by supervisors. However, there is one exception. If the supervisor's harassment caused a hostile work environment, then the employer can escape liability—and paying the victim money—if it can show two things:

1. The employer took reasonable steps to prevent and quickly correct the harassment, *and*
2. You, the employee, *unreasonably* failed to take advantage of the preventative or corrective resources offered by the employer.

We will discuss strategies in more detail in part IV. But for now, know that communicating with human resources or a manager about the problem typically beats this defense.

Harassment by Non-Supervisors

The default rule is that your employer is not automatically responsible for harassment from non-supervisors. Non-supervisors include your peers, but also vendors, contractors, clients, and visitors. However, employers would be liable for a hostile work environment created by non-supervisors if they knew or should have known about the harassment and failed to take the appropriate action. Communicating with human resources or a manager about the problem is always your best defense.

REPORTING HARASSMENT

You have a limited amount of time to report unlawful harassment. Generally, you must file a charge of discrimination with the Equal Employment Opportunity Commission (EEOC) within 180 calendar days of the last time the harassment occurred. However, you can also get a private attorney (like me) to handle the claims for you. In some states, your statute of limitations can be longer.

But before you get there, you really should notify your employer of what is happening so they have a chance to fix it. Even if you have the worst, most untrustworthy HR rep in the world, it is in your best interest to make a paper trail showing that you reported the harassment. Keep a copy for yourself so they cannot pretend you never notified them of the problem.

Sample Email Template: Reporting Harassment (Age)

Dear Human Resources,

I am writing to report harassment from my supervisor, Bill Lumbergh, because of my age. On January 18, Bill told me that I am getting "too old" for my department. He keeps pressuring me to retire. On one occasion, he asked me if I was sad about my "childhood friend" Betty White passing away.

The constant jokes and comments about my age are severe, pervasive, and they are creating a hostile work environment for me.

What will the company do to help?

Respectfully,
Employee

Sample Email Template: Reporting Harassment (National Origin)

Dear Human Resources,

I am writing to report harassment from my coworker, Todd Packer. I was born in the US and grew up here, and I am of Indian descent. Todd continues to ask me invasive, offensive questions about my race and national origin.

On March 11, he asked if we eat dogs for lunch in my country.

On May 1, he drew a red dot on his forehead and asked me if I liked it (I did not).

Throughout my employment, he has spoken to me in an offensive pseudo-Indian accent.

The constant jokes and taunting about my race and national origin are severe and pervasive, and they are causing a hostile work environment for me.

What will the company do to help?

Respectfully,
Employee

CASE STUDY: *ATTORNEY RYAN V. KING NOTHING*

I once had a case against a real estate investor who fancied himself a king. We'll call him King Nothing.

King Nothing had a few unsavory character traits. For starters, he was a cheapskate. His company earned millions every year, but his office was old, dingy, and filled with ancient computers that took over fifteen minutes to boot up. He skimped on everything, from the single-ply toilet paper in the bathroom to the pitiful wages on employees' checks.

Another vice King Nothing had was equal parts lust and contempt for the women who worked for him. He insisted on a strict dress code—women were required to be done up with full hair and makeup every morning, and only high heels were permitted at work. As you probably guessed, King Nothing only hired young, attractive women.

One of my clients worked for King Nothing, and she was terrified of him. King Nothing had frequent, uncontrolled outbursts of anger whenever he didn't get his way. He would berate, belittle, and insult the women in the office one day, only to flirt with them the next. His rapid transitions from bully to creep made his employees afraid of him. But they also despised him.

When my client found out she was pregnant, she was scared of how he would react. Still, she asked for FMLA leave to focus on her health (we will learn more about FMLA leave in part III). Of course, King Nothing was livid.

"I'm not paying for you to take a vacation," he scoffed.

I want to fact-check King Nothing for a moment. For starters, FMLA is unpaid. Second, any parent will tell you that raising a child is NOT a vacation. But that's beside the point.

The next day, King Nothing instructed his HR manager to fire my client. When she refused, he fired the HR rep, then he fired my client.

I'm sure he felt very tough. He really showed those women who the big bad boss was, right?

Wrong.

My client hired me to pursue her FMLA retaliation, gender discrimination, and wrongful termination case. When I got a hold of the HR rep, she had a *mountain* of evidence to offer—in addition to her own claim for wrongful termination.

As we followed up with witnesses, I found an army of former employees who were more than happy to testify against King Nothing. He was hated, and there was no shortage of people waiting for their shot at him.

By the time the case ended, we had six witnesses backed up by hundreds of texts and emails. As it turned out, they had all been waiting for the bully to stumble. When the castle fell, King Nothing had no one to rule over, and no one to blame but himself. I think Metallica said it best:

Where's your crown, King Nothing?

[Summary]

- Bullying is not illegal by itself, but it can be under certain circumstances. The difference is whether the bullying is motivated by your protected characteristics.

- Protected characteristics include your race, color, national origin, religion, disability, age (40+), sex, and pregnancy.
- Malicious intent is common, but it is not required to prove harassment.
- Harassment causes a hostile work environment when it is severe (meaning it is so outrageous it has no place in civil society) and/or pervasive (meaning it occurs frequently).
- Isolated instances of harassing behavior are usually not enough to establish a hostile work environment.
- Generally, employers are automatically liable for harassment from supervisors. They are *not* liable for harassment from non-supervisors, unless they knew or reasonably should have known you were being harassed and they failed to help.
- A written complaint of harassment makes it harder for the employer to escape responsibility.

[CHAPTER 5]

Sexual Harassment

LET'S GO SELL YOUR FACE

My client, who we will call Emily, worked in business-to-business (B2B) sales. Without giving too much away, her job was to close large software sales with businesses in the real estate management space. These were competitive deals that required lots of traveling and face time with prospective customers.

Her boss was the top salesman for years before being promoted to management. He was an old-school sales bro, reminiscent of Greg Weinstein (played by Nicky Katt) in the 2000 film *Boiler Room*.

Emily's boss, who we will call Greg, acted just like the character in the movie. Slick talker, shiny Rolex, expensive BMW, and *lots* of misogyny.

On sales calls, Greg would say to Emily, "I need you dolled up at these meetings. It's the sex factor that wins at these things."

Of course, he insisted that she had full hair and makeup for every meeting. He forbade her from wearing pants or flat shoes. It had to be skirts and heels. Emily had to keep an eye on Greg. He ogled her constantly, which isn't illegal on its own, but he also liked to get extremely close so that his hands could brush against her legs. Though Emily became a master of the last-minute lean to avoid being groped, she was not always successful. Greg thought he was slick with these "accidents," but it was a persistent problem Emily was forced to endure to keep her job.

Oh, and one more thing Greg required:

"These guys like when you show a little cleavage. Not so much that it's slutty, just enough to get them interested. That's how we edge out the losers at our competitors."

Unfortunately, my client Emily was very young. She went along with Greg's abuse because it was clear that her job depended on following his instructions, no matter how humiliating and degrading they were. But as time went on, his sexually charged behavior became worse (and more frequent).

During a sales call in San Francisco, Greg said to Emily, "Let's go sell your face."

They went to an office downtown, where Greg led a sales presentation. Emily was instructed to "look pretty" and take notes. During a short break for lunch, Greg pulled her aside. "The client keeps checking you out. If you flirt with him, we'll get the deal."

"That's gross," Emily said, nearing the end of her patience.

Greg shrugged her off. "I'm just saying you can take one for the team."

Later that month, at a company happy hour, Greg had a few too many drinks. And he got handsy. While posing for a group picture, he slid his hand across Emily's lower back, then squeezed her hip.

Emily had had enough.

She swatted his hand away. "I'm done. I'm fucking done with this," Emily said, holding back tears. "You can't treat people like this. I'm a person, Greg!"

Greg smirked at her. "If you're not gonna play the game, then you're not gonna make it in this industry."

Later, as the drinks continued to flow, Greg sent a series of texts that really sealed his fate.

> You could have had a shot with me. You know how much I make. I could have put you in a G-Wagon. But ur nothin now.

> Stuck up bitch.
>
> You think ur special cuz you got big tits?
>
> Stay broke.
>
> You're not gonna make it.
>
> Hot chicks are cheap merch in this industry.
>
> Replaceable like the rest.

Yikes. Quite the Prince Charming, isn't he?

Needless to say, Emily resigned the next morning. But in her rage, she spilled ALL the beans about Greg's disgusting behavior with HR—including screenshots of his misogynistic text messages.* When she applied for unemployment, the company tried to fight it because she resigned. This was true, and the state initially denied her unemployment claim.

BUT.

Remember constructive dismissal from earlier in this book? With some evidence of the sexual harassment Emily experienced, we were able to show she was forced to quit due to Greg's constant groping and sexual comments. That got her some unemployment while we worked on the case.

During litigation, we showed that Emily's rights were violated by Greg and the company in a number of ways:

- Greg's constant comments about Emily's appearance, his absurd demands that she sexualize herself to get sales, plus his constant touching and ogling, all resulted in a hostile work environment.
- Greg made it clear that submitting to his degrading requirements (showing cleavage, full hair and makeup, skirts or dresses only,

*Turns out, Emily was following me on social media before she became a client. She kept copies of her complaint to HR and all the screenshots!

unwanted touching) was a *condition* of remaining employed. The "this in exchange or that" nature of his expectations created a quid pro quo form of harassment.
- The constant sexualization and touching was so outrageous that any reasonable person would feel forced to quit, thus making Emily's sudden resignation a constructive dismissal.
- Greg targeted Emily for harassment specially because she was a woman. This was discrimination and illegal harassment, not merely bullying.
- Greg was a supervisor with hiring and firing power. In California, the company was automatically liable for his conduct.

Altogether, we recovered a large settlement for Emily. She now lives a very happy life in Southern California, where she is working on an advanced degree.

WHAT IS SEXUAL HARASSMENT?

Sexual harassment is illegal in all fifty states. It generally comes in two forms: hostile work environment and quid pro quo. Coincidentally, Greg's actions are an example of both of these illegal forms of harassment.

When people imagine a sexual harassment case, they often think of a 1960s *Mad Men* kind of environment: a few horny men chasing after the pretty young women in the office. Yes, that happens. But sexual harassment comes in many forms, some of which may surprise you. Here are a few cases I handled recently:

- Straight male harassed another straight male by spanking him with tools.
- Straight female harassed another straight female by constantly grabbing her butt and trying to kiss her.
- Male boss set female subordinate's username to FakeBewbz on a work program.

- Male coworkers played pranks by putting gay pornography on each other's work computers.
- Male coworker repeatedly asked female coworker on dates; he sent her over four hundred text messages in a month. (He seesawed between flattering her and calling her a "bitch," depending on his mood.)
- Female HR rep fired for reporting sexual harassment on behalf of someone else. This is considered retaliation, even though the HR rep was not directly harassed.
- Male boss pressured female subordinate to hook up at a company event. The boss hugged her, squeezed her when she tried to pull away, and whispered, "I'm so in love with you."

These are just a few examples. The point is that sexual harassment takes many forms. So let's hit the key facts you need to know.

- **SEXUAL DESIRE IS IRRELEVANT.** Most sexual harassment occurs because the harasser is attracted to the victim. But it's not a legal requirement. It is the *conduct*, not the intent, that matters.
- **BEING OF THE SAME GENDER IS NO EXCUSE.** Especially in blue-collar jobs, I handle a lot of cases where a heterosexual man sexually harassed another heterosexual man (taunting, name-calling, unwanted slapping, etc.).
- **IT DOESN'T MATTER IF IT'S "JUST A JOKE."** Again, the intent is irrelevant. Many abusers are surprised to learn that their "pranks" actually crossed the line between being merely rude and being illegal.
- **CONSENT IS KEY.** No matter how sexually explicit the conduct is, it is not illegal if you consent to it. Remember: The harassment begins when the consent ends. But having a long, documented history of consenting to or tolerating the conduct can make it harder to prove your case.
- **THE COMPANY IS NOT AUTOMATICALLY LIABLE IN MOST CASES.** You don't win a case just by making the allegation. In most situations, you have to show that the company knew of the harassment

and failed to intervene. In some cases, the company may be automatically liable—but you need evidence (such as a written complaint) to establish liability.

The stigma is backward. Standing up to abusers takes courage. Some of my clients are afraid that their reputation will be harmed if they say no. But the *harasser* is the one who is wrong, not you. The *harasser* should be worried about their reputation, not you. Anyone who looks down on you for standing up to an abuser is not someone you want in your circle. **Harassers are counting on your silence. Don't let them win!** They win when you stay silent. And the longer you tolerate the abuse, the worse it is likely to get.

Knowing your rights is half the battle. In this chapter, we will arm you with the knowledge you need to take harassers to task.

SEXUAL HARASSMENT HAS NASTY RIPPLE EFFECTS

A study by Stop Street Harassment found that **81 percent of US women and 43 percent of US men have experienced some form of sexual harassment** in their lifetime.* The Equal Employment Opportunity Commission (EEOC) has said that about one-quarter to one-third of *all* discrimination claims involved some form of sexual harassment.† Over three in every four women over the age of eighteen will experience sexual harassment at work.‡

With these stats in mind, let's dive into what sexual harassment in

*Holly Kearl, *The Facts Behind the #MeToo Movement: A National Study on Sexual Harassment and Assault* (Stop Street Harassment, 2018), stopstreetharassment.org/wp-content/uploads/2018/01/Full-Report-2018-National-Study-on-Sexual-Harassment-and-Assault.pdf.

†United States Equal Employment Opportunity Commission, "EEOC Proposes Updated Workplace Harassment Guidance to Protect Workers," press release, September 29, 2023, eeoc.gov/newsroom/eeoc-proposes-updated-workplace-harassment-guidance-protect-workers.

‡United States Equal Employment Opportunity Commission, "Sexual Harassment in Our Nation's Workplaces," April 2022, eeoc.gov/data/sexual-harassment-our-nations-workplaces.

the workplace typically looks like. All sexual harassment comes in one of two broad categories: hostile work environment and quid pro quo.

HOSTILE WORK ENVIRONMENT

If you flip back to chapter 4, where we talked about harassment, you'll recall that a hostile work environment involves:

- Unwelcome, unwanted, or nonconsensual conduct
- Harassment motivated by a protected characteristic (in sexual harassment cases, your gender is typically the motivating factor, even if the harasser is not attracted to you)
- Harassment so severe that it has no place in civil society, and/or it is occurring so frequently that it is pervasive
- A negative effect on the victim's ability to work or on their employment, such as demotion, termination, failure to promote or hire, or lost wages

Being "motivated" by your gender simply means you are being targeted because of your gender. I know this can be confusing, especially when the harasser is clearly *not* sexually attracted to you. So let's look at an example from one of my prior cases.

Case Study: "Hey, Gaywad!"

Brendan worked in a metal fabrication shop. His boss was extremely insecure and wanted everyone to think he was an "alpha male." The boss liked to bully other men with crude, sexual jokes to embarrass them.

For example, he liked to call Brendan "gaywad" when greeting him.

He also liked to call Brendan a "cuck" when he was angry. Other times, he'd hold up a tool and say, "Want me to spit on it first, gaywad?"*

*For anyone unfamiliar, the "spit on it first" statement implies that he will shove the tool into Brendan's butt. Sexually harassing statements do not need to literally spell out the harasser's intentions to be illegal—innuendo like this is equally unacceptable.

Brendan was *not* gay. And his manager was *not* sexually attracted to him.

Still sexual harassment? Absolutely. A hostile work environment? Yes.

Brendan's boss used abusive language which Brendan did not consent to. He was motivated by Brendan's gender, attempting to insult him by implying he was gay. He also "joked" about shoving tools into Brendan's anus. Again, the boss was motivated by Brendan's gender, because he presumed that making jokes about Brendan's body parts and sexuality would undermine his confidence as a man.

Finally, the conduct was so severe and pervasive that it made it hard for Brendan to feel safe at work. Therefore, this became a hostile work environment.

QUID PRO QUO

The Latin term *quid pro quo* translates to "this for that" in English. In the context of a sexual harassment case, *quid pro quo* means you were forced to submit to sexual harassment *as a condition* of keeping your job, avoiding a punishment, or gaining a benefit at work. Often it is a combination of those things. A simple example would be a boss who promises a raise if you sleep with him. The raise is the *quid,* and the sexual act is the *quo.* The law prohibits employers from abusing their power to extract sexual gratification from their employees.

Now, a boss is probably not going to say, "If you don't have sex with me, then you are fired." I wouldn't put it past some of the weirdos I've sued, but it's not likely. Rather, quid pro quo harassment is generally more subtle. Here is an example from a case I recently handled.

The owner of a business liked to take the youngest and prettiest women at the office on "shopping dates" to help him pick clothes for himself. While trying on clothes, he often "accidentally" exposed himself. In the summer, he held "business trips" in Las Vegas, where he expected women to wear revealing bikinis at pool parties. Those who attended were pressured to hook up with him. Any employees who did not attend were disqualified from promotions, raises, or new accounts.

Here, the "quid" was going on awkward errands, tolerating the boss exposing himself, and going to Vegas, where they were expected to wear revealing swimsuits. The "quo" was being eligible for bonuses and new accounts.

You might be thinking, *Wait a minute, this still sounds like a hostile work environment.* If so, you are absolutely correct! Quid pro quo harassment almost always creates a hostile work environment, but not all hostile work environments involve quid pro quo. Remember, severe and pervasive abuse creates a hostile work environment. Quid pro quo, on the other hand, is when a job, benefit, or punishment is given in exchange for submitting to sexual abuse.

SEXUAL HARASSMENT LAWS PROTECT VICTIMS *AND* WHISTLEBLOWERS

In 2022 a Los Angeles jury awarded a whopping $460 million verdict to two former employees of the utilities company Southern California Edison (SCE). Both employees complained about pervasive sexual and racial harassment. After filing their complaints, they were subjected to mafia-style retaliation until they were forced to quit.* The company tried to argue that these men had manufactured their complaints to score an easy payday. But after hearing all the facts and evidence, the jury didn't buy it.

Here's the play-by-play:

- Alfredo Martinez and Justin Page worked at SCE in Los Angeles County.

*Astute readers might be thinking, "Constructive dismissal!" If that's you, then you get a giant gold star, because you are correct. The plaintiffs proved constructive dismissal to get this massive verdict.

- Page blew the whistle after seeing a supervisor harass female employees.
- Martinez made two whistleblower complaints about supervisors harassing women.
- The SCE Ethics department investigated the complaints. The investigation revealed a pattern of sexual misconduct (including one supervisor masturbating in the office).
- Three supervisors were terminated. However, their allies remained employed.
- Those allies launched a retaliatory campaign against Page and Martinez, including threats, shoving, and false accusations of misconduct.
- Martinez was slapped with *seven* different investigations after he blew the whistle. The sham investigations resulted in Martinez being referred for termination.
- Meanwhile, Page was diagnosed with PTSD due to the abuse from supervisors and the company.
- The company insisted that they had taken appropriate action by terminating the supervisors. They also claimed that Martinez and Page were lying about the retaliation. However, the jury saw the truth. SCE got slapped with a grand total of $464,577,265 in damages for the whistleblowers.

I'm not saying everyone who reports harassment will get a Powerball lottery payout. Verdicts like this only occur in cases with substantial evidence and exceptionally heinous conduct. But there's still an important lesson here. Martinez and Page were not *direct* victims of the harassment. They saw bad things happening, so they blew the whistle. I think the jury wanted to reward their courage just as much as they wanted to punish the harassers.

Remember, doing the right thing doesn't always mean you'll score a huge payday. *That's not the point of standing up for what's right.* But if you are smart, if you know the law, if you make a paper trail, then your odds of success are better.

Sample Email Template: Reporting Sexual Harassment You Witnessed

Dear Manager,

I am writing to report sexual harassment I witnessed against my coworker, Gabi, by our supervisor, Paul. On Tuesday, May 18, I witnessed Paul asking Gabi if she was "into chicks" and if she'd ever been in a threesome. Gabi was clearly uncomfortable, but Paul keeps making jokes about Gabi's sexuality, including disgusting comments about whether she'd engage in a three-way with Paul and another woman.

This conduct is severe and pervasive, and I believe it is causing a hostile work environment. What will the company do to help?

Respectfully,
Employee

WARNING SIGNS

It is *not* your fault if you get harassed at work. But if we can spot warning signs before the abuse starts, then we should pay attention!

Beware of bosses who ask lots of personal questions right out the gate: "Do you have a boyfriend?" "Are you married?" "What's your type?" None of these are appropriate in a job interview, and they are a clear sign that the boss is interested in something beyond an employment relationship.

Watch their eyes. Yes, we are all human and we may check each other out from time to time. But millions of years of evolution has blessed us with a sixth sense. That burning feeling you get someone is staring at you? That's your DNA warning you of a predator. Pay attention to people whose gaze makes you uncomfortable.

And that's the key point here: Trust your gut. If someone creeps you out, there's a high probability it will get worse. Avoid them if possible. Report unwanted conduct *in writing* as early as possible. You'll see plenty of examples about how to do this later in this book!

ADDRESSING COMMON FEARS ABOUT STANDING UP TO HARASSERS

To close this chapter, let's take a moment to address the two biggest fears that keep you trapped when you feel harassed, and the facts that will set you free.

FEAR: No one will hire me if I sue a boss for harassment.

FACT: I have *never* had a client who was unable to find work because they sued a harasser. I'm not saying it's *impossible* the lawsuit will affect your future employment. I'm saying that these fears are overexaggerated. Besides, do you really want to work for someone who only hires people who tolerate sexual harassment?

FEAR: What if people don't believe me?

FACT: The first thing most abusers do is deny the abuse. This *is* something I see quite often. But it's very simple to protect yourself. The evidence matters. Keep copies of texts and emails. Make a note of who witnesses the harassment. Keep copies of all your complaints.

The company can lie, the abuser can make excuses, but when confronted with a paper trail, their façade withers.

The age of fear is over. We know our rights, and we are embracing our power.

Summary

- Sexual harassment comes in two main forms: hostile work environment and quid pro quo.
- Hostile work environment harassment can occur when there is severe and/or pervasive sexual misconduct.
- Quid pro quo harassment is when a job, benefit, or punishment is conditioned on whether or not you submit to sexual abuse.
- Consent is key. The harassment begins when the consent ends. You should make it clear as early as possible that you do *not* welcome the harassment.
- Desire is irrelevant. Sexual attraction is not required. Intent is irrelevant. It does not matter if the harasser was "just kidding."
- The law protects the direct victims of harassment as well as whistleblowers who stand up for them.
- Fears of blacklisting or reputational harm are understandable. However, they are generally overestimated. Knowing your rights and making a paper trail is key to preventing these problems.
- Trust your gut. Your instincts can warn you that someone is bad news long before they start acting out.

[CHAPTER 6]

Discrimination

SHORTCHANGED

In 2019 Disney employee LaRonda Rasmussen made an infuriating discovery. One that eventually led to a $43 million lawsuit.

LaRonda was a highly respected product development manager who had worked at Disney for over eleven years. In that time, she went above and beyond, missing weekends, birthdays, and family gatherings in order to prioritize her job. She was a true believer in "Disney magic." And she worked tirelessly to deliver that magic.

Being a woman in the cutthroat Los Angeles entertainment industry is hard; being a woman of color is even harder. But LaRonda was a team player. For years, she had received high marks and was praised for her work.

But the rumor around the office was that—despite her good work—she was the *lowest paid* product development manager.

How could that be? After all she'd sacrificed, all the years of hard work, would Disney really do this to her?

LaRonda looked for answers. She sent an inquiry to HR with a simple question: How did her pay stack up against other employees with similar jobs and experience? What she learned made her feel sick.

Despite being one of the most senior employees, she was the lowest paid in her role. The hits didn't stop there. She wasn't just underpaid; she was *grossly* underpaid.

In 2017 LaRonda earned $109,958. An impressive salary, to be sure, but in that same year, *each* of the six men with the same job title (senior product manager) had considerably higher base pay, at least $16,000 more in base salary alone. Comparing her pay to the *average* base salary of the male senior product managers, LaRonda was being shorted over $50,000 per year.

But then things got worse.

Not only was she paid less than the lowest-paid man, but she was paid less than her own subordinate employees. One of the male senior product managers, a new hire, had several years *less* experience than LaRonda, but he was paid $20,000 more than her annually.

LaRonda's shock turned to outrage. She was doing the same work as the men, yet she was being paid substantially less than any of them. Was she really being shortchanged just because she was a woman? It was such an egregious and unjustifiable offense.

In response to LaRonda's questions about pay equity, Disney's human resources tried to claim the reason she was underpaid was *not* due to her gender but could not offer any other explanation for the massive pay gap. Obviously, HR was just covering for the blatant discrimination. So LaRonda filed suit along with several other Disney employees who had been shorted due to their gender.

During the lawsuit, experts estimated (but did not conclusively confirm) that Disney had underpaid female employees by about $150 million compared to men. Ultimately, after several years of litigation, Disney caved. They agreed to pay $43 million to women like LaRonda. They also agreed to hire experts to prevent future gender discrimination based on pay.

While LaRonda eventually got justice for herself and other women like her, the truth is that discrimination is far more rampant at work than many realize. According to the US Department of Labor, women working the *same* jobs as men typically earn just 84 percent of what their male peers earn.*

---

*United States Bureau of Labor Statistics, "Women's Earnings Were 83.6 Percent of Men's in 2023," *TED: The Economics Daily,* March 12, 2024, bls.gov/opub/ted/2024/womens-earnings-were-83-6-percent-of-mens-in-2023.htm.

But as staggering as these statistics are, let's not lose sight of the forest for all the trees. The primary problem with discrimination is that it robs *you* of your money and your inherent right to be treated as a human being. You are entitled to a fair shot. You deserve to be paid according to the value you bring, not by your race, sex, age, or anything else.

WHAT IS DISCRIMINATION?

The D-word gets thrown around quite a bit. I've had many employees come to me and say, "My boss shows favoritism to his buddies, is this discrimination?"

Probably not.

Here's a quick test to see if you might be suffering from illegal discrimination at work:

1. You suffered an adverse employment action (recall this term from chapter 3).
2. You suffered the adverse employment action *because* of discriminatory reasons, such as your protected class (also called protected characteristics earlier in the book).
3. The adverse employment action, which was motivated by discriminatory reasons, resulted in some kind of measurable harm, such as lost wages.

Remember, it is *not* illegal to be an asshole. If your boss is a giant jerk to you just because they don't like you personally, then it's not discrimination. It becomes *illegal* discrimination when these things happen because of your protected class.

Adverse Employment Actions

Legally, discrimination is when you suffer an adverse employment action *because* of your protected class. As you might remember, *adverse employment action* means you were denied some right or benefit at your job. Examples include:

- Being denied a job you are qualified to do
- Being paid less than similarly qualified candidates for the same work
- Getting fired, demoted, or given undesirable assignments
- Being held to unreasonable performance standards not expected of other employees
- Severe and frequent harassment, such as slurs, jokes at your expense, threats, or other bullying behaviors motivated by your protected characteristics

Protected Classes

Discrimination becomes illegal when a protected class is involved. Several federal statutes *specifically prohibit* discrimination against certain protected classes. As you'll recall, protected classes include race, national origin, gender, disability, religion, LGBTQ+ identity, and age (40+). Everyone has a protected class of some sort.

Are you dealing with a disability, even temporarily? Protected class.

Are you a man, woman, or something in between? Protected class.

Do you practice a religion? Protected class.

Are you pregnant or might you become pregnant? Protected class.

Are you over forty? You guessed it, protected class.

(And before you ask, yes, discrimination against white people, cis men, heterosexuals, or other historically privileged groups is rare, but it does happen! When it does, it is equally unlawful and subject to the same protections as anyone else. And if I may take the soapbox for a moment, this is why I take offense to any notion that antidiscrimination laws give "special" rights to some but not others. It is simply not true. You are protected from discrimination based on your protected class, regardless of whether you are a member of a historically marginalized group or not.)

Here are some examples of the statutes that have created protected classes:

- **TITLE VII OF THE CIVIL RIGHTS ACT OF 1964 (TITLE VII):** Prohibits employment discrimination based on race, color, religion, sex, and national origin.
- **EQUAL PAY ACT OF 1963 (EPA):** Requires equal pay for substantially similar work.
- **AGE DISCRIMINATION IN EMPLOYMENT ACT OF 1967 (ADEA):** Prohibits discrimination against people who are 40+ years old.
- **AMERICANS WITH DISABILITIES ACT OF 1990 (ADA):** Prohibits discrimination against qualified individuals with disabilities in employment. Requires employers of fifteen or more workers to provide reasonable accommodations unless doing so would impose an undue hardship.
- **GENETIC INFORMATION NONDISCRIMINATION ACT OF 2008 (GINA):** Prohibits discrimination based on genetic information in hiring, firing, promotions, and benefits. Specifically, this prohibits discrimination based on family medical history and genetic testing results.
- **PREGNANCY DISCRIMINATION ACT OF 1978 (PDA):** Prohibits discrimination based on pregnancy, childbirth, or related medical conditions.
- **UNIFORMED SERVICES EMPLOYMENT AND REEMPLOYMENT RIGHTS ACT OF 1994 (USERRA):** Prohibits discrimination against individuals who serve or have served in the military.
- **FAMILY AND MEDICAL LEAVE ACT OF 1993 (FMLA):** Prohibits retaliation against employees who take protected family or medical leave. Applies to employees who work at a location where their employer has fifty or more people within a seventy-five-mile radius.

Virtually all government employers and labor unions are required to follow these antidiscrimination laws. Most private employers are covered as well, but small employers may be excused. If the employer has *fifteen or more employees,* then it is covered by antidiscrimination rules on the basis of race, color, religion, sex (including pregnancy), national origin, disability, or genetic information. State laws may apply to smaller employers. And if the employer has twenty or more employees, then it is covered by antidiscrimination rules on the basis of age (40+). Again, additional state laws may apply to smaller employers to protect employees.

States are free to make their own antidiscrimination laws so long as they offer *more* protections than the federal rules. For example, under federal law, employers of fifteen or more workers must provide reasonable accommodations. But in California, we have additional state laws that require employers of five or more employees to provide reasonable accommodations.

WHEN IS DISCRIMINATION *LEGAL*?

I have seen employers refuse to hire applicants *specifically because they were women*. Illegal, right? Not so fast. Like most laws, there are exceptions. Discrimination is *legal* in certain situations. Broadly speaking, there are four scenarios in which discrimination is legal.

1. **CHURCHES AND RELIGIOUS ORGANIZATIONS** are allowed to discriminate as part of their religious practice. This is because all laws are *not* created equal in the US. The Free Exercise Clause of the First Amendment trumps Title VII of the Civil Rights Act.

   EXAMPLE: A Catholic charity can refuse to hire non-Catholics.

2. **BONA FIDE OCCUPATIONAL QUALIFICATIONS (BFOQs)** allow employers to discriminate when doing so is reasonably necessary for the operation of the business.

   EXAMPLE: A production company can legally refuse to hire a woman to play the role of King Shaka Zulu in a theatrical production about his life.

3. **UNDUE HARDSHIPS** are an exception to the general rule that employers covered by workplace disability laws must provide reasonable accommodations for certain conditions.

   EXAMPLE: A sewing company can refuse to hire an applicant with no hands if finding a way to accommodate them would be too expensive or complicated. Again, there are limits to this exception, which we will discuss in chapters 14 and 15.

4. **DISPARATE IMPACT CASES** occur when an employment policy affects members of a protected group more than others. Disparate impact cases can get *really* interesting (not to mention scandalous). Discrimination based on disparate impact is sometimes legal. It is legal when (1) the policy is justified as a business necessity and (2) a less discriminatory policy isn't feasible.

   EXAMPLE: A fire department can require applicants to be able to lift fifty pounds unassisted. This will disproportionately impact candidates who are women, older workers, and people with disabilities. But because firefighters must regularly lift heavy equipment, this policy is legal.

HOW DO I PROVE DISCRIMINATION?

This may shock you, but in all my years as a lawyer, I have *never* had an employer tell one of my clients, "I am firing you because you are Black." Even the stupidest bosses in the world know that would get them in trouble. So when a bad boss wants to illegally discriminate against you, they will resort to a few common tactics. These include but are not limited to:

- Setting unrealistic standards for you but not for others.
- Unfairly enforcing work policies against you but not others.

- Excluding you from opportunities to gain training, advancement, or raises.
- Harassing, bullying, and degrading you until you quit out of frustration.

To prove illegal discrimination has occurred, you must be able to prove that you experienced *unequal treatment*. Let's look at another example.

My client, who we will call Todd, worked for a law firm (yes, I sue law firms too sometimes). Todd was a paralegal, and he was taught to save client files a certain way by his manager, who we will call Biff.

Biff was obnoxious. He got his job by being the loudest, most confident man in the room, not because of his skills, which were sorely lacking. Biff loved to swear. Everything was "fuck this" and "fuck that." He also had a general disregard for rules, thinking he was somehow above them. Biff had no tolerance for people who questioned him.

"There's two ways of doing things," he told Todd. "You do it my way, or you don't do it at all, because you'll be fired."

Not much room for negotiation there, right? And that became a problem, because Biff ordered Todd to organize client files in a way that violated the firm's policies (this became a big problem, so remember this fact). Anyway, Biff and his paralegals attended a company dinner not long after this. During the dinner, Biff got drunk and started making offensive jokes.

"I'm glad we can say f*g again," he slurred, his breath stinking from booze. "Doesn't mean anything against gay people, but if someone's being a little f*ggy you gotta tell 'em."

Obviously, this was gross behavior, but it got worse.

"Hey, Biff," Todd said quietly, "I don't know if you knew this, but I'm married to a man. I'm not really a fan of that word."

"Oh, come on, Todd." Biff scoffed. "It's not an antigay thing. It's just a joke, like, 'Oh, quit being a little f*g.'"

Repulsed, Todd sent an email to HR the next day. The subject line was *Harassment and Discrimination*. He complained that Biff was using language that unfairly discriminated against gay employees. Todd was smart; he saved a copy of the email as a PDF to his personal hard drive.

And thank goodness he did, because the following Friday, he was fired. The letter accused him of "falsifying records against company policy."

But was that really what happened? Todd didn't falsify anything. He saved files under a naming protocol that Biff ordered him and the other paralegals to use. To cover their tracks, HR wrote up all the other paralegals who had followed Biff's orders, but Todd was the only one who was fired.

Why? Because Todd was gay and he reported Biff's use of the word "f*g" at a company event. The firm claimed Todd was fired for violating policy, but his unequal treatment compared to the other employees made the truth undeniable: Biff and the firm were substantially motivated by Todd's protected class. We sued them for wrongful termination, harassment, retaliation, and discrimination on the basis of sex. (In 2020 the US Supreme Court held in *Bostock v. Clayton County, Georgia* that firing an employee merely for being gay violates Title VII of the Civil Rights Act of 1964. Until that time, it was legal in some states to discriminate against gay employees.)

WHAT IF THEY DON'T SAY WHY I WAS FIRED?

Oh, and if an employer refuses to say why you've been fired? If discrimination is involved, it doesn't matter *what* the reason they give is, or if they give no reason at all. I once sued a pizza shop for wrongfully terminating a pregnant employee. My client requested a modified schedule to accommodate her pregnancy. Other employees had gotten accommodations for other reasons in the past, so she figured it wasn't a big deal. But the boss *really* did not want to accommodate her. He said her position was eliminated "at will." My client asked why she was fired. The boss insisted that he did not have to say why.

Although the boss declined to say *why* he fired my client, it was clear he would not have done so if she had not been pregnant. He had made accommodations for other employees in the past, but for some stupid reason, he drew the line at pregnancy.

My client didn't want special treatment. She wanted the *same* treatment that everyone else got. But instead of treating her the same, he slapped her with an adverse employment action in the form of a termination. The point: You do not need a "confession" to enforce your rights; the facts and the evidence will speak for themselves!

THE ELEPHANT IN THE ROOM

Let's say a new manager recently took over. They won't say it out loud, but secretly, they don't want Black employees in their department. They know better than to just fire them, so the new manager concocts a plan: *I can't fire them for being Black, but if I watch these employees like a hawk, I can eventually catch them violating company policy. Then I can use that as my "legal reason" to fire them.*

You may have seen bosses do this in your career, perhaps even to you. The boss is motivated by a discriminatory purpose, but they are watching for alleged "violations." And this raises an important question: If you make mistakes at work, doesn't that make it *legal* to fire you, even if the boss has discriminatory motives?

The answer may surprise you.

Case Study: Flexing on a Racist Employer

Bodybuilder Röbynn Europe had it all, or so it seemed. She was a successful athlete, winning recognition from *Muscle & Fitness* magazine for her achievements in competitive fitness. Her notoriety scored her a dream job. She was selected as a personal training manager at one of the most prestigious gyms on Manhattan's Upper East Side: Equinox.

But what started as a dream soon turned into a nightmare. Röbynn was a Black woman in a luxury gym surrounded by old money and old ideas.

One of her subordinates, a white man, refused to acknowledge her authority as his boss. We will call him Racist Jock, or RJ for short. RJ undermined Röbynn in front of staff and customers, challenging her authority and deliberately calling her expertise into question. RJ disobeyed Röbynn's instructions, leaving work unfinished and creating problems for her to deal with. All along the way, RJ pointed to the problems he created as proof that she "didn't belong." RJ didn't just have a problem with Röbynn but with every nonwhite staff member. He called these employees "lazy" and vowed to get them fired.

But RJ's contempt for Röbynn was not limited to their working relationship.

RJ objectified Black women in front of Röbynn, talking openly about which ones he found sexually attractive. One evening, he even asked Röbynn to help him flirt with a Black woman at a nearby café. How or why he thought Röbynn would want to help him get laid, we may never know. But the point was the same. Röbynn's authority was challenged, and she was being sexually harassed, *because* she was a Black woman.

Röbynn knew this behavior was unacceptable. She reported it to the general manager. But they ignored her concerns. When a client demanded a white personal trainer instead of Röbynn, the general manager complied with the discriminatory request. Röbynn complained, but nothing came of it. Clearly, the company cared more about racist customers than their own employees.

Shortly after Röbynn spoke up, a troubling pattern emerged. She was disciplined for minor issues like tardiness—even though other managers at her level were never required to log their start and end times. Her complaints about discrimination and harassment were met with silence, but her supposed "tardiness" issues were used as a *pretext* for poor performance. Ultimately, Equinox terminated her.

But Röbynn was a fighter. Years of hardcore training had strengthened her mind as well as her body. She took a stand. She filed a federal lawsuit against Equinox for race and gender discrimination, disability discrimination, and retaliation. The legal process was grueling, and notably, Equinox was able to get the disability and retaliation claims tossed before trial.* But the race and gender discrimination claims survived—meaning a jury *would* hear the evidence and make a verdict. Röbynn and her lawyers pressed on.

The trial was a dogfight. Röbynn presented proof of discrimination, but to discredit her, the company presented over forty documented instances of "tardiness." Their strategy was simple—by showing that Röbynn was not a "perfect" employee, they hoped the jury would believe she was fired for legitimate, nondiscriminatory reasons. But the evidence spoke for itself. The jury heard about RJ's racially motivated insubordination, his sexual comments about Black women's bodies, and the company's refusal to protect Röbynn.

On May 16, 2023, the jury delivered a hammerblow to Equinox. They found the company liable for race and gender discrimination and for maintaining a hostile work environment. Röbynn was awarded $1.25 million in compensatory damages and an additional $10 million in punitive damages—a total of $11.25 million plus attorneys' fees, costs, and interest.

Röbynn's story shows that you have the right to be free from discrimination *even if you have made mistakes at work*. There is no requirement that you be a "perfect" employee to win.

DISPARATE IMPACT DISCRIMINATION: NOT SO INNOCENT

Not all discrimination is intentional, but it is still harmful (and illegal). When an employer has a policy that appears neutral but disproportionately impacts people based on their protected class, we call it *disparate impact discrimination*. Here are some examples so you know what to look for:

- **HIRING PRACTICES:** A company requires all applicants to pass a physical strength test that disproportionately excludes women.

*For my law nerds, Equinox filed successful motions for summary judgment as to those claims.

If the strength test isn't directly related to job performance, this could be considered disparate impact discrimination.

- **EDUCATIONAL REQUIREMENTS:** Requiring a college degree for an entry-level warehouse job when the qualifications are not reasonably related to the job duties. This can cause historically marginalized groups who do not have equal access to higher education to be excluded.
- **HEIGHT AND WEIGHT REQUIREMENTS:** Requiring a minimum height of six feet for firefighters may disproportionately exclude women and certain ethnicities with lower average heights. (Note from a former firefighter: Having a diverse crew with varying heights and weights makes fire crews more effective for various rescue scenarios—bigger is *not* always better!)
- **EMPLOYEE TESTING:** Using a test that favors one group over another, without clear evidence that it predicts job performance.
- **GROOMING POLICIES:** A policy that prohibits natural hairstyles such as braids, locs, or afros will disproportionately impact Black employees. In 2019 California passed the Creating a Respectful and Open Workplace for Natural Hair Act (CROWN Act), which prohibits discrimination based on hair style and texture. A federal CROWN Act was introduced but never passed into law. However, despite the lack of a clear federal statute, discrimination based on race-specific hair textures can still lead to a disparate impact discrimination claim.

Case Study: *Griggs v. Duke Power Co.*

By the mid-1960s, the Civil Rights Movement was in full swing. In 1954 the Supreme Court ruled in *Brown v. Board of Education* that racial segregation in schools was unconstitutional. In 1963 Dr. Martin Luther King Jr. led the March on Washington for Jobs and Freedom. One year later, the Civil Rights Act of 1964 was signed into law by President Lyndon B. Johnson. But the battle for civil rights was still raging. Since racial discrimination was illegal, some employers found subtle ways to protect the old status quo.

Enter Duke Power and one of its Black employees, Willie Griggs.

Willie worked at Duke Power's Dan River hydroelectric plant in Draper, North Carolina. The company had five departments: Labor, Coal Handling, Operations, Maintenance, and Laboratory and Test. Prior to 1965 (the effective date of the Civil Rights Act), the company had an open policy of anti-Black discrimination: Black employees like Willie Griggs were *only* eligible to work in the Labor department. Notably, the *highest paid* jobs in the Labor department received less than the *lowest paid* jobs in the other four departments, where only white employees were allowed. Even after the Civil Rights Act had passed, Duke did not want Black employees in the "whites only" departments. So the leadership at Duke concocted a scheme.

They made an "aptitude test" that—officially—applied to all employees. However, there was a catch. Duke knew that Black employees had less access to public resources, such as a high school education. So they made a test that would exclude Black workers without specifically saying anything about race. The tests were carefully designed to *look* neutral while giving a consistent advantage to white employees. For example, the mechanical comprehension component tested applicants on concepts that generally only white employees would have been taught. It was diabolical enough to work and subtle enough to get away with.

Or so they thought.

Willie Griggs and twelve other Black employees saw through the scheme. They filed a lawsuit alleging Duke's "aptitude tests" were designed to exclude Black employees. In its defense, Duke claimed that the tests applied equally to all.

The Supreme Court was not convinced by Duke's arguments. First, the court shot down the idea that standardized tests were an effective tool for measuring employee aptitude: "History is filled with examples of men and women who rendered highly effective performance without the conventional badges of accomplishment in terms of certificates, diplomas, or degrees,"* the court said. Second, the court ruled that

*Griggs v. Duke Power Co., 401 U.S. 424, 434 (1971).

even when discriminatory intent does not exist, the *impact* of a policy can be discriminatory nonetheless.

It is interesting to note that this case went through three federal courts: a district court (which heard the case first), a court of appeals, and then the Supreme Court. But as the case churned through the courts, the *impact* of the policy became more important than its *intent*.

The Supreme Court then issued its landmark decision that forever changed discrimination law in the US: Even if there is no discriminatory intent, employers may not impose requirements that effectively exclude people based on their protected class.

Employers who impose requirements like this must show that (1) the policy is job-related and justified by business necessity and (2) less discriminatory alternatives are not possible.

HOW DO I KNOW IF IT'S DISPARATE IMPACT DISCRIMINATION?

Disparate impact discrimination tends to get swept under the rug. Sometimes the discrimination is not *intentional,* but like the saying goes, "The road to hell is paved with good intentions." It's no excuse to say the employer did not *intend* to discriminate against you.

Here are the warning signs that a policy is discriminatory, even if the discrimination is not intentional:

- The policy makes *assumptions* about your abilities based on your race, age, sex, pregnancy status, or disability.
- The policy deals with groups as a whole, rather than accounting for individual merit and ability.
- The same business needs could easily be served with a less restrictive policy. For example, giving pregnant employees an opportunity to request light duty if needed serves the same purpose as but is less restrictive than automatically removing them from full duty.

Case Study: US Customs and Border Protection

In 2024 US Customs and Border Protection (CBP) paid $45 million to settle workplace discrimination claims against about one thousand former and current CBP employees.*

For years, CBP had a policy that allowed sick or injured workers to request light duty for their assignments. Light duty was an option for people too injured to fulfill their normal duties, especially in the short term. But it came at a price: fewer advancement opportunities, lower performance metrics, and sometimes less pay. For an injured worker, requesting light duty was no small decision.

But there was a disturbing catch to CBP's light duty rules.

When an employee became pregnant, they were *automatically* assigned to light duty. Pregnant workers assigned to light duty were given little to no say in the matter—even if they were still able to fulfill their normal duties. The result was disastrous. Pregnant employees assigned to light duty got substantially fewer opportunities for overtime, promotion, and training.

In a statement about the case, lead plaintiff Roberta Gabaldon said, "Announcing my pregnancy to my colleagues and supervisor should have been a happy occasion—but it quickly became clear that such news was not welcome. The assumption was that I could no longer effectively do my job, just because I was pregnant. It was traumatizing, frustrating and demoralizing."†

According to CBP, the policy was a safety precaution and no discriminatory impact was intended. Still, the loss of income, training, and promotion opportunities meant that employees were effectively punished for being pregnant.

**Roberta Gabaldon et al. v. Secretary Alejandro Mayorkas*, U.S. Department of Homeland Security (CBP), EEOC No. 450-2017-00086X.

†Cohen Milstein, "Customs & Border Protection Employees Reach $45 Million Settlement After Uncovering Widespread Pregnancy Discrimination," press release, August 13, 2024, cohenmilstein.com/customs-border-protection-employees-reach-45-million-settlement-after-uncovering-widespread-pregnancy-discrimination.

In addition to the $45 million settlement, CBP was required to make significant changes to its light duty policies:

- The policy must assume pregnant employees can continue performing their regular duties unless they request light duty.
- CBP was required to publish a list of accommodations available to pregnant employees.
- The agency also agreed to provide mandatory training for supervisors about pregnancy discrimination and reasonable accommodation rights.

Pay attention to policies at your job. Make sure that unequal enforcement or unequal rules have a legitimate business-related purpose. And if they don't, then it's time to speak up.

HOW DO I REPORT DISCRIMINATION?

It can seem impossible to fight back when things that make you feel powerless, like discrimination, happen. But as I've said over and over in this book, the solution is to know the warning signs and create a paper trail!

Be on the lookout for any sign that *you* are being held to a different standard than other employees. If so, then ask, "Is there a plausible, nondiscriminatory reason?" If not, then the reason may be discriminatory. From there, look for other signs. In the Equinox case study, Röbynn knew RJ had biases against people of color because he called them "lazy." She also knew the unequal treatment was racially motivated because clients in her gym requested not to have a Black trainer. She did the right thing by speaking up! Without the paper trail of protected complaints, it would have been easier for Equinox to claim she was fired for violating the attendance policy even though no other manager was held to that standard.

Keep a record of everything—emails, incidents, and your efforts to address the issues. A protected complaint to management or HR *in writing* helps establish that you are being targeted. Here is a sample email to help you get started:

Sample Email Template: Reporting Discrimination

Dear Human Resources,

I am writing to report discrimination I am experiencing at work.

On [DATE], I experienced an adverse employment action in the form of [describe what happened—keep your tone neutral and stick to the facts].

I sincerely believe the adverse employment action was motivated by my [race, sex, religion, national origin, etc.].

The discrimination I am experiencing is severe and pervasive, and among other things, it is creating a hostile work environment for me.

What will the company do to help?

Respectfully,
Employee

Summary

- Discrimination is when you are targeted for adverse employment actions because of your protected class.
- Adverse employment actions are things like refusal to hire you, termination, demotion, retaliation, or harassment.
- Protected classes include but are not necessarily limited to race, color, sex, religion, national origin, genetic information, pregnancy, age (40+), disability, and military service.

- Historically dominant groups, such as straight white men, are equally protected by antidiscrimination laws.
- Companies will sometimes use a pretext, such as poor performance, to conceal illegal discrimination. Your written complaint of discrimination helps protect you from this tactic.
- Telltale signs of illegal discrimination include unequal treatment, unequal enforcement of company policy, setting impossible (or very difficult) expectations not required of other employees, and offensive statements about your protected class.
- Disparate impact discrimination is when an employment policy appears neutral on its face but tends to negatively impact certain groups more than others. This can be intentional or unintentional.
- Warning signs that you are being singled out by a policy include: (1) It makes assumptions about your abilities based on your protected class; (2) it deals with groups as a whole, without regard for individual merit or ability; and (3) it could easily be replaced with a less restrictive policy.
- You should report discrimination right away, in writing, to your manager or HR.

PART II

Protect Your Money

LIE: Loyalty and hard work will be rewarded.

TRUTH: The silent workhorse will work until they collapse, then they will be unceremoniously replaced.

WHALES AND WAGE THEFT

I represented a woman who was wrongfully denied proper pay. This employee went above and beyond, working twelve-plus-hour days to finish a sales pitch for a new client. Her boss emphasized that this client was a "whale."

"If we bag this whale, we are in the money," he said. "Give this pitch everything you've got."

She sacrificed her sleep, her social life, her morning workouts—everything—to make the deal happen.

But when payday came, her check was the same as it had always been.

Naturally, she felt pissed off. Was there some mistake? Where was the extra money? What about overtime pay? She had worked herself nearly to death to help her boss win a big contract—surely he simply forgot to pay for her extra hours.

She approached her boss and asked, "Don't I get overtime pay?"

The boss scrunched his nose as if she had just farted in his office.

"Everyone's always got their hands out," he huffed to himself. "I had to work for years to get here, and you want all this money because why? Because you worked hard for a week?"

"Shouldn't I be paid for the extra time I put in?"

The boss glared at her. "You're paid a salary, not hourly. I don't have to pay overtime, and even if I did, what does it say about *you* that every time you think you put in some effort, you come in here looking for free money? Think about what kind of reputation you want in this industry."

Quite the peach, that guy was.

The boss manipulated my client with half-truths. Yes, salaried employees are generally not eligible for overtime pay. But a boss can't just *say* you are salaried exempt to avoid paying overtime! There are special requirements an employee must meet to be exempt from overtime pay. As it turned out, the boss didn't pay attention to any of those requirements—he was just stealing from his employees!

Wage theft takes many forms; over the next four chapters, we will learn to spot them. Sometimes it's an intentional scheme to enrich the employer at your expense. Other times it's an honest mistake. (You still need to know your rights so you can fix the mistake!)

We are not going to assume all employers are stealing. We will take a practical, informed approach to the question of whether you are being paid what you have earned, and whether it accurately reflects your worth. You work for money. There's no honor in sacrificing your well-being for a company. In the United States, we tend to celebrate "the grind," glorifying the idea that the world owes us nothing. You must sacrifice endlessly, for years, maybe even your whole life, just for a shot that *maybe* one day you will get to be the boss.

That "one day" is the carrot on a stick. If you ever caught the carrot, then your boss would have nothing left to dangle in front of you. They want you always chasing, always reaching. Too close to the carrot to give up now, but just far enough that you'll never catch it. And chasing that damn carrot will cost you a lot of time and energy over the course of your career.

The popular narrative in the US is that you must always give 110 percent, wake up early, stay up late, work through lunch, say yes to every project.

My friends, this is the path to burnout. This line will likely get me some flak, but it needs to be said: **Hard work has no intrinsic value. It serves no purpose at all if it is not serving *you*.** In part II, we're going to make sure you get paid for your work. In the preface of this book, I shared my own experience with wage theft as an EMT. The financial cuts added up terribly over my six months at that job.

Wage theft takes billions of dollars from hardworking people every year, making it among the costliest crimes in the United States. The Economic Policy Institute, a nonpartisan think tank devoted to researching issues that affect working-class people, made the following findings about wage theft in the US:

> *[The] failure to pay what workers are legally entitled to can be called wage theft; in essence, it involves employers taking money that belongs to their employees and keeping it for themselves. Amounts that seem small, such as not paying for time spent preparing a work station at the start of a shift, or for cleaning up and closing up at the end of a shift, can add up. When a worker earns only a minimum wage ($290 for a 40-hour week), shaving a mere half hour a day from the paycheck means a loss of more than $1,400 a year, including overtime premiums. That could be nearly 10 percent of a minimum-wage employee's annual earnings—the difference between paying the rent and utilities or risking eviction and the loss of gas, water, or electric service.**

The problem with wage theft is that many Americans are taught from a young age *not* to talk about money. We are told that asking for pay transparency comes off as "rude." We are told that asking for a raise is "greedy." We are told that demanding equal pay for equal work is "entitled."

Not so.

IN THE FOLLOWING PAGES, we will learn what employers must pay you, when they must pay it, and how they should treat you along the way.

Part II covers two broad topics. First, we need to make sure you get paid what you've earned. At a bare minimum, **you deserve (and are**

---

*Brady Meixell and Ross Eisenbrey, *An Epidemic of Wage Theft Is Costing Workers Hundreds of Millions of Dollars a Year* (Economic Policy Institute, 2014), epi.org/publication/epidemic-wage-theft-costing-workers-hundreds. See also David Cooper and Teresa Kroger, *Employers Steal Billions from Worker's Paychecks Each Year* (Economic Policy Institute, 2017), epi.org/publication/employers-steal-billions-from-workers-paychecks-each-year.

legally entitled) to be paid for every hour worked. Second, we need to ensure you are paid **the correct amount for those hours**.

Companies often refuse to pay employees for the correct number of hours they work. Unpaid training, unpaid overtime, or making you work through breaks are all common examples.

Other times, you are paid for the correct *quantity* of time, but the *amount* is incorrect. Paying you your regular rate for overtime, paying less than minimum wage, or taking a portion of your tips are examples I see quite often.

To unlock your full financial potential, first you must learn when you are entitled to be paid, how much you should be paid, and what legal exceptions exist for these rules. Then, armed with this knowledge, you can avoid being underpaid, abused, or straight-up stolen from.

[CHAPTER 7]

Get Paid What You've Earned

CONFESSIONS AT THE TAQUERIA

In 2022 a Mexican restaurant in Northern California was investigated for widespread wage theft against its thirty-five employees. It was called Taqueria Garibaldi, and the case against it became legendary at the US Department of Labor (DOL).

The taqueria had three owners, Eduardo, Hector, and Alejandro (collectively, the "Three Stooges"). They got into some hot water for hiring a fake priest to spy on their employees. In 2023 the US Department of Labor filed a lawsuit against the Three Stooges *not only* for stealing from their workers but also for their clumsy attempts to interfere with the investigation.

The Stooges mostly employed undocumented people. This allowed them to use intimidation tactics to keep workers quiet. The Stooges (illegally) told the employees that if they cooperated with the Department of Labor's investigation, they would get deported.* They also threatened their employees, saying they'd be fired unless they told

*As I write this book, immigration retaliation like this is illegal in California. The logic of these laws is to prevent human trafficking, modern slavery, and human rights abuses. But as you can see in this case, it is far too easy for abusive business owners to hold undocumented immigrants hostage for low pay. However, despite the laws on the books, recent anti-immigrant activity by the Trump administration has seriously jeopardized these protections. Always talk to a local attorney about your options.

investigators that they worked only forty hours a week and were always paid in full.

But that couldn't have been further from the truth. Employees worked long, grueling hours but were not given proper overtime pay. Other times, they were paid nothing at all. They were also expected to work without breaks.

The Stooges were essentially holding the employees hostage while paying less than minimum wage. But messing with people's money never ends well. Despite the threats, some employees fought back. The Stooges were furious to find that many employees were cooperating with the feds.

That's when they got one of the stupidest ideas of all time.

The workers at Taqueria Garibaldi were primarily Catholic. So the Stooges hired a fake priest to conduct confessions at the restaurant. Instead of discussing greed, lust, pride, et cetera, this priest was only interested in work-related "sins."

One employee, Maria, suspected something was off. During her confession, the priest asked, "Do you sometimes have *bad thoughts* about your employer?"

As if we all haven't wanted to give our boss the finger before.

In a stern voice, the priest warned Maria that it was a grave sin to steal from her employer. He then asked if she'd ever stolen, clocked out early, or done anything to harm the restaurant. As a lifelong Catholic, Maria knew this was no normal confession. She immediately reported the strange priest to the Department of Labor investigators.

As weird as the Three Stooges' plan was, some of the employees caved. For fear of eternal damnation, some confessed to minor workplace infractions that hardly justified having their wages stolen, much less getting fired. Fortunately, the Department of Labor caught on pretty fast. They contacted the diocese to ask if any priests had been at Taqueria Garibaldi. Once the diocese confirmed the priest was a fake, attorneys for the DOL called witnesses to expose the bizarre questions this "priest" had asked the employees.

The Three Stooges' plot to cover their tracks collapsed. Ultimately, they got hit with $140,000 in unpaid overtime and liquidated damages, plus another $50,000 in back wages for the affected employees. The DOL also slapped another $5,000 on top of that for the fake priest stunt.*

So what's the point of this story? Why am I talking about Three Stooges and a fake priest in a chapter called "Get Paid What You've Earned"? Because this chapter is all about learning your rights under the Fair Labor Standards Act (FLSA). The employees at the taqueria were all nonexempt, meaning they were entitled to the full rights and protections of the FLSA. Most American workers are nonexempt. And knowing the rules better than your boss is your best weapon against wage theft.

We work for money. A boss who shames you for working "just for the paycheck" is a big-stupid-goober. No human dreams of labor. You need to pay us to make it worth our time.

And time is what this is all really about.

Your time is an irreplaceable resource. Do not give it away for free.

WHAT IS THE FAIR LABOR STANDARDS ACT?

In the 1930s the United States was in turmoil. The Great Depression had ravaged the US economy. Shantytowns—improvised communities of makeshift shelters—sprouted up all around the country as families lost their homes. Lines for soup kitchens snarled around city blocks as laid-off workers struggled to survive. The American economy was on life support because its working class was on life support. And America's troubles could not have come at a worse time.

Across the Atlantic, Hitler's armies prepared for lightning war across Europe. In the Pacific, the Imperial Japanese Navy ruled the waves. Sooner or later, the United States would have to take a stand. But before it could do so, it needed to regain its strength.

---

*I'm aware these damages sound minor considering how gross the Stooges' conduct was, but when we consider the size and revenue of the taqueria, plus the relatively meager means of its owners, I feel assured that justice was served here.

That's why President Franklin D. Roosevelt signed the Fair Labor Standards Act in 1938. The Act, which radically transformed US labor rights as part of the New Deal, was created to give working-class Americans better wages and work conditions. FDR believed that the power of the US economy could be unlocked only if the American people could rely on livable wages, a decent standard of living, and guarantees against abusive labor practices: "A self-supporting and self-respecting democracy can plead no justification for the existence of child labor, no economic reason for chiseling workers' wages or stretching workers' hours."*

The point is that learning your labor rights is not any small thing. I'd argue it's your patriotic duty to be as informed of your rights as possible. So let's take a look at the guarantees under the FLSA in order to understand when you must be paid and how much, and what you can do if a wage thief tries to stiff you.

The rights laid out by the FLSA were designed to get Americans back to work under dignified conditions. By raising the living standard of the working class, the United States had the economic might to outmuscle the Axis powers in World War II. And we retain many of the original rights of the FLSA today, though some have evolved over time:

- You must be paid at least the minimum wage. Currently, the federal minimum wage is $7.25 per hour. If your state or city has a higher minimum wage, then you must be paid that amount.
- The FLSA describes in detail when it is legal to pay less than minimum wage.
- You must be paid for all hours worked. That means any time the employer knows you are working, allows you to work, or exercises control over your time, you must be paid.

*Franklin D. Roosevelt, "Message to Congress on Establishing Minimum Wages and Maximum Hours," May 24, 1937, American Presidency Project, UC Santa Barbara, transcript, presidency.ucsb.edu/documents/message-congress-establishing-minimum-wages-and-maximum-hours.

- Federal law requires that nonexempt workers be paid 1.5 times their regular rate for every hour above their regular forty-hour week. Some exceptions apply, and in some states, like California, you can get overtime sooner.
- Federal law does not require any breaks. But if a break occurs, then there are some rules. Short breaks under twenty minutes generally must be paid. This specifically applies to rest, bathroom, and smoke breaks, but any short break usually counts.
- The FLSA has significant protections and limitations against child labor.

The rights and protections of the FLSA extend to all nonexempt workers in the United States. Nonexempt workers tend to work for hourly wages and/or perform more manual or technical labor. (If you are a salaried worker, you might be classified as exempt, meaning the rights from the FLSA do not apply to you. But we'll talk more about exempt workers' rights in the next chapter.) For now, remember that these are *rights*. They are not optional. If you are a nonexempt worker in the United States, your employer must honor these rules.

MINIMUM WAGE

Most Americans have the right to be paid no less than the minimum wage.* The Fair Labor Standards Act established the first federal minimum wage in the United States. (At the time, the minimum wage was $0.25 per hour.) The Act did not contain an automatic mechanism for raising the minimum wage. Only an act of Congress can raise the minimum wage. Currently, the federal minimum wage is $7.25 per hour. This amount has not changed since Congress voted to raise the minimum wage in response to the Great Recession in 2009.†

*Exceptions exist, which we will discuss later.

†Given fierce opposition in Congress, it is unlikely the federal minimum wage will rise again unless the US faces a national emergency similar to the Great Depression or Great Recession. Generally, labor rights protections are part of a congressional rescue package when the US economy is in trouble.

Despite a few very loud (and wrong) critics, the intent of the minimum wage was always to give employees a living wage, as Roosevelt said:

> *It seems to me . . . that no business which depends for existence on paying less than living wages to its workers has any right to continue in this country. . . . And by living wages I mean more than a bare subsistence level—I mean the wages of decent living.**

As I write this book, the federal minimum wage cannot sustain a simple two-bedroom-apartment lifestyle in *any US state.*† Fortunately, as we learned in chapter 1, the Tenth Amendment to the US Constitution gives states the right to enact their own laws in addition to federal protections, so long as the laws do not conflict with each other. Because of this, many states have higher minimum wages than the federal minimum. States that have no minimum-wage laws default to the federal minimum wage of $7.25 per hour.

SUBMINIMUM WAGES

There are a few circumstances where it is *legal* to pay less than minimum wage. Taking off my lawyer hat for moment, I will say this—just because something is legal doesn't make it right. And if you ask me, no business that pays less than minimum wage, even if they have a legal right to do so, deserves your labor (or your business, for that matter). That said, it is important to know if your job falls into a key minimum-wage exception.

1099 Workers / Independent Contractors

Independent contractors are not entitled to at least the minimum wage because they are not employees. A true 1099 contractor is in busi-

---

*Franklin D. Roosevelt, "Statement on N.I.R.A.," June 16, 1933, American Presidency Project, UC Santa Barbara, transcript, presidency.ucsb.edu/documents/statement-nira.

†"Out of Reach: About the Report," National Low Income Housing Coalition, nlihc.org/oor/about.

ness for themselves, and they are not protected by the Fair Labor Standards Act.

You may be thinking, *But wait! My boss hired me as a 1099 employee!* Buckle up, because I am about to blow your mind.

There is no such thing as a "1099 employee," not legally at least. If you are a "1099 employee," then what's likely happened is you are really an employee, but your employer has illegally misclassified you as a 1099 independent contractor. Employers do this to skirt payroll taxes, avoid paying overtime, avoid labor rights owed to employees, and make it easier to fire you. We'll discuss independent contractors in more detail in chapter 10.

For now, just know that under federal law, it is legal for an independent contractor to earn less than minimum wage.

Disabled Workers

Federal law allows employers to pay disabled employees less than minimum wage. To do this, they must get something called a 14(c) certificate. That's because section 14(c) of the Fair Labor Standards Act allows employers to pay less than minimum wage *only if*:

- The employee has a disability that directly reduces their productivity compared to nondisabled workers in the same role.
- The employer applies for and receives a 14(c) certificate from the Wage and Hour Division of the US Department of Labor (DOL).
- The alternative wage is based on measured productivity, not an arbitrary number.

But don't panic! Your employer cannot slash your pay to below minimum wage just because you are or become disabled. These special conditions must be met, and any employer who automatically slashes your pay due to your disability is likely breaking multiple state, federal, and local laws. Also, be aware that some states have outlawed subminimum wages for disabled workers.

Youth Minimum Wage

Section 6(g) of the Fair Labor Standards Act allows employers to pay young workers as little as $4.25 per hour. We call this the youth minimum wage. Employees under age twenty can be paid $4.25 per hour for the first ninety calendar days of employment. If the employee turns twenty before the ninety days are up, then they automatically must be paid the full minimum wage.

This practice is legal under federal law, but it has been outlawed in several states, including (at the time of writing) California, Delaware, Nebraska, New Mexico, New York, North Carolina, Oregon, and Wisconsin.

Tipped Minimum Wage

Employers may legally pay less than minimum wage when you earn at least thirty dollars per month in tips. **But pay attention, because I see this violation a lot:** You still must receive *at least* minimum wage on your paycheck. Here is how it works:

Under federal law, your employer may pay as low as $2.13 per hour, then use your tips to bring you up to the full minimum wage. If the tips are not enough to meet the full minimum, your employer must pay the difference.

Tipped minimum wages are controversial. The employer basically gets to use your tips to cover their own minimum-wage obligation. And the tipped minimum wage of $2.13, which was set in the 1990s, has never been adjusted for inflation. Some states have their own higher tipped wage. Other have banned tipped minimum wages. We will talk more about tips in chapter 9.

Tipped minimum wages are not legal if your employer has a tip pool. That's when everyone's tips are collected into a pool and then distributed after the shift.

Internships

It is my opinion, based on my experience as a workers' rights lawyer, that most unpaid internships in the private sector are actually illegal.

Not all, but most. That's because, while unpaid internships are allowed, employers must meet special requirements to legally do this, and most employers do not meet the criteria. To legally hire an unpaid intern, the intern must be the *primary beneficiary* of the job. In English, that means the learning opportunities provided to the intern must be worth more than whatever labor the intern produces for the employer. There is a multifactor test for this (which most unpaid internships fail), but as a general rule, a LEGAL unpaid internship has these characteristics:

- The intern is there primarily to learn and gain experience.
- The intern's work is not used as a substitute for regular, paid employees.

If the intern is used for regular work, they must be paid at least minimum wage!

Be very suspicious of all unpaid work. My office pays student interns. Not just because it helps us attract talent, but because it's morally wrong to make people work for free.

"HOURS WORKED" UNDER THE FLSA

Under FLSA regulation, you must be paid for all "hours worked." Sounds simple, right? In my opinion, it *is* simple. If you work, you should get paid. But thanks to a few unscrupulous companies (not to mention those pesky lawyer people), we have to fight about what "hours worked" really means. What-ifs and weird situations come up all the time.

If you're curious whether you must be paid for something you do at work, ask yourself three questions:

1. Am I currently under my employer's control?
2. Is this activity mandatory?
3. Is this activity a necessary or essential part of my job?

If the answer to all of these is YES, it is very likely you must be paid. There are, however, limits to what federal law says must be paid. Here are some common examples of what time is *not* considered "hours worked" under federal law, and therefore is not legally entitled to compensation:

- Time spent commuting to and from work.
    - **Exception:** Employees dropping off mail for the employer after work generally must be paid.
    - **Exception:** Employees dropping off checks or cash at the employer's bank after work generally must be paid.
    - **Exception:** If you are hauling equipment to or from a jobsite, you generally must be paid, even though it is technically a "commute."
- Time spent in security screenings before or after shifts.
- Waiting for an employee shuttle on company property.
- Changing into uniforms usually is not paid either.
    - **Exception:** Time spent donning and doffing (putting on and taking off) protective equipment that is necessary for work must be paid. A common example is a chemical plant worker donning protective gear before their shift.

Waiting Time and On-Call Time

As a firefighter, I was paid for every hour I spent at the fire station. I wasn't always responding to emergency calls. Sometimes I did chores around the station; sometimes I worked out with my crew. Other times, I was sleeping, eating, or showering. I was paid for all these hours because I was ***on call***.

- I had to remain on fire department property during my shift.
- I was forbidden from consuming drugs or alcohol.
- I was required to maintain a state of readiness to quickly respond to calls.

- There were disciplinary measures in place if I did not respond to a call. (Don't worry, this never happened. But we still had rules just in case.)

Not everyone who reads this book is a firefighter, so why should you care? Because all of these firefighter rules also apply to other employees who are on call. When the employer restricts what activities you are allowed to do, places a time limit on how quickly you must respond, and has disciplinary measures for a failure to respond, then it is very likely you must be paid, even if you are "just waiting" for a call.

We call this being *engaged to wait*. Another good example is a receptionist waiting for calls during a slow shift.

There is a flip side to this. Generally, if you are allowed to go home, and if the employer is not placing strict rules on your on-call time, then you may not legally need to be paid. When in doubt, just remember, the more control the employer places on your on-call time, the more likely it is you must be paid.

OVERTIME

Federal law requires employers to pay 1.5 times a nonexempt employee's regular rate for every hour after forty hours worked in a week.

I had a case once against a very famous fast-food restaurant. The franchise owners had about a dozen locations in California. They were successful. They had a new Cadillac Escalade, wore designer clothes, and took expensive vacations.

That lavish lifestyle didn't come cheap, so they found a way to put a little extra cash in their Louis Vuitton wallets—they stole from the kids who worked for them. Here's how the scheme worked:

Instead of following federal law, the owners asked their staff to "volunteer" for overtime. Volunteers were then rewarded for their "good work ethic" with gift cards *to the restaurant*, usually worth only twenty or twenty-five dollars, no matter how much the employees worked.

By the time we'd unraveled the scam, the owners had stolen thousands of dollars from their workers. But those who fuck around must eventually find out. We sued them not just for failure to pay overtime but also failure to pay minimum wage (for the many unpaid hours), failure to provide proper pay statements for the overtime, violation of California child labor laws, violation of California final paycheck rules, and unlawful business practices.

So remember: Nonexempt employees *must* be paid for overtime work. They must be paid in real money, not gifts. And they cannot be asked to "volunteer" for unpaid overtime shifts (or any unpaid shifts!). Otherwise, the employer is committing wage theft.

If you worked overtime hours but were not paid, or were only paid your regular hourly wage, you should first contact your HR and payroll departments. If your company then refuses to pay your correct overtime wage, consider consulting a lawyer.

Sample Email Template: Reporting Unpaid Wages

Dear Human Resources / Payroll,

I am writing to report unpaid wages. My last paycheck was for [TOTAL PAY] and recorded [NUMBER] hours.

This is incorrect. I actually worked [NUMBER] hours, and my regular rate of pay for those hours should be [your regular hourly rate].

If you are missing overtime pay: Also, I worked overtime this pay period. I worked [NUMBER] of overtime hours, and these must be paid at 1.5 times my regular rate, for a total of [1.5 × your regular hourly rate × number of overtime hours].

Please let me know when we can get this corrected and I can collect my correct pay.

Respectfully,
Employee

Note: For most hourly nonexempt employees, your overtime (OT) hours are all hours you worked after forty regular hours in a workweek.

So if you worked a total of forty-six hours in a given week, six would be OT hours (46 total hours − 40 regular hours). Some states, such as Alaska and California, have daily OT rules. In those two states, you can earn OT after working eight regular hours. *Always* consult your state rules to ensure you get every penny you earned!

Unauthorized Overtime

Employers may sometimes discipline workers for something called "unauthorized" overtime. This is when you work beyond your scheduled hours without prior approval from your employer. They are within their rights to discipline you for working without approval, but there is a catch. They still must pay you so long as they knew (or reasonably should have known) you were working and didn't stop you. They must pay even if they are upset. However, if you are sneaking into work to clock extra hours, that may not be legally protected.

Mandatory Overtime

Generally, your employer may require mandatory overtime so long as you are paid properly. If you refuse the mandatory overtime, it may be legal to fire you.

MEAL AND REST BREAKS

Federal law generally does not require any meal or rest breaks no matter how long your shift is. However, if a break occurs, then it must be paid unless (1) you are totally relieved of your duties and (2) the break is twenty minutes or longer.

This means an employer who makes you clock out to use the bathroom is breaking the law.

Some states have their own required meal and rest break rules. In Illinois, for example, employees who work more than seven and a half hours generally must get a twenty-minute unpaid meal break within the first five hours of work. In California, employees who work an eight-hour shift must receive two paid ten-minute breaks and one unpaid thirty-minute meal break.

OTHER POLICIES COVERED (AND NOT COVERED) BY THE FLSA

Labor law can be complicated, but the issues we just discussed are some of the most common concerns you will come across at work. At a minimum, knowing these rules puts you ahead of 95 percent of the population (including your boss!). With that in mind, here are a few more scenarios where it pays to know the law. I personally got ripped off on uniform costs when I was starting out, so let's talk about those first.

Uniforms and Equipment

Any decent company will provide uniforms to employees free of charge. However, there are a lot of cheapskates out there, and sometimes we have to work with them. As a general rule, federal law allows employers to make you pay for your own uniforms.

But there is a HUGE exception!

The uniform costs cannot bring your pay below the federal minimum wage. Here's an example of how the math works on that. Let's say you earn $8 an hour and work 40 hours a week ($320 total pay). Suppose your employer charges you $50 for a work uniform. That would bring your total pay down to $270 for the week ($320 − $50 = $270).

That's a problem. Because minimum wage is $290 per week ($7.25 per hour × 40 hours = $290).

So even though you earned $8 an hour, the $50 uniform brings your effective hourly rate to less than minimum wage, and that is not allowed.

Astute readers (or math whizzes) may have noticed that, based on this formula, you cannot be forced to pay for uniforms if you earn minimum wage. That's correct! Because even if your uniform cost just one dollar, it would bring your total pay down below minimum wage.

Some states have forbidden employers from charging you for uniforms. As I write this book, those include California, Illinois, and New York, plus the District of Columbia.

But in all states, employers can have a store available if you want to supplement your uniform (Cal Fire did this when I was a firefighter, and frankly I did not mind). This is legal, with one little caveat. Employers cannot force you to buy uniforms from a specific vendor if the required clothing is available elsewhere.

Training

Franchises tend to be the worst wage and hour violators I see. In 2022 Subway got absolutely wrecked online when a memo by one of its franchise owners went viral. The memo, allegedly from a Subway store in Michigan, had the following rules:

1. Employees are at will and can be fired at any time, but must provide two weeks' notice to quit.
2. If an employee does *not* provide two weeks' notice, their pay is dropped to minimum wage.
3. The employee will have $200 docked from their final check for training and uniform costs.

I spit out my coffee when I read that memo. There are a *lot* of labor violations here, but let's focus on number 3 for this section. You already know that if you are paid minimum wage, you should not be charged for uniforms. Deducting a uniform expense while dropping you to minimum wage is a no-go.

But what about training?

Training must be paid. The viral Subway memo is illegal because it charges you for something that you should have been paid to do! No matter what your boss says, on-the-job training generally must be paid. There are three major exceptions that you should know about:

1. **VALID INTERNSHIPS AND APPRENTICESHIPS:** So long as they meet the primary beneficiary test we talked about earlier.
2. **CERTIFICATE PROGRAMS:** Training related to your profession but not limited to just your employer doesn't have to be paid. That might sound kind of "legalese," so let me clarify. For example, an EMT taking an afternoon to get a CPR certificate from the Red Cross doesn't have to be paid for that time. But if the ambulance company puts on a mandatory CPR course for its EMTs, then it generally must be paid.
3. **VOLUNTARY TRAINING:** Training does not have to be paid if (1) it is voluntary, (2) it is outside normal work hours, and (3) any work done during the training was primarily for your benefit rather than the employer's.

Rounding Your Time

A rounding policy is when employers take your time and round you up or down to the nearest number. Usually they do this in fifteen-minute intervals. For example, if you clock out at 6:03 p.m., your employer may round you down to 6:00. If you work until 6:08, they may round you up to 6:15.

But some employers use rounding policies to keep your pay low, even when you work long hours. That is wage theft!

I've sued large corporations for improper rounding policies in the past. Remember that a rounding policy is legal only if it generally results in a wash for the employee. That means the rounding sometimes brings you up, sometimes brings you down, but does not result in a net loss over time.

Case Study: Timmy Tooth and the Final Paycheck

You are always entitled to your full final paycheck. Even if you are fired for cause, even if you are fired for misconduct. You must be paid for the hours you worked.

We've all had a know-it-all boss. The kind who very confidently (and loudly) tells people what they think the law is. Unfortunately, they are often wrong.

Such was the case when a sleazy boss fired my client for "poor performance." Really, he just didn't like her personality. That's not illegal, but what *was* illegal was refusing to pay her final check!

My client worked as a receptionist at a small dental office. Her boss, who we will call Timmy Tooth, told her she had to "make up" her unpaid lunch break by staying late. He paid her, but only at her regular rate. He did this even when he should have been paying overtime. She did not know this was illegal, and in fact, she never would have sued Timmy Tooth if he hadn't stiffed her on her final two days of work.

She was owed a little under $550. But when she told me about Timmy Tooth's little "make up" overtime games, I took notes.

As I went through the case with her, we found several big problems.

1. Timmy Tooth made her answer calls while on lunch. This means she was working, which also meant that the break didn't count, and it was illegal not to pay her. That added up to about five hours that she was not paid for each two-week pay period.
2. Because she was still working, the extra thirty minutes at the end of her shift added up to five hours of unpaid overtime every two-week pay period.
3. In California, employers who fail to provide proper meal breaks must pay you an additional hour of pay at your regular rate. This added up to five full hours of extra pay every pay period.

My client had worked at that dental office for about twelve months. As you might guess, these damages added up fast. But I was not done with Timmy Tooth yet!

In California, employers who do not provide your full final pay on your last day incur a penalty. The penalty is equal to one full day of pay for every calendar day the money is late (up to thirty days). Because Timmy Tooth stiffed my client on her last two days of work, and because of all the unpaid hours we discovered, he was on the hook for those penalties.

Now, employers don't just sit there politely while I sue the shit out of them. Timmy Tooth raised some defenses that reduced his total damages. But when the dust cleared and we signed the final settlement, all the damages and attorney's fees against Timmy Tooth added up to about $33,000. All because of a failure to pay a final $550 paycheck!

DO SALARIED EMPLOYEES HAVE RIGHTS TOO? WHAT IF YOU ARE AN EXEMPT EMPLOYEE?

We talked a lot about the rights nonexempt employees get. But what about salaried employees? Specifically, what about those *salaried exempt* employees?

Being *exempt* means you do not get the full protections of the FLSA. That matters, because if an exempt employee works a fifty-, sixty-, or even eighty-hour week, they are not legally entitled to overtime pay.

Most salaried employees are exempt—which is why their pay stays the same week to week even if their hours fluctuate. But being salaried *by itself* does *not* make you exempt. Otherwise, every employer would pay a salary rather than hourly to avoid paying overtime.

What Makes You Exempt?

The most common exemption is the *administrative professional* exemption. If that description makes you picture a regular, salaried office job, then you are on the right track. Under federal law, you must be paid *at least* $35,568 per year* *and* your work must be primarily office-based administrative work. Most manual labor jobs cannot be exempt under this rule. If you are paid less than this threshold, or if you don't per-

*Under the Biden administration, this minimum threshold was raised. However, a Trump-appointed judge struck down the increase shortly before the Trump administration's second term. As of this writing, there are no plans by the Trump administration to raise this minimum salary.

form mostly office or administrative work, then you cannot be considered exempt. That means the FLSA protections we talked about apply to you.

What If I Am Misclassified as Exempt?

Remember that simply *calling* you exempt—or paying you a salary rather than hourly—doesn't make you exempt. If you are mostly doing manual labor, or if you are paid less than the minimum salary, you might be getting ripped off. Unfortunately, this is a common problem. We'll spend the entire next chapter on exempt vs. nonexempt work, and what your options are if you think you've been misclassified.

[Summary]

- The Fair Labor Standards Act (FLSA) gives nonexempt workers in the United States important rights, like the rights to a minimum wage and overtime pay, and it sets standards for when it's legal (or illegal) for work to be unpaid.
- The FLSA requires nonexempt employees be paid for "all hours worked." Generally, *hours worked* means you are subject to the employer's control, the activity is mandatory, and it's necessary for your job.
- You usually must be paid for on-call time, even when not actively working, if you are subject to a high degree of restrictions or control by the employer during the time spent on call.
- There are some circumstances in which paying less than minimum wage is legal. Disabled workers,

employees under age twenty in their first ninety days, 1099 independent contractors, interns and apprentices, and staff who receive tipped minimum wages are examples of workers who may legally make subminimum wages. Some states have outlawed subminimum-wage practices like these. Note that "legal" and "ethical" are not the same thing in this regard!

- Training must be paid when it is mandatory for your job.
- Employers can charge for uniforms so long as doing so doesn't bring your effective pay down to less than minimum wage. Some states have forbidden employers from making staff purchase their own required work uniforms.
- While there is no federal meal or rest break requirement, you generally must be paid for short breaks under twenty minutes.
- You are always entitled to your final paycheck.
- Exempt employees are not covered by the protections of the FLSA. These are often salaried administrative workers.

[CHAPTER 8]

Salary vs. Hourly

THE SALARY SCAM

I got scammed.

The scammers made off with about $3,500 of my hard-earned money. No, I didn't lose it in a crypto coin or online sports betting (though I hear the odds of losing money are about the same for both). Rather, it was because I did not know my rights and the corporation I worked for used that against me. While I was investing my labor to help them make money, they were stealing a couple hundred bucks from every paycheck. How I got that job is an interesting story. How they ripped me off is even more interesting.

Shortly after I left the fire department to pursue a law degree, I ran into a problem. I applied to over a dozen law schools. Do you know how many I got accepted into?

Zero. None. Zilch.

I was devastated. I had left a steady career as a firefighter to chase this dream. But when I opened the thirteenth small envelope from the thirteenth (and final) law school to reject my application, I cried.

Had I just irreversibly fucked up my life? What was I going to do?

With few options left, I scrambled for a job, any job, to pay bills while I prepared a new round of law school applications. (At eighty to one hundred dollars a pop, this was no small undertaking.)* I landed a job in an office that did temporary staffing for health care workers. I would call leads, read a script, and fill out a preprinted template if I won a contract. This meant that the way I performed my job was tightly controlled—an important detail for how this scam worked.

At first, the job felt like a big upgrade from the fire service. I got to wear sneakers instead of boots. I had a cubicle of my own. The coffee wasn't great, but it was free, and I could have as much as I wanted. And as a former wildland firefighter, this is the part I *really* got psyched about: I got to sit inside, in the shade, with air conditioning. *Air conditioning!*

And best of all, they paid me a whole $48,000 a year for this! I thought I'd scored a great job. Maybe I wouldn't need to go to law school after all?

Boy, was I wrong.

Despite long hours, my paychecks barely covered the cost of living in San Diego.

The company said I didn't get overtime because I got a salary. One day, my manager pulled me aside and said, "You really should come in on Saturdays. The extra day of work ensures we will meet quota early, and the team needs you to hit those numbers as fast as possible every month."

To say I was disillusioned is an understatement. Even though I had a "cushy" indoor job, none of my extra work was improving my life. I was going *backward.* This was especially painful when I looked back at the overtime pay I had received as a firefighter. My hourly pay might not have been particularly high, but the overtime from long shifts and wildfire assignments at least gave me financial stability. Now I was in a restrictive job with long hours but less pay.

I eventually did get into law school. Ironically, it was a school that had rejected me the first time around. But on my second attempt, they offered a scholarship to let me attend. I quit the office job right away.

---

*Personally, I think college and graduate school application fees are a scam of their own, but that's another story.

Then, while I was in my second year of law school, I got a funny letter in the mail.

My old office job had been sued for misclassifying its workers as salaried exempt, and I got a check from the class action settlement. It turned out that I should have been paid overtime for all those evenings and weekends I worked.

As a broke law student, I was thrilled to get some mailbox money. But getting scammed never feels good.

Here's where the company went wrong: I didn't have any independent discretion in that job (recall the prewritten script!). I was not a manager. I was just an ordinary frontline office worker. Because of this, I should have been classified as nonexempt. That matters, because it meant I should have gotten overtime pay. Misclassifying employees as exempt to avoid paying overtime is a common scam that employers pull. But if you know your rights, you'll be able to spot it!

Shady employers steal more from their employees than employees could ever dream of stealing from their employers. And they do it with scams like this.

HOT TAKE: Based on my years of experience as a workers' rights lawyer, most people are better off making an hourly rate than a salary. But in this chapter, we'll cover what your rights are if you are a salaried (a.k.a. exempt) worker, and what to do if you've been misclassified.

DO SALARIED EXEMPT EMPLOYEES HAVE ANY RIGHTS?

YES. You still have rights as a salaried exempt employee. Almost everything in this book applies to you, with one big exception. Salaried exempt employees are, well, *exempt* from many of the rights and protections of the Fair Labor Standards Act: They are not entitled to overtime pay, no matter how much they work, and they are not entitled to pay for on-call time. Salaried exempt employees are, however, entitled to an annual salary of at least $35,568, and they typically do not need to track their hours. They are still paid the same if they work slightly *less* than regularly scheduled. Did you leave early one day to pick up your kid from soccer practice? Your salary should be the same. Was it a slow week at the office? Salary stays the same.

WHAT, LEGALLY, MAKES YOU AN EXEMPT EMPLOYEE?

To become legally exempt from overtime pay, you must have (1) the correct minimum salary and (2) the correct job duties. We call this the *exemption test.*

The Administrative Professional Exemption Test

The administrative professional exemption rule is the most common way to make employees exempt from overtime pay. To take advantage of this rule, your employer must meet the following criteria:

1. You must be paid at least $684 per week (equivalent to an annual salary of $35,568);*

and

2. Your job must be mostly office work (not manual labor), and it has to be directly related to management or the employer's general business operations;

and

3. Your primary duties must allow you to have discretion and independent judgment in how you do your job.

*This number could be changed by the US Department of Labor, but as of this writing, there are no plans to do so.

The minimum salary part of the test is easy. You just look at your paycheck to make sure you are getting at least $684 per week of gross pay.*

But the job duties part of the analysis can be confusing, especially if you feel like you have *some* freedom to make decisions at work. Employers use this ambiguity to steal from you. So here are some examples of who is exempt and who is not under the job duties test:

PROBABLY EXEMPT

- A customer service professional who is free to offer discounts, refunds, or other creative solutions to help customers
- An office manager with a budget who is free to make certain purchasing decisions
- A warehouse manager who sets employee schedules, plans workflows, and is free to make executive decisions about how best to organize the warehouse

PROBABLY NOT EXEMPT

- A customer service professional who reads a script to answer questions or address customer-related problems
- An office manager who must follow strict policy procedures without deviating from them
- A warehouse manager who spends about half their time loading pallets and doing other manual labor

You might have picked up a couple of themes in these examples:

- If you are doing manual labor, you are probably not exempt, and that means you should get overtime.
- If you are not making decisions on how to do your job, or if you

*Some states have a higher minimum salary-exempt threshold, but the job duties part of the test is the same. In California, for example, you must earn at least double the state minimum wage to meet the minimum pay part of the exemption test.

don't have independent discretion on how to solve problems, then you are also probably not exempt and you should get overtime.

I know this can be complicated, but it *matters*. Companies steal millions from people like you every day by muddying the waters on this topic.

Case Study: Assistant (to the) Branch Manager

One way companies try to fake their way through an overtime exemption test is by just calling you a "manager." But remember: Just calling you a manager and paying you a salary does *not* automatically make you exempt from being paid for all hours or earning overtime pay!

Employers who switch frontline employees to a salary, a change generally accompanied by a title such as "assistant manager" or "associate manager," sometimes do so to steal from them.

JPMorganChase tried to skirt the rules, so they learned about the administrative professional exemption test the hard way. The bank gave several thousand employees the title "assistant branch manager." At first glance, this seemed like a position of authority—someone who ranked just below the branch manager. One would think this title would come with some decision-making power. Not so.

Instead, the assistant branch managers had almost zero managerial duties. They spent most of their time performing the same tasks as the hourly employees. When problems came up, they had to read from a script or immediately get a "real" manager to deal with it. They had no authority and no independent discretion, but were expected to "set an example" by working extra hard, often off the clock. And unlike the people they allegedly supervised, the assistant branch managers were not paid a single penny of overtime.

After a while, the employees caught on that they were not really managers at all. So they filed a class action lawsuit alleging that JPMorganChase had systematically misclassified them—and thousands of others—under both federal and state overtime laws. The employees argued that the company had deliberately used inflated job titles to avoid paying overtime hours.

The case spanned multiple states, where lawyers for the assistant branch managers alleged violations of both federal and state labor laws. In the face of mounting legal pressure, JPMorganChase ultimately agreed to a *$16 million settlement* for the employees' unpaid wages.

And JPMorganChase wasn't an outlier. Across the financial industry, major banks have been caught many times using the same tactics—assigning impressive-sounding job titles to avoid paying overtime.

MISCLASSIFICATION IS A CALCULATED GAMBLE FOR EMPLOYERS

The reality behind misclassification schemes—like the one JPMorganChase pulled—is that companies are making a bet. They're gambling that you won't know your rights or that you'll be too scared to push back. They know the odds are in their favor because most employees do not understand the salary exemption rules. By illegally misclassifying their employees, companies can cut labor costs and squeeze more hours out of workers for free. Assuming they can avoid a class action for long enough, shady employers think the potential profits are worth the risk.

The administrative exemption is the most commonly abused classification because regular office work is so common in the United States. But there are a few other jobs *not* entitled to overtime pay you should know about. Jobs like outside sales, information technology (IT), and computer professionals have special requirements to be exempt. But watch out! Shady employers love to skirt the rules. So, let's take a closer look at the requirements of the other exemptions.

Outside Sales Exemption

Sales is an interesting profession. Few jobs promise such high rewards for hard work while also providing such minimal base pay. Many sales employees earn their living entirely on commissions—if you don't sell, you don't eat.

Because sales is notoriously feast-or-famine, there are special rules your employer must follow before refusing to pay for your hours or your overtime.

To qualify for the outside sales employee exemption, *both* of these tests must be met:

1. Your primary job must be making sales or securing orders or contracts for services;

AND

2. You must be regularly making sales, generating leads, or making calls away from the employer's usual place of business.

If number 2 is confusing, think about it like this. You are an *outside* salesperson if you are spending most of your time *outside* the office: going to trade shows, knocking on doors, meeting clients at their places of business, attending seminars and lunches with prospects. These are all examples of outside salespeople. Generally, most people meet this exemption if they do these duties for at least 51 percent of their work. If your sales job does not meet those qualifications, then you are NOT exempt and therefore are entitled to the full rights and protections of the FLSA, including the right to a minimum wage and overtime pay.

Computer Professional Exemption

As information technology (IT) and programming jobs continue to grow, I am seeing more and more people fall into this exemption. But don't get it twisted! Just because you work with computers doesn't mean you are exempt from overtime. For example, a retail employee at a store that sells computers is not a "computer professional" under this rule.

So who is? To qualify for the computer employee exemption, your employer needs to show that you meet *all three* of these tests:

1. Pay requirements
   - You must be paid a salary of at least $684 per week—*or*, if you are paid hourly, your rate must be at least $27.63 per hour. Remember, paying you a salary does not automatically make you overtime exempt, and paying you hourly doesn't automatically make you nonexempt.

2. Job role requirements
   - You must be a computer systems analyst, computer programmer, or software engineer, or hold a similar skilled role, and you must have the following duties:
     - Using systems analysis, including consulting with users, to figure out specifications
     - Designing, developing, documenting, analyzing, creating, testing, or modifying computer systems or programs (including prototypes) based on user or system design
     - Designing, documenting, testing, creating, or modifying computer programs for machine operating systems
     - A mix of these duties that require similar skills

Employers Often Misuse Exemptions to Avoid Paying What You Are Owed!

Unfortunately, the above exemptions are prime targets for abuse. If you are not earning overtime, then you should look at your job with a healthy level of suspicion. Don't be paranoid—just be smart!

KEY POINT: Simply paying you a salary does not automatically make you exempt from the Fair Labor Standards Act. Nor can an employer weasel out of paying overtime just by *saying* you are exempt.

WHAT IF YOU ARE MISCLASSIFIED?

The problem with misclassifying you as exempt, when you should legally be nonexempt, is that it almost always results in you being underpaid. This leaves workers with longer hours, lost wages, and a meaningless "manager" title that feels more insulting than encouraging. The best way to make sure this is not happening is to *talk about your pay*!

This point bears repeating. I even considered printing the phrase *TALK ABOUT YOUR PAY* in bold red letters on every page of this book. (That may have been a bit aggressive, so we scrapped the idea.) Catching wage theft, misclassification, discrimination, or other violations is hard to do by yourself.

You have a federally protected right to talk about pay and work conditions with coworkers, so long as those discussions are not disruptive to your work. Under the National Labor Relations Act, employees have the right to engage in "concerted activities" for "mutual aid or protection." In English, this means you aren't just *allowed* to discuss your pay, but that an employer who tries to stop you is violating federal law!

Still, discretion is important. You don't necessarily have to hide these discussions about pay, but you should use common sense. A quick chat about who got raises this year is legally protected, but shouting "Denise got a raise and everyone else is getting screwed!" from a bullhorn probably isn't.

Your employee handbook may have a policy that says you will be fired or punished if caught discussing your pay. Keep a copy. If you are retaliated against for discussing pay in a *nondisruptive way,* then that policy is evidence of the employer's illegal motive. Handbooks are not the law!

Once you've had these discussions and have determined that you might be misclassified as an exempt employee, you have a few options. Generally, you can file a complaint with your state labor board or the US Department of Labor, or find a private lawyer (like me!) to help understand your options.

Summary

- A salary is when you are paid a set amount every pay period. It generally does not change based on your hours. Many salaried employees are exempt from earning overtime.
- My personal opinion, although it does not apply to all situations, is that it is generally better to be an hourly nonexempt employee than a salaried exempt employee.
- To make you exempt, your employer must show that you pass the exemption test. You must have the correct minimum salary and the correct job duties.
- Administrative professionals are the most common type of exempt employee, but companies try to cheat this system all the time.
- You may be owed serious money if you are illegally misclassified.
- Talk about your pay and work conditions with coworkers. It's your federally protected right to do so, and it's the best way to make sure you are not getting hustled!

[CHAPTER 9]

Tips

GORDON RAMSAY VS. AMY'S BAKING COMPANY

Following a televised visit from chef Gordon Ramsay, a small bakery in Scottsdale became the most hated restaurant in America. On a now-infamous episode of *Kitchen Nightmares,* Ramsay was so outraged by a restaurant's labor violations that he walked out on the owners. This was a historic first for the show.

The restaurant was called Amy's Baking Company. It was owned by Amy and her husband, Samy, a self-proclaimed "Vegas playboy." The couple invested over a million dollars into their bakery. Despite the investment, they suffered from years of poor reviews. But the problem wasn't the cakes and muffins. It was the owners.

Reviewers told stories of being berated by the couple. Samy reportedly screamed at, threatened, and banned customers from the restaurant. Others complained about his wife, Amy, who some people called Amy Crazy Eyes. Unlike Samy, Amy appeared to have a soft side. She said she had three children who were "trapped in cats' bodies." (She also claimed to be fluent in feline, and she demonstrated her proficiency by meowing for the cameras.)

But all wasn't kittens and smiles with Amy.

Hell broke loose when a local food critic wrote a negative review about Amy's pizza. In response to the criticism, Amy said, and I quote, "Do us a favor and keep your ugly face and ugly opinions to yourself."

Not a great look. Still, Ramsay accepted the owners' calls for help.

Things started out okay during the initial inspection. Ramsay complimented the owners on how tidy the kitchen was—rare praise for a *Kitchen Nightmares* episode. But the employees warned Ramsay that all was not as it seemed.

In whispered voices, they said Samy routinely seized the servers' tips rather than letting them keep what they earned. When Ramsay confronted Samy, the owner insisted it was his right to pocket the tips—an excuse that infuriated the employees and Ramsay alike.

Ramsay couldn't believe his ears. The employees worked for those tips! The owners had no right to steal from them. Ramsay observed as a table of customers left a tip for their server, only for Samy to scoop it up. In front of the customers and the cameras, Ramsay demanded to know what Samy intended to do with the money. Without flinching, Samy declared that the tips go to the house (himself) because the employees got paid hourly.

The customers were furious. "We left that money for *her*!" they yelled, pointing to the waitress who had served them.

As Ramsay's inspection continued, the toxic atmosphere worsened. Staff told Ramsay they were afraid to speak up about the tip theft. Amy had a strict rule against employees speaking to one another. One server even commented, "This is the only kitchen I've worked in where employees can't speak."

Ramsay, in his typical fashion, gave the owners an expletive-laced scolding. Instead of acknowledging their wrongdoing, they deflected. They claimed their actions were justified because the staff didn't "deserve" the tips.*

And this led to another disturbing revelation about Amy and Samy's behavior.

---

*It was at this point that I spit out my drink. At my partner's recommendation, I took a short walk to calm down before finishing the episode.

Ramsay sat down with two former employees. One said Samy made them wash his car. Another revealed that in just eighteen months, the owners had fired at least fifty people.

At that point, Ramsay had seen enough. He confronted Amy and Samy about the mass firings, tip theft, and bullying. Surprisingly, the couple broke down in tears. When Ramsay called them out, they finally realized the error of their ways. They admitted they were wrong and apologized.

Just kidding! Literally it was the exact opposite of that.

Amy went *full demon mode*. She screamed and swore at Ramsay with the force of an atom bomb. Speaking of bombs, Samy exploded. He bragged that he had not just fired fifty employees—no, it was *one hundred* employees!

Somewhere in the middle of this, Ramsay realized that perhaps this couple wasn't open to constructive criticism. Knowing a lost cause when he saw it, he walked off the episode early—officially giving up on a restaurant for the first time on his show.

But Amy's Baking Company couldn't outrun karma forever. After years of online feuds, a cringe-inducing appearance on *Dr. Phil*, and thousands of negative reviews, Amy's Baking Company shut down for good on September 1, 2015. Amy and Samy reportedly split shortly after.

Couldn't have happened to a nicer couple.

Lessons from Amy's Baking Company

You don't need a law degree to know that stealing tips is wrong. But tip theft remains one of the most common labor law violations I see. In this chapter, we're going to learn all about tips, tipped wages, and common tip-theft schemes. Here are a few quick facts to keep in mind:

- Tips are your property. There is no excuse for an employer taking your tips. It makes no difference if they say you do not "deserve" the tip.

- Confiscating tips for things like broken dishes, broken equipment, or a dine and dash is also illegal.
- Your base hourly rate is not a replacement for the tips you earned.
- Employees have the right to discuss pay and work conditions with coworkers. Forbidding employees from having these discussions violates the National Labor Relations Act.

Tiny tyrants like Amy and Samy can be found in almost every town in America. So let's learn our rights so they can't get away with it!

TIPPED MINIMUM WAGE

Federal law allows employers to pay as little as $2.13 per hour to some tipped employees. If that sounds ridiculously low, it's because it is! Here is how it works:

- The employer pays you $2.13 per hour for the time you work.
- So long as you earn at least $30 per month in tips, the employer can use your tips to make up the difference to the full minimum wage.
- Put simply—the employer is allowed to use your tips to help them cover the cost of paying the full minimum wage.*
- If your tips are not enough to cover the difference, then your employer must pay enough to bring your total wages for all hours to at least the minimum wage.

Some states have raised the tipped minimum wage to higher than $2.13 per hour. Seven states (Alaska, California, Minnesota, Montana,

*Personally, I think this is cheap. Any employer who can't afford the minimum wage needs to do the work themselves until they can afford to properly compensate workers without taking their tips. But hey, that's just my opinion.

Nevada, Oregon, and Washington) have prohibited tipped minimum wages altogether. You must be paid the same minimum whether you are a tipped or non-tipped employee in those states.

Because of the variety of state rules on this issue, it is wise to look up whether your state allows tipped minimum wages, and if so, how much that tipped minimum really is. There is a fair probability it is higher than $2.13 per hour!

The United States has a strong tipping culture, primarily because minimum wages have stagnated for so long that tips are the primary source of income for many workers. Has tipping culture gone too far? Perhaps.

You shop in a convenience store, pick out your own products, bag them yourself, then at checkout a clerk spins an iPad around and says, "It's gonna ask you a couple of questions." And they have the *nerve* to ask for up to a 30 percent tip when you did all the shopping yourself!

Americans can't be blamed for feeling cheated. But low wages are what got us here, not the people earning low wages. Greedy employers caused workers to become dependent on tips.

Why am I on this soapbox? Because too many Americans are mad at the wrong people. Are some tip requests absurd? Surely. Is tipping out of control? Perhaps.

But so long as mouths must be fed and rent must be paid, workers will depend on these tips to survive.

WHAT ARE THE MOST COMMON TIP-THEFT SCHEMES?

I've shaken down many tip thieves in my career. Some were cleverer than others; they relied on deceptive policies, confusing contracts, or total lies to scam their employees. Others, like Samy from *Kitchen Nightmares,* used brute force and intimidation. But in the end, they all paid dearly! Here are the most common tip-theft schemes I've seen:

- Managers claim a percent of all tips "for the house."
- A boss takes your tips as punishment for tardiness, slow work, or other infractions.
- Managers say you "forfeit" your tips if you quit without notice.
- A store owner accepts tips but refuses to distribute them to employees because they are "already paid hourly."
- Taking your tips to cover a dine and dash, broken plates, or replacement costs for equipment.
- Using your tips to bring your pay up to minimum wage but keeping any amount over that for themselves.

The law around tips is crystal clear. The federal Fair Labor Standards Act states that tips are solely the property of the employee who earns them, not the employer. Once you accept a tip, the money is yours. Bosses cannot take tips except in specific and carefully regulated situations.

However, some bosses will lie about the law to their employees. Others will make illegal policies, such as taking a percentage of your tips, and basically dare you to call them out.

For the record, I *love* busting greedy bosses who steal tips. For example, I had a case where a restaurant owner stole employees' tips to cover the cost of a new dishwasher. How did he justify the theft? This frickin' clown claimed that because employees "didn't rinse the plates good," that meant he was entitled to have them buy a new machine for him.

Preposterous. As most tip-theft schemes are.

REMEMBER: Your tips are your property. There are almost zero excuses for a boss putting their grubby hands on your tips.

TIP SHARES AND TIP POOLS

I just said, several times, that your tips are your property and bosses cannot take them for you. Several readers in the service industry may be thinking, *Wait a minute, my boss makes me share my tips with my coworkers. Is that illegal?*

Not necessarily. And no, this is not a contradiction. Allow me to explain.

A tip pool (sometimes called a tip share) is when an employer pools everyone's tips and then distributes them after the shift. Tip pools are controversial.

People who like tip pools point out that gratuities can be random. A particular customer's generosity is often a bigger factor than the employee's performance. And sadly, some customers refuse to tip no matter how great the service was. For this reason, one employee might get a huge tip while another gets stiffed. A tip pool helps the team share unusually high tips while protecting against unusually low tips.

Another factor tip-pool advocates point out is the inclusion of back-of-house workers. At a restaurant, the server is not the only person who makes that hot food appear at your table. With a tip pool, the line cooks, the dishwashers, and the bussers who contribute to the business can also get a share of the tips.

Critics of tip pools point out that servers are effectively punished for good service, since they lose a share of their earnings no matter how hard they work. Others argue that the percentage splits will always leave someone feeling unsatisfied.

Whether you love tip pools or hate them, the employer generally has a right to set them up. But they *must* follow the rules!

- Managers with hiring and firing power may *not* participate in a tip pool.
- Tips must be distributed *promptly*. Cash tips generally must be distributed that same day. Electronic tips can be paid no later than the next pay period.
- A tip pool is *not* allowed if the employer uses the tipped minimum wage.
- No matter how much you earn in tips, you must also earn the minimum wage for your hours worked. A boss who gives you a $0.00 paycheck because you "earned too much in tips" is stealing from you.

ARE THERE OTHER SITUATIONS WHERE EMPLOYERS CAN LEGALLY TAKE TIPS?

Tip pools are common situations in which unscrupulous employers might try to break the rules. But there are a few specific and carefully regulated circumstances when a boss can legally take an employee's tips. Let's talk about those scenarios now so you can protect your hard-earned cash.

Credit Card Fees on Tips

When a customer pays a tip with a credit card, the credit card company charges your employer a fee. Usually it's a small percentage of the transaction. On most transactions, like a lunch tab, this fee comes out to a few bucks.

Some bosses are *so cheap* they try to make *employees* pay this fee for them!

Federal law allows employers to take the credit card transaction fee out of your tips. However, they cannot take the *whole* fee from you. It can only be a proportionate amount.

Here's a rough example to make sure you aren't getting scammed by your employer:

- A customer buys lunch and their total tab is $40.
- The customer pays with a credit card.
- At checkout, the customer adds a $10 tip.
- The credit card company charges a 3 percent fee on transactions.

What happens next? Here are the *legal* and *illegal* moves an employer might make:

LEGAL: The employer may take 3 percent of the $10 tip, or about 30 cents.

ILLEGAL: The employer may *not* take 3 percent of the whole $50 transaction from you (about $1.50). Even if the employer deducts the right amount, doing so is not allowed if it would cause your total pay to drop below minimum wage.

I know this sounds like a small amount of money, but those dollars and cents add up fast! While taking a percentage of credit card fees out of your tips may be legal in most states, you deserve better than a cheapskate boss nickel-and-diming you every shift. (Note that in several states, taking credit card fees from your tips is illegal; it is worth doing a quick internet search to confirm your state's rules.)

Case Study: Karen Café

Here's an example from a case I worked on; we call it the case of Karen Café. The boss owned a chain of small cafés in corporate office parks throughout California. Among multiple wage theft violations, she was also a tip thief. Karen Café claimed that since employees' tips were part of the total transaction, that meant they had the right to take the *whole* credit card fee out of the employees' paychecks.

This was funny for three reasons:

1. The employer was taking 100 percent of the credit card fee from employees (which was *wayyy* too much).
2. Even if the employer had charged their employees a fair percentage, which they had not, that would still have been illegal because taking tips to cover credit card fees is banned in California.
3. The owner had a reputation for bragging about how expensive her designer clothes and accessories were. It was a weird flex, since she was stealing from her own staff. (Personally I thought her style was tacky, but I guess money can't buy class.)

Federal law lets employers take the credit card processing fee from your tips. But it has to be proportionate. They cannot use your tips to cover the whole fee. And in several states, taking credit card fees from your tips is illegal.

Prohibitions Against Tips

It is legal for employers to ban employees from accepting tips. However, this does *not* mean your boss can "confiscate" your tips if a customer tries to leave a tip anyway!

If your employer does not allow you to accept tips but a customer still gives you one, then federal law clearly states that the tip is your property. An employer may discipline you for accepting the tip (which, let's be honest, would be insanely petty). However, they cannot take any portion of the tip as punishment for accepting the tip.

Taking Tips as Punishment

Speaking of taking tips away as a punishment, it is technically legal to take employee tips in cases of "gross negligence" or "fraud."

However, I have two things to say to any slimy corporate defense lawyer trying to justify this:

Ahem

First of all, on the issue of *gross negligence* . . . Shut up, nerd. You dork. You dweeb. You pencil-pushing, bean-counting corporate dunce.

Sure, gross negligence can be a valid reason to take an employees' tip. But gross negligence is a high bar to meet. We both know the employee in question needs to *royally* fuck up before you can justify taking tips. Sure, if the employee starts playing hacky sack with your glassware, then fuck it, take the tips. The law is probably with you on that one.

But if a boss runs around screaming "gross negligence" every time they are unhappy with an employee's work, then they'll be stealing more often than not. And that'll put them on the wrong end of a lawsuit.

Takes a deep breath

Second, on the issue of *fraud*... You dingbat. You dimwit. You pearl-clutching, finger-wagging weirdo.

Yes, fraud is a valid reason to confiscate a tip. If an employee concocts some scheme to make extra tips by defrauding you or a customer, then *obviously* the law will not protect those tips. Obviously. But a boss cannot just throw wild accusations around without proof. If they suspect an employee is committing fraud, then they need to call the police. Employers have no right to be judge, jury, and executioner on whether an employee's earnings are "fraud."

Withholding your tips because you were late? Illegal.

Taking your tips because you had a "bad attitude"? Illegal.

Confiscating a tip because you "didn't work hard enough"? Illegal.

Taking a tip because you accidentally dropped some glassware? Illegal.

I rest my case.

[Summary]

- If you received tipped minimum wages, your employer can pay less than minimum wage (base) but then use your tips to bring you to the full minimum wage.
- The tipped minimum wage is $2.13 per hour. It has not changed since the 1990s.
- If your tips aren't enough to bring you to the full minimum wage, your employer must pay the difference. You are entitled to at least the full minimum wage one way or another.
- Tips are your property. Once earned, there are only a few *very* specific situations where they can be taken.

- A tip pool is when employees' tips are gathered into one big pot, then shared according to a predetermined split after the shift. If your employer has a tip pool, they cannot pay a tipped minimum wage, and they must pay you at least the minimum wage plus your share of the tip pool.
- Managers with hiring and firing power cannot join a tip pool.
- Managers cannot steal your tips as punishment for a mistake.
- Employers will make up all kinds of crazy excuses for stealing tips. Learn to spot them, and don't let bad bosses rip you off!

CHAPTER 10

"1099 Employees" and Independent Contractors

ATTORNEY RYAN V. BROJACK

My consultation with Dylan was unusual. His girlfriend arranged his appointment with me because, despite being part of Gen Z, Dylan did not have an email address, and he didn't know how to fill out forms on a computer. He had a basic flip phone for calls, but that was it.

What he lacked in tech skills, he more than made up for in his expertise as a handyman. At only twenty-three years old, the kid could build a dream backyard on his own. Electrical work, water features, landscaping, outdoor kitchens, he could do it all (so long as no emails were involved).

Dylan came from a proud blue-collar background. His tattered blue jeans were like a tapestry chronicling his years of hard work. He carried an old banker's box full of documents under one arm. Like a gentleman, he removed his John Deere cap when he entered the office. "Nice to meet you, Mr. Stygar," he said, looking me right in the eye as he shook my hand.

"Please, call me Ryan," I said. "How can I help you?"

Dylan twisted his ball cap in his hands. "I'm not one to complain," he said. "I'm not asking for any handouts. But I think my boss is scamming me."

Dylan explained that he worked for a contractor who specialized in residential landscaping. It was big business. Dylan worked ten to twelve hours per shift, sometimes six days straight before getting a day off. His boss, who we will call BroJack, was an ex-cop who was *obsessed* with "work ethic." But as much as BroJack preached about hard work, he sure had a shady business model.

For starters, he hired Dylan as a "1099 employee." (That's in quotes for a reason; more on that later.)

Here's how BroJack explained the deal to Dylan: "You'll need your own trailer. We can lease one to you for a good deal. Once you have that, you'll need some tools, and you can buy those from us as well. I'll give you the jobs, and you'll get 40 percent of the invoices, minus the deductions for tools and equipment."

If that sounds fishy, it's because it was!

I flipped through the papers Dylan had brought. I found something suspicious. It turned out BroJack had no receipts to prove that the tools cost what he deducted from Dylan's paychecks. Instead, he took random, inflated amounts, usually round numbers. For example, he deducted thirty dollars for a hammer, one hundred for a box of nails. But BroJack could not provide any receipts to justify these deductions (probably because he made them up).

When Dylan finished a job, customers paid BroJack for the work via one of his invoices. BroJack took 60 percent the invoice for himself, then deducted hundreds of dollars for "expenses" like the trailer and tools. Dylan kept whatever pittance remained.

Then we talked about Dylan's hours. I asked, "Did you get any overtime pay?"

"No," he answered. "BroJack said I don't get overtime."

Oof. That was a big violation.

"What about breaks?" I asked.

Dylan chuckled and shook his head. "I had so many jobs to do each day, if I took a break I would have fallen behind. So, I just ate while I worked. I didn't really take breaks."

"And mileage? Did you ever get reimbursed for driving between jobsites?"

"Never."

Dylan and I ran the numbers. After all the hours and deductions, Dylan was earning *less than minimum wage*!

It was already a bad situation. But then tax season came. That's when Dylan got the worst surprise of his life.

He owed thousands of dollars in taxes for the prior year.

"I can't afford that," he said. "They also said I owe self-employment tax, but I'm not self-employed. How did this happen?"

"See here?" I said, tapping the tax forms. "Your boss reported your earnings on a Form 1099. That means he told the IRS you're an independent contractor. Basically, he said you are not an employee, but a self-employed person he subcontracted with for those jobs."

Dylan shook his head. "You mean he lied?"

I nodded yes.

"He told me I was a 1099 employee . . ." Dylan said quietly.

"I'm sorry, but that doesn't exist," I explained. "A 1099 is an independent contractor. It looks like your boss called you a 1099 to avoid payroll taxes, then used the money he paid you as a tax write-off for himself."

"What about me?" Dylan asked. "Do I get a tax write-off too?"

I shook my head. "You have a problem, because when you got paid, your boss didn't do any tax withholdings for you, so you owe taxes on all the income you earned."

Dylan slumped in his seat. The look of betrayal on his face was heartbreaking.

"What can I do?" he asked.

"First," I began, "don't beat yourself up. I see this all the time. If you were illegally misclassified as an independent contractor, then you might be owed a *lot* of money. But I need to run through some questions with you first. This is called the *economic realities test*." I pulled out a pen and notepad. "Question one: Did you have any opportunities to turn a profit, or did you risk a loss? This is based on your business skills, not necessarily how hard you worked."

Dylan thought a moment. "Well, if I worked hard, I could do more jobs, but BroJack got all the customers. I didn't do sales or anything.

So . . . I guess I didn't have much opportunity to turn a profit. I was just working."

"What about losses?"

"Well, I lost a lot from the deductions, but I wasn't running a business or anything."

I jotted down the answer, then said, "Question two: Did you make any investments to get new customers, increase profits, or reduce costs?"

Dylan shook his head. "No, I just paid my boss for the trailer and the tools."

"Question three: Were you hired to finish a specific number of jobs, or were you hired on a more permanent basis?"

"I thought I'd work for BroJack for a few years," Dylan said. "He made it sound like I could earn a lot if I worked hard."

"Would you say it was a permanent position then?"

"Oh, for sure."

"Okay, question four," I continued. "How much control did BroJack have over your work?"

"Not much. I worked alone most days."

"Did he set your schedule?"

"Sort of. Every week he handed me the job invoices with the addresses, and he told me to get them done by a certain time. Sometimes he came to the jobsite but not much."

"Okay, so you had some flexibility in how to do your job?"

"Yes, definitely."

"All right, that weighs in favor of you being an independent contractor," I explained. "But the other factors seem to lean toward you being an employee. No single factor in this test is conclusive on its own. So, let's continue. Question five: Were these landscaping projects integral to BroJack's business?"

"What do you mean, 'integral'?"

"More like . . . was the work a key component of the business, or were you doing stuff that was outside his normal operations?"

"Oh, it was landscaping work, and that's all we do. I'd say it's integral, yeah."

"Okay, question six: Did you use any business skills, such as making bids for new work, or planning ways to grow the business?"

Dylan laughed. "No, sir, I just did the landscaping."

"Well, that's good enough for me," I said, putting my pen down. "Dylan, I am positive you were illegally misclassified. So, the real question is, do you want to sue this guy to get your money back?"

Dylan frowned. After thinking awhile, he asked, "How much do you think he owes me?"

"Well," I said, "because you were an employee, you should have at least gotten minimum wage and overtime. You also should have been reimbursed for mileage. Not to mention all the statutory penalties for not getting any wage statements. Looking at your hours, how long you worked there, your expenses, and how little he actually paid you, I'd say somewhere around $50,000, if our math is right."

Dylan's jaw dropped. "I don't want to take advantage . . ." he began.

"Let me be clear," I said. "This guy lied to you. He said you were an independent contractor when you weren't. By doing that, he underpaid you, caused you to get a huge tax bill, and deducted bogus expenses from you. This guy ripped *you* off, Dylan. *He's* the bad guy, not you."

Dylan cracked a smile. "All right, let's get him."

Ultimately, we sued BroJack for failure to pay minimum wage, failure to pay overtime, failure to provide meal and rest breaks, failure to furnish itemized wage statements, waiting time penalties, unreimbursed expenses, breach of contract, and unfair competition.

Oh, and we slapped some interest on all that for good measure.*

Remember, "1099 employees" do not exist. Calling you a "1099 employee" is often a red flag that your boss is doing something illegal.

Dylan's situation was egregious, but by no means unique. It's very likely that you or someone you know has been misclassified as a 1099 independent contractor at some point in your career. Heck, it even happened to *me*!

Whether your boss *calls* you an "independent contractor" or a "1099

*No mercy for wage thieves. ☺

employee" has no legal effect whatsoever. Actions speak louder than words.

WHAT IS AN INDEPENDENT CONTRACTOR?

Independent contractors are self-employed people in business for themselves. When someone hires an independent contractor for a job, the earnings are reported on an IRS Form 1099. This is why they are sometimes called a 1099, a 1099 worker, or a 1099 independent contractor. But they are not employees.

Independent contractors have lots of freedom about how to do their job because they are *economically independent*. Technically, the "employers" are actually their clients.

Because independent contractors are not employees, they do *not* have important rights that employees have:

- The right to a minimum wage
- The right to overtime pay
- The right to be paid for all hours worked
- The right to be reimbursed for certain business expenses
- In many cases, the right to be covered by protected leave, paid sick leave, or workers' compensation if they get hurt

Because independent contractors are self-employed, they are also liable for their own taxes.

Here are some examples of true independent contractors:

- An electrician doing repairs at your office
- A singer performing at a fundraising event
- A mechanic repairing your delivery truck
- A lawyer drafting legal contracts for your business

You might have noticed some themes here, which become *very* important to ensure you are not getting ripped off. First, all the people in these examples were hired to do a specific job with a well-established scope of work (help with taxes, repair an office, perform at an event, repair a truck, draft a contract). There is no expectation of continued employment once the job is done, though I am sure all these contractors would love repeat business.

You'll also notice that these jobs are not doing work as part of the hirer's core business. In legalese, we say that the independent contractor's work is not "germane" to the business.

Germane is a funny word that doesn't get used much, so here's an example. If I need help with court appearances full time, I will hire an associate attorney as an employee. This is because court appearances are germane to my core business—we are a law office, after all.

But if the lights go out in my office, I will need an electrician. I provide legal services, not electrical services, so I need an independent contractor to do this job for me. Once the job is done, the business relationship will end until I need an electrician again.

The Economic Realities Test

As we saw in Dylan's story, just because your boss says you're an independent contractor doesn't make it so. What you are *called* is much less important than the economic reality. The *economic reality test* weighs six factors to see whether you are an independent contractor or a misclassified employee. No single factor decides the test by itself. Instead, we weigh all the factors like stones on a scale.

1. **OPPORTUNITY FOR PROFIT OR LOSS:** Can the worker make more money based on their business skills?*
2. **INVESTMENT IN EQUIPMENT OR MATERIALS:** Does the worker supply their own tools and materials, or does the employer provide them?
3. **PERMANENCY OF THE RELATIONSHIP:** Is the work project-based/temporary, or something more permanent?

*Note that this measures your business acumen, not necessarily your effort or work ethic.

4. **DEGREE OF CONTROL:** Does the employer control how, when, and where the work is done?
5. **INTEGRAL PART OF THE BUSINESS:** Is the worker's role *germane,* or essential, to the employer's business?
6. **SKILL AND INITIATIVE:** Does the worker use specialized skills in an independent business, or are they trained by the employer?

Remember, Dylan had some factors that weighed in favor of him being an independent contractor—but the majority of factors leaned in favor of him being an employee. It is a balancing test based on the totality of circumstances.

Employers are fighting uphill if they classify you as 1099, because the default position is that you generally are an employee unless proven otherwise.

What Are the Benefits of Being an Independent Contractor?

Don't get me wrong, there are good reasons to be an independent contractor, if that's what you really are. While independent contractors lose the stability, benefits, and legal rights employees have, they get *freedom.* Freedom to set your own hours, work at your own pace, choose your jobs, and decline work that does not align with your goals. As a self-employed person, there is (theoretically) no cap to how much you can earn.

The flexibility and the potential to earn more money are powerful incentives on their own. But as a self-employed independent contractor, you also have opportunities to obtain tax benefits for running your business.

For many professionals, being an independent contractor makes sense! But you should know what being self-employed means. If you are genuinely self-employed, you do your own marketing, management, and sales. You have lots of freedom in how to do your work, and you should have multiple clients (rather than just one employer). If being self-employed is important to you, make sure you really are.

Real Estate Agents

One common question I get is whether real estate agents can properly be classified as 1099 independent contractors.

As a longtime fan of *Million Dollar Listing*, I can see why people get the impression that agents are employees. They apply for jobs at a brokerage, the broker is their boss, and they generally present themselves as being part of a larger organization that employs them. (For example, the eccentric power broker Fredrik Eklund worked for Douglas Elliman.)

So are real estate agents employees? Generally not. Using the economic realities test, we can see why:

1. **OPPORTUNITY FOR PROFIT OR LOSS:** Agents earn commissions rather than salaries, meaning their income depends on their ability to grow a book of business, rather than how many hours they work.
2. **INVESTMENT IN EQUIPMENT OR MATERIALS:** Many agents cover their own business costs, including office space, advertising, licensing fees, and professional memberships.
3. **PERMANENCY OF THE RELATIONSHIP:** Agents can typically work with different brokers over time, and they may even have a separate brand outside the brokerage.
4. **DEGREE OF CONTROL:** While brokerages oversee real estate agents, most agents get a lot of freedom in how to do their work. They set their own schedules, choose clients, and decide on marketing strategies.
5. **INTEGRAL PART OF THE BUSINESS:** While real estate agents are key to a brokerage's success, they often operate their own businesses within the brokerage framework. For example, in the show, while Fredrik Eklund was part of Douglas Elliman, he had his own division (the Eklund Gomes Team), which operated at least semi-independently.
6. **SKILL AND INITIATIVE:** Success in real estate depends on the

agent's sales skills, market knowledge, and networking, which suggest an independent business model.

So while we can point to several factors hinting that real estate agents ought to be considered employees, the balance of all these factors consistently leans in favor of an independent contractor relationship.

Employers have a strong financial temptation to misclassify employees. Some think they can get away with it by making you sign a contract saying you are an independent contractor. Funny enough, BroJack made Dylan a contract like this. It expressly stated that Dylan was an independent contractor, not an employee.

But what you are *called* makes no legal difference. And an independent contractor agreement does *not* conclusively prove you are a 1099. You cannot waive most of your labor rights under the Fair Labor Standards Act. And all workers start with the default presumption that they are employees, not independent contractors. The economic realities test is the real benchmark—not your job title, not your employment agreement, and definitely not your boss's personal opinion.

WHAT ABOUT GIG WORKERS, LIKE DELIVERY DRIVERS?

Whenever I discuss independent contractors online, I get *hundreds* of comments asking how it's legal for companies such as Uber, DoorDash, and Lyft to treat their workers as independent contractors, even though the economic realities test makes it pretty clear they should be employees.

Take Uber, for example. It has substantial control over how its drivers operate. It controls their customers, their prices, even their hours in some scenarios. The drivers have very little discretion in how to do their jobs; the company establishes rules, maps out routes, and even sets limits on where drivers can or cannot accept rides.

When we consider all the factors, it is hard to see how an Uber driver is anything but an employee. However, the business continues to operate with most of its workers as independent contractors.

How can that be?

These companies have waged a multimillion-dollar, multiyear campaign to win special exceptions, privileges, and carve-outs for their business model.

In 2020 special interest groups in California introduced Proposition 22, which allowed gig economy platforms such as Uber to classify workers as independent contractors instead of employees. This law essentially said, "Hey, you should probably be an employee, but we made a special exception for this specific industry."

There was an uproar at the time because the language in Prop 22 was deceptive, and many voters thought they were giving *more* rights to gig economy workers. The reality was the opposite. By allowing a special exception, millions of gig workers actually *lost* rights and protections under this rule. Part of the problem is that the people who made the rules—legislators and judges—are at least twenty years behind in terms of regulating these industries.

Now, enter the gig economy. While the business model is not new, its popularity and accessibility with new technology is. We are witnessing a patchwork of state and local regulations because the federal government has not caught up.* For most of its history, Uber owned no cars. It had no fleet of vehicles of its own. That's because the company—Uber's lawyers have argued—is not a taxi service, but rather a platform that connects drivers to riders. So with a little lobbying, some political ads, and a few well-worded legal arguments, you will see a lot of "gig workers" being treated as independent contractors rather than employees.

Let's call it what it is. The gig economy is exploding because wages in general are not keeping up with the cost of living. This is forcing workers to supplement their income with gig work. In an interesting case out of New York, an unemployment insurance appeals board ruled that three Uber drivers were "employees" for the purpose of getting unem-

*Remember, this is the same federal government that thinks a minimum wage of $7.25 per hour should be enough to live on . . . since 2009.

ployment insurance. This ruling applies only to unemployment cases in New York, but at the time, the administrative law judge said on the record that "the overriding evidence establishes that Uber exercised sufficient supervision, direction, and control" to create an employer-employee relationship.*

KEEP IT SIMPLE

All these rules, exceptions, tests, and legal theories can be complicated. But there's a simple question you can ask yourself if you're unsure whether you are an employee or an independent contractor: "Am I self-employed?" It's not always consistent, but nine times out of ten, if your answer is no, then you are probably an employee.

If you are really unsure, it's worth having an experienced employment lawyer take a look at the situation.

*Dana Rubinstein, "State Labor Judge Finds Uber an 'Employer,'" *Politico*, June 13, 2017, politico.com/states/new-york/city-hall/story/2017/06/13/state-labor-court-finds-uber-an-employer-112733.

Summary

- An independent contractor is a self-employed person in business for themselves. Their earnings are reported on an IRS Form 1099. They are sometimes called 1099s, 1099 contractors, or (incorrectly) 1099 employees.
- Independent contractors are responsible for their own taxes. Being improperly misclassified can lead to serious tax consequences for the employee.
- Independent contractors do not have the same legal rights employees do, such as the right to a minimum wage, the right to overtime pay, protected medical leave, sick leave, paid time off, severance, and other benefits.
- The default position is that workers are employees unless proven otherwise. The economic realities test balances six factors to see if you are an independent contractor.
- Real estate agents may *appear* to be employees. But on careful examination, most agents meet the economic realities test for independent contractors.
- Employees may be entitled to substantial financial damages if they are illegally misclassified.
- "1099 employees" do not exist. Whether an employer calls you a 1099, even if they make you sign a contract or set up an LLC, is not relevant to the economic realities test.
- In spite of the economic realities test, some gig workers, such as Uber, Lyft, and DoorDash drivers, are usually

considered independent contractors. These jobs are an exception to the general rule.

- Keep it simple. Ask yourself, "Am I self-employed?" If the answer is no, then you are probably an employee.

PART III

Protect Your Health

LIE: If you don't put your job first, you will get left behind.

TRUTH: You are replaceable at work; you are *not* replaceable at home.

THE RIGHT ENVIRONMENT

A plant cannot thrive in bad soil, and *you* will not thrive in a toxic workplace; it will ruin your self-esteem, convince you that you are ordinary and replaceable, and cause stress to seep into your home life. But the problem is the environment, not you!

Consider the following story.

Joshua Bell is a legendary violinist. His talents earned him a debut at Carnegie Hall at the young age of seventeen. His work has been featured in Hollywood films, including a collaboration with Hans Zimmer for the movie *Angels & Demons* starring Tom Hanks. In short, Joshua Bell is one of the greatest violinists of all time.

In 2007 Joshua and *The Washington Post* decided to conduct a social experiment. Joshua traveled to a subway station in Washington, DC, where hidden cameras observed him from afar. Disguised as a street performer, Joshua played for forty-five minutes to the bustling metro crowd. Live music from such an iconic performer was expected to move the crowd to tears—perhaps even shut down the subway.

But what happened was even more newsworthy.

Of over one thousand travelers, only seven people stopped to listen to the music for even a short time. Of the seven, only one recognized the great Joshua Bell. During the whole performance, Joshua earned just $52.17 in tips—$20 of which came from the one and only person who recognized him.

Concertgoers could expect to pay a premium for a Joshua Bell concert. But here, in a subway station surrounded by commuters, his music faded into white noise.

The results of the experiment are quite telling: No matter how great you are, no matter how worthy or wonderful, you will be treated as ordinary, even disposable, in the wrong environment.

You must not allow a toxic, degrading workplace to define you. Rather, you must learn how to deal with difficult bosses. When push comes to shove, you must learn to assert yourself. Like Joshua, you cannot measure your worth by the way a workplace responds to your efforts. Unlike Joshua (in this experiment), you have legal rights that empower you to stand up and say, "I deserve better."

By understanding what rights protect your health at work, you regain control over your life. You will gain the freedom to enjoy important life events; you will have time to care for your health; you will have the strength to push back when someone bullies you.

By combining *knowledge* of your rights with *strategies* to enforce them, you can improve your quality of life. Bullies at work lose their power. Threats from managers won't frighten you anymore. Your irreplaceable time is no longer given for free. You create time and space for your health, for your family, and for the life you truly want to live.

The truth is, for many people, the number one barrier to getting what they really deserve at work is *themselves,* not their boss:

"I'm not lazy!"

"I don't want to take advantage."

"I'm not asking for a handout."

"I feel guilty taking time off work."

I've heard it all. So that's why I need everyone who reads this book to understand that the rights I will teach you about in the following chapters are *essential* to a balanced life. You can have balance. You can prioritize your health. You can put your family and your happiness first.

Just don't let any outdated ideas like "hustle culture" get in your way. In part II, I said that hustle culture keeps you broke, and I advise anyone who reads this book to dump it. Left unchecked, it will leave you isolated, anxious, unfulfilled, and even make you sick. And for what?

Money, perhaps. But as I've said before, hard work has no intrinsic value. Celebrating "the grind" for its own sake is foolish. A car spinning its wheels in mud goes nowhere but burns its fuel anyway.

HOW HUSTLE CULTURE CONSUMES ITS FOLLOWERS

Rooted in the Puritan ideology of its earliest colonists, the US has long associated hard work with *morality* and *worthiness*, making rest *immoral* by default. The idea being that if you are resting, you should feel bad about yourself. Employers know this. And they manipulate our work ethic to suit their own goals. Often the toll it takes on employees is disastrous.

EXPLOITATION DISGUISED AS AMBITION: Companies use hustle culture to squeeze more labor out of you for little or no extra pay.

BURNOUT AND MENTAL HEALTH DECLINE: Hustle culture normalizes chronic stress and exhaustion. It guilt-trips you for taking time to enjoy the good parts of life, like a vacation or a quiet evening with your family.

MISSED MEMORIES: Moments of joy during your short time on this floating space rock are precious. They are the essence of life. You were not born to produce cheap labor for a greedy boss. You do that work to earn enough money to enjoy your life outside work. Hustle culture demands you sacrifice irreplaceable memories to stay late at the office.

FALSE NARRATIVES OF SUCCESS: Take it from a guy with millions of social media followers: What you see isn't always the full story. Those "hustle influencers" rarely show the privilege or plain luck that led to their success. Others are not successful at all—they're just lying for clicks! The reality? Most people grinding 24/7 don't become millionaires.

They just end up tired.

THE GUILT TRIP: Hustle culture doesn't just glorify overwork. It makes you *feel bad* when you do anything else—like take a break, sleep in, or (God forbid) play a video game after a long day. Simply relaxing feels like a failure because we've been conditioned to believe every minute should be *productive*.

Guilt keeps people trapped in the cycle: too exhausted to break free but too ashamed to stop. You deserve better than this. Rest is not something you "earn." It is an essential requirement for life.

HOW TO BREAK FREE

The strategies for protecting your legal rights are half the battle. The other half is your mindset. So here are a few mindset shifts to free yourself from hustle culture:

- **REDEFINE SUCCESS:** Success isn't just about how hard you work. It's about health, relationships, and personal fulfillment.
- **UNLEARN GUILT AROUND REST:** Rest is productive. It's necessary. You do not "earn" rest. You need it. And even if you don't feel productive, a moment enjoyed is never a moment wasted.
- **RECOGNIZE EXPLOITATION:** Is your labor helping you reach your goals, or do you feel like you're just spinning your wheels? If you're spinning, step back and ask if something is missing. Are your labor rights being honored? Is your pay correct? Is it time to ask for a raise? Regular check-ins like this help recognize and prevent exploitation at work.

TRUE WEALTH IS *TIME*—PROTECT IT!

It's *time*, not money, that makes a rich life. In the hustle of the modern world, we sometimes forget why we started chasing "success" in the first place—to have the time and freedom to live on our terms.

I can't hand you a check for life-changing money (not unless you're a client I've won a case for, at least). But what I *can* offer is a few chapters about how to protect your time from a greedy job. Because believe me, they will take every moment they can from you if you let them.

[CHAPTER 11]

FMLA Leave for Yourself or a Family Member

ATTORNEY RYAN V. EVIL INC.

"What radicalized you?"

It's a common joke in my circle that every lawyer eventually has a case that "radicalizes" us. A case where we witnessed such injustice, such cruelty, that it essentially fuels us for the rest of our careers.

For me, it was the flat tire case.

Brace yourself, because this was the most barbaric way I have ever seen a company act.

My client was a very sweet woman named Grace. Grace worked as an account manager at a staffing company, which we will call Evil Inc. Her job was to make new sales, maintain existing accounts, and grow her book of business. She worked full time at Evil Inc.'s main office for years, where she had earned a sort of "office mom" reputation among her coworkers.

But then in March 2020, everything changed. The Covid-19 pandemic ripped through the US. People were scared. This invisible disease was infecting millions, and there was no telling how long the crisis would last. Even Evil Inc. got spooked. Like many companies, Evil Inc. emptied its office to prevent Covid from spreading to its workers (not that the company cared; this was about protecting earnings, not people).

"Two weeks to flatten the curve!" they said.

But two weeks became two months, then four, then eight.

Grace and her coworkers worked remotely for almost a year. In that time, Grace was still expected to meet her sales goals. Each day was a grind. Grace made calls in the morning, drafted new contracts in the afternoon, and ended each day with a Zoom meeting to discuss progress with her team. Despite the uncertainty of the Covid era, Grace's sales actually *increased.*

Working remotely meant less time commuting, less time in unproductive office chats, and more time chasing new sales. Not to mention the reduced risk of catching a deadly virus at work.

But then Grace got terrible news: She was diagnosed with breast cancer. It hit her like a wrecking ball, but she didn't despair. She was determined to fight her way through it.

She knew she needed immediate chemotherapy to survive. Fortunately, she had followed me on social media, so she knew that she was legally entitled to Family and Medical Leave Act (FMLA) leave for her cancer treatments. If approved, it would give her up to twelve weeks of time off. Grace emailed human resources requesting Thursdays off for her chemotherapy appointments. She promised to make up for the lost time on weekends.

It was a simple request. By law, all Evil Inc. had to do was approve the intermittent FMLA and wish Grace well. Instead, they hopped in a handbasket and booked a one-way ticket to hell.

By the time Grace submitted her FMLA request, it had been almost one year since the company sent workers home due to Covid. But then Evil Inc. issued a company-wide mandate: All employees were *required* to return to the office full time—no exceptions.

Grace followed up with HR about her FMLA request. After consulting with management, HR responded with the suggestion that Grace could resign her position now, then return when she "felt better."

Grace was hurt by how cold HR was acting. By law, she was entitled to take time off for her chemotherapy, but she also should have been allowed to work remotely. The Americans with Disabilities Act, or ADA, entitled her to such accommodations. Grace reminded HR that she had cancer and her treatment left her vulnerable to infection. She needed to work remotely (as she had done successfully for months) while undergoing and recovering from chemo.

Once she processed the shock of what was happening, she decided to fight back. She sent HR a copy of the FMLA rules she found on the US Department of Labor website. Begrudgingly, HR caved. Grace was approved to take intermittent FMLA for her chemo—but if she did not report to work *in person*, despite the risk to her health, then she would be fired.*

This arrangement lasted for about six weeks. Grace told me these were the worst, most painful, and most exhausting weeks of her life. While undergoing chemotherapy, she was forced to drag her weakened body to the office early in the morning and work under bright fluorescent lights, surrounded by people who could potentially be carrying Covid (or other germs).

Eventually, it was too much to bear. Grace asked for the rest of her FMLA to be done consecutively rather than intermittently.† She took nine consecutive weeks of FMLA to finish her fight with cancer, which I am thrilled to report she won.

But then things went downhill. Grace returned to mixed reactions at Evil Inc. Her coworkers showered her with kindness, offering a welcome party, gifts, and lots of sweet treats to celebrate her recovery. One card even said, *I am so happy to have my office mom back.* ☺

But as Grace's coworkers rallied around her, the higher-ups scowled from their corner offices. They saw her cancer diagnosis as a financial liability—and they didn't want her working remotely either, lest any of the other employees get big ideas about working from home. Twirling their mustaches like a group of cartoon villains, they pondered: *How do we make this Grace problem go away?*

One of them had the demonic idea to simply overwhelm Grace with work until she quit.

---

*Like I said, these people booked themselves a ticket straight to hell.

†She had used only six days of intermittent leave, so she had plenty of FMLA remaining.

They increased her workload by almost 50 percent, but without an increase in pay or any help. When she complained, management *again* pushed her to resign: "If you can't keep up with the pace of business, maybe we need to consider a separation."

The leadership at Evil Inc. were a bunch of ghouls. *Ghouls,* I tell you.

Anyway, Grace saw the writing on the wall, so she began applying to other jobs. Still, the bills wouldn't pay themselves, and she needed her health insurance now more than ever.* She tried to stick it out for a while longer. But in that time, she got slapped with the first poor performance review of her career.

The charges? Failure to grow her book of business, failure to upsell new accounts, failure to keep up with account reports.

Grace protested that the added accounts were making it hard to keep up. She needed help with the workload. But Evil Inc. shrugged her off. After a second poor performance review, they hit her with a title demotion and slashed her pay by $20,000 per year.

Now she was struggling to pay rent.

A third poor performance review followed. By that time, Grace had had enough. She had fought cancer and won, she had battled retaliation and harassment from Evil Inc., but now she wasn't earning enough to survive. To make matters worse, she worried about her ability to get a new job if she was fired. So she did what any reasonable person would do.

She resigned.

Admittedly, resigning did not help Grace's case. She was worried about her reputation, so she wrote a long email thanking the company for being so kind and accommodating to her. This was not true, but again, she was scared for her future employment prospects.†

Luckily, Grace reached out to us soon after. Once we took her on as a client, we filed a lawsuit against Evil Inc. for retaliation, harassment, constructive wrongful termination, and half a dozen other violations.

---

*Making access to health care conditional based on your employment is a barbaric practice that I hope to see the end of in my lifetime, but that issue is for another book.

†This email got thrown in my face a *lot* during the lawsuit. It wasn't the only problem we had to deal with, but it was a major issue.

During the litigation, the company dumped thousands of documents on us. Frankly, I didn't mind. Sorting through the evidence while listening to music was kind of relaxing. Most of the documents were useless, but late one night I found something peculiar: Dozens of emails between Grace's bosses described a "flat tire" in the sales department.

Interesting . . .

The next day, I asked Grace what she thought about the emails. At first, she had no idea who (or what) the "flat tire" was. But she noticed that several accounts in those "flat tire" emails were *her accounts*.

Then it hit us. *Flat tire* was code for *Grace*.

I confronted Evil Inc.'s lawyers with this discovery. Their response triggered one of the most heated exchanges of my career.

I am paraphrasing, but I said something to the effect of "What the fuck is this?"

To which they replied, "The company has to pay attention to sales, and they needed longevity in the sales team. The flat tire statements . . . they're a bad look, but it's a metaphor for the burden Grace put on the company."

"Excuse me?" I gasped.

"Well, when we look at her declining performance record—"

I cut him off. "She was fine until the company forced a performance issue by increasing her workload without support."

The Evil lawyer threw up his hands. "I think you're mischaracterizing the facts here."

"As for longevity," I continued, "are you saying that *because* she had cancer, the company didn't want her around in case she died at an inconvenient time? Is that really what you're saying?"

The Evil lawyer realized he'd painted himself into a corner. Shifting in his chair, he said, "Your client has our sympathy, but for business reasons—"

"Sympathy doesn't pay the bills," I interrupted. "The timeline doesn't lie. This is textbook retaliation for taking FMLA leave."

The Evil lawyer grimaced, then smirked. "She resigned willingly, and she made a point to thank the company for being so accommodating. You and I both know that's a problem for you."

Well, shit, I thought. *He's a sleazeball, but he's a sleazeball with a point.*

"Yeah, she resigned," I conceded, "and she said some things she didn't mean to protect her career. But this 'flat tire' shit really makes the company's intentions clear, don't you think?"

We slugged it out in court for over a year. Finally, the case went to mediation. Mediation is a structured negotiation between both sides with the help of a retired judge. It was a long, challenging day, but I am proud to say that Grace won a substantial cash settlement.

As we continue in this chapter, my goal is to help you protect your job while getting the leave you deserve. Most employers will honor these rights. But if they try to mess with you like Evil Inc. did, I want you to have an airtight paper trail so you can get justice.

WHAT IS FMLA?

FMLA is one of the most important labor rights you have. So important that I've devoted two chapters to it. By understanding FMLA, you can enforce the boundary between your personal life and your work life. FMLA will help you be present when your family needs you. It will also give you the flexibility to take care of your health.

Remember—hustle culture will leave you broke and broken. FMLA can help prevent this.

So what exactly is FMLA, and how does it work?

FMLA leave grants you up to twelve weeks of protected time off to recover from a serious health condition or to care for a family member with a serious health condition. These rights come from the federal Family and Medical Leave Act of 1993. The leave is unpaid, but you are protected against retaliation when you take it. (Note that some employers will offer paid leave; others will have you use your paid time off [PTO] hours if you have them.)*

*You might be asking, "Wait, if I am too sick to work, how will I pay bills?" This is an excellent question. The United States is extremely unusual in that it does not offer federally protected paid leave for workers. I hope to see this change one day.

In this chapter, we will discuss your rights to take time off to care for a serious medical condition for yourself or a family member.

Time Off for a Serious Health Condition

When taking FMLA to care for yourself, you must have a qualifying condition. Specifically, it must be a *serious health condition* as defined by the FMLA statute.*

A serious health condition is a medical condition that substantially interferes with major life activities (such as work). According to the US Department of Labor, "A serious health condition means an illness, injury, impairment or physical or mental condition that involves inpatient care . . . or continuing treatment by a health care provider."

While this definition can be somewhat broad, a *serious health condition* usually looks like one or more of these common situations:

- A medical issue that makes you unable to work or perform daily activities for more than three consecutive days.
- A health status that requires continuing treatment by a health care provider. (Routine examinations generally don't count.)
- Chronic conditions, including permanent or long-term conditions, that require medical supervision.

FMLA applies when your condition is so serious that it prevents you from performing essential functions in your job, even if it is temporary. For example, if you deliver packages for work, a broken ankle will probably interfere with essential functions of that job. Likewise, if you suffer a stroke, you will certainly need some recovery time before returning to an office job.

The serious health condition can be temporary or permanent, physical or mental. Yes, mental health conditions count as well! Some bosses have extremely ignorant views on mental health. They may not

---

*29 C.F.R. § 825.113, for any who wish to see the full text of the law.

understand that conditions like depression, anxiety, and PTSD are very real. Still, your privacy matters, and using FMLA for a mental health condition needs to be done the right way.

The DOL has confirmed that such disorders may qualify for FMLA if they meet the requirements to be considered a *serious mental health condition*.* Under FMLA, this is defined as a condition that requires inpatient care or continuing treatment by a health care provider.

- **INPATIENT CARE** means you had an overnight stay in a hospital or other medical facility. This can include a treatment center for drug or alcohol addiction or for eating disorders.
- **CONTINUING TREATMENT** means conditions that make you unable to work for three consecutive days, and which require ongoing medical treatment (such as multiple appointments). It can include chronic conditions like depression or anxiety.

Just like any other serious health condition, your employer can require certification from a health care provider to support the need for FMLA leave, but a diagnosis is not required.

What About Stress Leave?

I want to make a special note about *stress leave*. **It is my opinion that most people should not request stress leave.** While I applaud people being proactive about managing stress, stress leave is a trap, as you'll see shortly. Stress by itself is not a serious health condition under FMLA because stress is generally considered a *symptom* rather than a *condition*.

*In 2024 the conservative majority in the Supreme Court overturned the long-held principle of *Chevron deference*. Basically, this reduced the power of agencies like the DOL to interpret the laws they enforce. As a consequence, a legal challenge to FMLA in a conservative-leaning court could result in these rights being narrowed down (or eliminated). Thus, it is *possible* we may see some of these FMLA rights restricted to fewer conditions. That said, this information is accurate and up-to-date as of this writing, but the law is always evolving. Check with an experienced workers' rights lawyer if you aren't sure if your condition qualifies.

If you are under so much stress that you need FMLA, then there is a smarter way to do this. Getting a diagnosis for anxiety, depression, or another underlying issue from a health care provider is better. If you ask your boss for stress leave, a few things may go wrong:

- Your request will be granted as sick leave or vacation, not FMLA.
- Your request will be denied, because stress alone is not legally a serious health condition.
- You may be subjected to heightened scrutiny, because some bosses wrongfully see stress as an indication that you can't handle your job.

You do not need to share a diagnosis with your employer, but you should ensure your official mental health condition is one that (1) has a diagnosis and (2) requires inpatient care or continuing treatment.

Intermittent FMLA Leave

FMLA leave can be taken all at once if you want. But that isn't always the best fit for your situation. Fortunately, it can be taken as *intermittent FMLA leave.* Intermittent leave means you are still working but taking some days or weeks off to deal with your health issue. This is helpful when you need the FMLA for medical treatment but still want to work.

Your employer must consider your preferences, but ultimately, they get to have some input as well. The law requires you to make a reasonable effort to schedule medical treatments at times that "minimize disruption" to the business.* If necessary, your employer is allowed to temporarily transfer you to an alternate position during this time.

But watch out! The new position cannot be a demotion (that would be illegal retaliation). It must have the same or substantially similar

*I don't make the rules, I just report them.

pay and benefits. It should also be clearly appropriate for accommodating intermittent leave.

You should work together with your manager to find an intermittent schedule that works for everyone.

Continued Health Benefits

If you have an employer-sponsored health plan, then those benefits must continue as if you were not on leave. If the employer covers a portion, but not all, of your health plan premiums, then you will have to continue paying your own contributions. I understand this can be a burden. The state of US family and medical leave is quite sad compared to other industrialized nations. However, there are some states where you can get paid leave. (We'll discuss this more in chapter 14.)

Other Qualifying Reasons for FMLA

This book aims to be a broad reference guide to your rights at work, and FMLA leave could be a book on its own. You can find more detailed reference guides for FMLA-specific situations on my Substack (substack.com/@attorneyryan).

Our focus in this chapter is using FMLA for serious health conditions. But note that FMLA can apply to other important situations, including:

- Caring for a spouse, child, or parent with a serious health condition
- Birth, adoption, or foster care placement of a child
- Military caregiver leave or qualifying exigency related to military service*

We'll cover some of these circumstances in later chapters.

*You can get up to twenty-six weeks of protected leave under these qualifying reasons for taking FMLA.

WHO GETS TO TAKE FMLA?

Having a serious health condition is required for FMLA, but it's not the only requirement. You must have also worked for a minimum amount of time in the twelve months *prior* to taking the leave. So, to qualify, you must have worked for the same employer for twelve months, and you must have worked at least 1,250 hours in those twelve months.

WHICH EMPLOYERS HAVE TO FOLLOW FMLA?

FMLA leave does not apply to all employers.

Under federal law, only *covered* employers must provide FMLA leave. What makes a covered employer under this rule? Basically, it boils down to three broad umbrellas:

1. **PRIVATE-SECTOR EMPLOYERS WITH FIFTY OR MORE WORKERS WITHIN A SEVENTY-FIVE-MILE RADIUS OF WHERE YOU WORK**

   I've had cases where employers tried to wriggle out of honoring FMLA because they had fewer than fifty employees at some point in the past year, or because they recently downsized. It's a petty and sneaky trick. Fortunately, the law has an answer. We look at the previous *and* current calendar years.

   If the employer had at least fifty workers for twenty workweeks in either the current or prior calendar year, then they have to honor FMLA.

2. **GOVERNMENT EMPLOYERS**

   This includes state and local governments regardless of size.

3. **LOCAL EDUCATIONAL AGENCIES**

   This includes public school boards, public elementary and high schools, and private elementary and secondary schools, regardless of size. It generally applies only to *instructional* employees, meaning those whose main job is teaching. This includes most classroom teachers. It can also include coaches, life skills instructors, and special education assistants.

Small employers with fewer than fifty employees do not have to abide by FMLA rules. The exception, of course, is if there is a state or local law covering small employers.

CAN I USE FMLA LEAVE TO CARE FOR SOMEONE ELSE?

Yes! FMLA isn't limited to just *your own* serious health condition.

In 2023 I had a case where my client's husband needed a hip replacement. If you weren't aware, hip replacements are *brutal.* (Squeamish readers should skip to "Case Study: FMLA to Support Your Spouse's Recovery.")

Still here? Okay, let the party begin.

First, the surgeon slices open the flesh around your hip, then literally *disassembles* your entire hip joint. But they're just getting started. They yank out your femur (or whatever is left of it) then *saw off the top of it.* When that's done, they set the femur aside for a moment, then pull out a drill.

Yes, a drill.

They *drill* a new hole in your hip, then install a metal or ceramic socket on top of your freshly shaved bone matter.

While this is happening, they prepare your femur for installation. To do this, they shove a metal rod down the shaft of your femur, smack a metal ball on top of that, then shove the whole thing into the socket they drilled into your hip.*

*I am told there is a more accurate medical term than *shoving,* but honestly, it all sounded like a bunch of shoving to me anyway.

Case Study: FMLA to Support Your Spouse's Recovery

When the fun is finally over, you've got a new hip! However, the road to recovery is long and difficult. My client's husband had to relearn how to walk. He was a trooper, but my client said he broke down in tears during physical therapy—the pain and frustration were almost unbearable.

When they got married, my client swore to stick by her husband in sickness and in health. She helped him get dressed, use the bathroom, and bathe. She made his meals, drove him to his doctor's appointments, and gave him a shoulder to lean on when the recovery was too painful to bear.

Needless to say, she had much more important things going on than attending weekly Zoom meetings about nothing with her bozo boss.

She put in for FMLA to care for her husband. At first, Mr. Bozo had no idea what FMLA was. But that didn't stop him from violating her rights.

"I'm very sorry to hear about your husband," Mr. Bozo said in an email. "I wish him a speedy recovery, but we don't offer spousal leave as a benefit. You will need to find a way to plan doctors' visits around your work schedule."

Oof. Let's go ahead and mark that as Exhibit A for the inevitable lawsuit.

Remember when I said *you* will have to take the driver's seat in getting your FMLA? This is why. Most managers have no clue what FMLA is, how to give it to you, or even what conditions qualify.

Devastated, my client asked me for help. Here's the email we drafted in reply. We copied the manager and human resources. You may want to keep this template handy, because it got the manager to back off immediately.

Sample Email Template: Response to Denial of Your FMLA Leave

Dear Mr. Bozo and Human Resources,

I am disappointed to hear my request for FMLA leave has been wrongfully denied. I qualify for the leave because I have worked for more than twelve months and 1,250 hours. The company has more than fifty employees within a seventy-five-mile radius of where I work.

Further, I have a qualifying reason for FMLA leave. The FMLA provides protected leave to care for a family member, including spouses, for a serious medical condition. My husband is recovering from surgery, and he needs my help.

Therefore, I would like to formally escalate this to human resources. Please inform me whether my leave is approved. If not, please inform me in writing why it is denied despite my legal right to take FMLA.

This is a time-sensitive request. Please provide more information before the end of the week so I can attend to my spouse's serious health condition.

Respectfully,
Employee

FMLA RETALIATION IS ILLEGAL!

Unfortunately, my client was in fact let go right in the middle of her FMLA leave. The company claimed that this termination was done as part of a "reduction in force." However, we didn't buy it. We sued for wrongful termination, FMLA retaliation, and a few other violations. Ultimately, the company could not prove that the "reduction in force" was real, or even necessary.

When my client left for FMLA, the company made it very clear they were not happy about it. They hired a temporary worker to cover for her. But here's what they didn't say when they fired my client—they promoted the temp employee to full time to replace her! That's not a reduction in force. That's the oldest trick in the FMLA retaliation book.

Your employer is well within their rights to hire a temporary replacement. But FMLA is *job-protected leave.* You must not be fired just for taking FMLA. When your FMLA leave is done, you must be reinstated to the same or a nearly identical position (with no loss in pay!).

Regardless of the reason you are taking FMLA, it is expressly protected from retaliation by your employer. Remember that retaliation is an adverse employment action motivated by your protected activity. That absolutely includes FMLA leave.

Wrongful termination for taking FMLA leave is one of the most common and high-value kinds of cases I work on. But you cannot protect your job (or get the maximum financial recovery) without a paper trail.

To make a good paper trail, *protected complaints* are one of the most important tools in your toolbox. When you have a reasonable suspicion that you are facing retaliation, call it out! Make that paper trail *early,* before the employer has an opportunity to conjure up a pretext (such as poor performance) to fire you.

Here is a template of what a protected complaint for FMLA retaliation looks like:

Sample Email Template: Protected Complaint of Retaliation for Taking/Requesting/Returning from FMLA Leave

Dear Human Resources,

I am writing to report retaliation I have experienced for [taking/requesting/returning from] FMLA leave.

I requested protected leave under the FMLA on [DATE]. I sent the request to [name everyone you sent it to]. Since then, I have experienced retaliation in the form of [reduced pay, write-ups, demotion, harassment, threats of termination].

It is clear these adverse employment actions are motivated by my request for FMLA leave, which is against federal law.

What can HR do to help make the retaliation stop? Also, I feel this situation necessitates additional training for management on the no-retaliation rules around FMLA. I would encourage such training to prevent others from experiencing the retaliation I have experienced.

This is a time-sensitive situation. Please keep me posted on what progress the company is making to address the retaliation.

Respectfully,
Employee

Not to toot my own horn, but this email slaps. It works because it calls out the retaliation with a few specific examples. All that is required is that you put the company on notice of the retaliation. So this email is a winner because it avoids the common trap of giving too much detail. Remember, HR works for the company, not for you. Sometimes they are looking for reasons to deny you or push you out. That's why it's important to keep your emails fairly short—because while everything you say will add to your paper trail, it could also be used against you.

FMLA INTERFERENCE IS ILLEGAL!

FMLA interference is when your employer intentionally blocks, slows down, hinders, or otherwise *interferes* with your ability to take FMLA leave. It can take several forms:

- Slow rolling or intentionally ignoring your requests for FMLA leave
- Making you jump through artificial hoops to request FMLA leave, such as requiring you to fill out mountains of unnecessary paperwork
- Demanding lots of unnecessary "proof" and additional medical information from your doctor

Speaking of unnecessary "proof," we need to talk about what kind of certification your employer can require. As a general rule, employers only need two things: Notice of when you need the leave, and a note from your doctor confirming the need for medical leave.

Everything else is just fluff, but within certain boundaries, the fluff is not illegal—just annoying. Therefore, you will have to play the medical certification game with your employer so long as they don't break any rules.

Employers may try to pry into your medical history. They may even press you for a diagnosis. If this happens, don't panic. Your doctor can describe the time off needed. They can also describe in broad terms how the medical necessity will limit your work abilities.

But no diagnosis is required. That's private.

Your employer is not your doctor. Human resources is not your doctor. None of these people have any need (or right) to pry into your personal medical information. They should *never* disclose your medical information to anyone without your consent either. They may be breaking multiple laws if they do so.

If your employer starts asking invasive questions about your medical condition or history, simply say, "The law protects my medical privacy. I am happy to share my needs as they relate to medical leave, such as my treatment schedule, but my diagnosis and specific treatment plan are private."

If they continue to press, ask, "How is this information necessary for approving, planning, or implementing my leave?"

Keep employers in their lane.

Caveat: Medical Certification

I never like it when employers demand doctor's notes to "prove" you need leave. Frankly, it feels childish. But as my niece would say, "Them's the rules." Employers can require medical certification from a health care provider confirming the need for FMLA leave. A medical certification like this doesn't have to be anything fancy. A simple letter from your doctor will suffice, saying something to the effect of:

> *[Employee] is a patient in my care. For medical reasons related to a serious health condition, for which I am providing continuing care, [employee] requires [number of weeks] of leave.*

The exact wording of the letter doesn't matter, so long as the doctor informs the employer of the expected duration of the leave.

Often, this will include intermittent FMLA. In that case, the letter from your doctor should include the frequency of visits and the duration of the leave. For example: "[Employee] will need intermittent leave for eighteen weeks, with Thursdays off for medical treatment."

Caveat: What Kind of Paperwork Can Employers Require for FMLA?

Because HR will absolutely lie about this, I'll be very clear: Federal law does not require any specific documentation for FMLA leave.

I've seen it too many times. Some HR rep you've never met denies your FMLA request because "you filled out form X, but you needed form Y *and* an original copy of your first-grade report card. Your time-off request for emergency surgery is denied."*

It's frustrating, confusing, and makes employees feel small and powerless. And that is the point. Some employers want you to get so frustrated with the process that you simply quit or give up. Don't let them win!

Employers are within their rights to create their own forms for an employee to fill out when requesting FMLA leave (within reason). And the US Department of Labor has created its own forms for employers to use. But these DOL forms are not legally required.

Yes, you should cooperate and fill out their forms (within reason). But once you make the request in writing, the process begins. This is true whether you do it in a text, email, Slack message—doesn't matter. (Though I prefer you do it in a way that ensures you always have a copy.)

The point is that your employer does *not* have free rein to do whatever they want. Dumping so much paperwork on you that requesting FMLA becomes a bureaucratic nightmare might be illegal interference. Employers who impose unreasonable paperwork demands or try to block your request can be held responsible. The system may feel absurd—but you still have rights.

---

*While this is a bit hyperbolic for the sake of illustration, it's not too far from the truth. No one has asked my clients for a first-grade report card, but you'd be shocked at some to the things HR thinks they are entitled to.

HOW TO REQUEST FMLA

I've talked a lot about the employers' responsibilities for FMLA. They can't interfere, they can't retaliate, and they must restore you to the same job when you return. However, I also said several times that *you* will have to take the lead in implementing your FMLA, and that comes with responsibilities as well.

The FMLA requires you to give reasonable notice to your employer that you need FMLA leave. *Reasonable notice* means that if the need for leave is foreseeable, like a scheduled surgery, you need to provide at least thirty days' notice. This helps you prepare for leave, and it helps the employer plan for your absence. More notice is a win-win.

But life is not always predictable. If your need for FMLA is *unforeseeable*, like a sudden illness, then your notice must be given as soon as possible. Usually this means within the same or next business day, or when it is safe for you to do so.

Heads up: Some employers will try to impose arbitrary notice requirements on your FMLA. They may even try to deny you (wrongfully) if you do not strictly follow those rules. Give notice as soon as you can, but if they deny your request because of "insufficient notice," it's time to talk to a lawyer. That's because short notice by itself is not a legal reason to deny the leave.

So how do you request FMLA leave in a way that protects you? Here are a couple templates you should keep handy.

Sample Email Template: Requesting FMLA Leave for Your Own Serious Medical Condition

Dear Manager / Human Resources,

I am writing to request FMLA leave for my serious medical condition. Please see the attached letter from my health care provider.

I'd like my leave to begin on [DATE] with an expected return date of [DATE].

Please let me know how the company would like to make arrangements for my leave. I am happy to assist with the transition.

Respectfully,
Employee

Sample Email Template: Requesting FMLA Leave for a Family Member's Health Condition

Dear Manager / Human Resources,

I am writing to request FMLA leave for my [spouse, child, parent, next of kin]'s serious medical condition. I will need to begin leave on [DATE] with an expected return date of [DATE].

If requesting intermittent leave: I would like intermittent leave, taking time off on the following repeating days and times to care for my family member: [List days and times].

Please let me know how the company would like to make arrangements for my leave. I am happy to assist with the transition.

Respectfully,
Employee

PREPARING FOR FMLA LEAVE

All right, you put in your notice for FMLA. Now what? Remember that while life comes first, you still need to cover your responsibilities at work. The more preparation you do before the leave, the easier the process will be. Further, it will make your case one hundred times stronger if you show that you prepared for FMLA leave responsibly but got punished anyway.

Fortunately, there's a simple way to help you prepare. You don't have to fly in the dark!

Here is a sample checklist you will want to keep handy when it's time to take FMLA leave. Every job is different, so your checklist may vary slightly. That said, this should help you get started.

Attorney Ryan's Ten-Step FMLA Leave Checklist

1. **CONFIRM ELIGIBILITY AND SUBMIT PAPERWORK:** Double-check FMLA eligibility and submit all required forms to HR as early as possible.
2. **NOTIFY YOUR MANAGER EARLY:** Provide written notice with expected leave dates and duration. Use the templates in this chapter if you aren't sure how to start.
3. **CREATE A TASK LIST:** Make a detailed list of your regular duties and any upcoming deadlines. Those deadlines are still your responsibility even if on leave, so make sure everyone knows about them and be *certain* that at least one person is clearly responsible for meeting each deadline.
4. **ASSIGN RESPONSIBILITIES:** Work with your manager to delegate key tasks and projects to appropriate team members. *Always* make sure there is a specific person (not a department, a person) who is going to take over each responsibility.
5. **DOCUMENT PROCESSES:** Provide clear instructions, guides, or templates for anything someone else will need to handle in your absence. Keep copies of these. This will prevent people from bugging you during your leave.
6. **SET OUT-OF-OFFICE RESPONSES:** Set up automatic out-of-office replies on your email. Update your voicemail as well. Both should say whom to contact for urgent matters. This helps prevent anyone from claiming you ghosted them while on leave.
7. **HAND-OFF MEETING (IF POSSIBLE):** Schedule a meeting with your team to walk through duties and answer questions. Make a recap email of the meeting and what was discussed. Keep copies.
8. **ORGANIZE FILES AND RESOURCES:** Make sure all documents, shared drives, and tools are easy to find and access. This step

will help prevent people from interrupting your leave with constant calls, texts, and emails looking for these things.

9. **PLAN FOR YOUR RETURN:** Leave notes for yourself on key projects and priorities to help you quickly get back up to speed.
10. **STAY IN CONTACT (IF POSSIBLE):** Checking in occasionally so that returning feels less overwhelming is a good idea. Also, if the employer asks for updates about your status during leave, you should cooperate. Failure to keep them updated *could* be legal grounds for termination under certain conditions, so play it safe by staying in touch.

Again, every job is different. But these steps will make a huge impact on how smooth your FMLA leave will go. Remember that the leave is temporary, and you'll want to be proactive so that returning to work is as painless as possible.

And don't forget to *document* every step. This will make your friendly workers' rights lawyer proud!

RETURNING FROM FMLA: HOW TO STICK THE LANDING

If you got this far, you are kicking ass. This is hard; the rules are complicated. But you are doing great and there is more to learn. So let's talk about what happens when you get back from FMLA.

When the leave is up, what happens next? Returning from FMLA will take some planning. Fortunately, you can do this in three easy steps.

1. **CONFIRM YOUR INTENT TO RETURN:** Send a note to your manager or human resources announcing your intent to return. Confirm your return date, time, and location for your first day back.
2. **PREPARE TO PICK UP WHERE YOU LEFT OFF:** This is your opportunity to get up to speed *before* you report back to work. Ask

whoever covered for you for a written hand-off report. You want to know what's being worked on, what's changed since you've been gone, and what priorities need your attention.

This is also a good time to request your login credentials be restored so you don't have issues getting into work programs on your first day back.

3. **BE ALERT, BUT NOT PARANOID:** Retaliation for taking FMLA often happens shortly *after* the employee returns from leave. Be alert for any unusual behavior from your boss, such as micromanagement, undue criticism, or even warnings about your performance.

   If you suspect you are being targeted for taking FMLA, then you should report it right away. Use the template from the "FMLA Retaliation Is Illegal!" section earlier in this chapter to help you report the retaliation if you are not sure how to start.

FMLA LEAVE MADE EASY

I understand this is a lot of information. No one expects you to be an expert on FMLA leave, but learning the basics always helps.

At the end of the day, using FMLA boils down to a very simple formula. Refer back to this list whenever you feel overwhelmed by the FMLA process, because it'll make things easier.

1. **EMPLOYEE REQUIREMENTS:** You have a qualifying reason for FMLA. And you have worked at least twelve months and 1,250 hours.
2. **EMPLOYER REQUIREMENTS:** Your employer has fifty or more employees within a seventy-five-mile radius of where you work.
3. **STATE LAW CHECK:** Some states make it easier to get FMLA by requiring more employers to provide it, expanding the

qualifying reasons for leave, or reducing work requirements. Some states might even offer paid leave.

4. **ANNOUNCE THE NEED FOR LEAVE:** No specific paperwork is needed, but you should cooperate with your employer's reasonable paperwork requirements. Always make the initial request in writing. Use my template for this.
5. **EMPLOYEE PREPARES FOR LEAVE:** Use my ten-step checklist to prepare for a successful FMLA leave period.
6. **EMPLOYEE RETURNS FROM LEAVE:** Use my three-step guide to stick the landing when you return.
7. **EMPLOYER MUST NOT RETALIATE:** Use my template for a protected complaint if you feel targeted after you return from leave.

[Summary]

- The federal Family and Medical Leave Act provides up to twelve weeks of unpaid but job-protected leave.
- You must be restored to the same or a substantially similar role when you return.
- FMLA can be used for a serious medical condition for yourself or a family member, for family leave (like having a baby), military caregiver leave, and military exigency leave.
- You qualify for FMLA if you have a qualifying reason *and* you have worked for at least twelve months and 1,250 hours for your employer. Your employer must have fifty or more employees within a seventy-five-mile radius of your work location.

- FMLA applies to government employers regardless of size.
- About a dozen states have their own FMLA equivalents, which apply to more employers.
- Retaliation for taking FMLA is illegal.
- Unlawful termination for FMLA is common. Be smart by making a paper trail. Make and complete a checklist to prepare for your leave.
- Interfering with your FMLA, like ignoring your request or burying you in paperwork, could be illegal.
- Use the ten-step FMLA preparation checklist to prepare for successful FMLA leave.
- Use the three-step stick the landing checklist when you return.
- Hustle culture is a scam. *Use FMLA for what it's intended for!* Your boss will not remember all the sacrifices you made by working long hours. But your family will remember. So never delay medical treatment because of work. Take FMLA leave and protect your health.

CHAPTER 12

FMLA for Family Leave

ATTACK OF THE BABY HATERZ

Welcoming a new baby into your life is one of the most important things you will ever do. It is exciting, rewarding, challenging, and wonderful all at once. You may be tempted to keep this part of your life private. Unfortunately, you will have to involve your employer at some point. *How* you do this will make the difference between protecting your job and possibly losing it.

Heed my warning: Do *not* assume your boss will be happy for you. I have seen some of the most absurd, callous, and straight up evil responses to baby announcements, like what happened to Melissa, who worked for a company we will call Baby Haterz, Inc.

Melissa was an account manager at Baby Haterz, a business-to-business (B2B) software sales company. She was good at her job, and her high salary reflected it. About two years into her career, she fell in love, got married, and started trying for her first child. When she got the news that she was pregnant, she was ecstatic. Melissa felt like all her dreams were coming true. She had a perfect career, a perfect husband, and soon she would have a perfect baby of her own.

Excited, she told her coworkers in a “work besties” group chat. They were thrilled. Melissa’s coworkers showered her with congratulations. They even threw a party with cake and gifts to celebrate the pregnancy.

In all the excitement, they posted pictures and videos of the "work besties baby shower" to their social media profiles.

When the party ended, Melissa and her friends started cleaning up. As she gathered paper plates and leftover cake, one of the more senior employees pulled Melissa aside.

"Keep this between us," the senior employee said quietly, "but Mr. Gekko [the CEO] has a history with pregnant women. He's not very understanding . . . to say the least."

A few days later, Melissa got a surprise. One of her coworkers—who was not part of the "work bestie" chat—dropped by her desk.

In an excited whisper, the coworker said, "I just want to say congrats! We're all so happy for you."

Melissa blushed. "Thanks so much, but we're kind of keeping it on the down-low until I'm past twelve weeks."

The coworker nodded. "Oh of course, it's all just so exciting. I'm surprised more people haven't come to congratulate you. Anyway, so happy for you." She floated away to chitchat with someone else. A moment later, Melissa's computer chimed.

It was an email from HR: "Please report to Gordon Gekko's office."

Melissa gulped. She had a bad feeling about this. She got up and walked to the corner office. It felt like she was walking to the gallows.

Nothing has happened yet, she thought to herself. *This could be about anything.*

She entered Gordon's office. Beside him sat Veronica, one of the human resources representatives. Neither smiled. Neither said a word as Melissa entered.

Gordon indicated that she should take a seat.

"Do you have something to tell us?" he said.

Melissa looked at Veronica, who looked like she was attending a funeral. "Actually, yes," Melissa said, trying to fake a smile. "I'm having a baby!"

Silence.

"I'm disappointed that you weren't more forthcoming about this," Gordon grumbled. "How long were you going to keep me in the dark?"

"I'm sorry," Melissa said, stunned at how cold he was behaving. "I don't feel like I did anything wrong, this is all pretty recent."

"You hid this from me," he growled. His hands shook with anger.

Veronica quickly chimed in. "You're not in trouble," she said, catching a sharp glare from her boss as she did so. "It's just . . . there's a right way and a wrong way to do these things. Being sneaky is never the right way. Are you planning on taking time off for this?"

Melissa was shocked. She felt a sting of anxiety in her belly. Her palms felt clammy. Then she thought of her baby, and she worried if the stress was harming her unborn child, which made her even more stressed. She felt dizzy.

Veronica's voice echoed through the haze. "Melissa?"

"I'm sorry?" Melissa stuttered, returning to the present.

"Are you planning on taking time off?" Veronica asked again.

"Well, I hadn't really thought about it. I'd like some time for my baby of course. But I thought it was too soon for that."

"These things take careful planning," Veronica said. "Under FMLA—"

"Two weeks," Gordon interrupted, barely containing his rage. "You get two weeks. Anything longer and you're asking me to change the whole company just for you."

Veronica frowned. Clearly, she was torn. Her loyalty was to the company, but deep down, she knew Gordon was wrong. "I'll work with you to make arrangements," Veronica said. "We'll be in touch."

Melissa was excused. As she left, she could hear Gordon muttering to himself.

"Unbelievable," he hissed. "Un-fucking-believable."*

A week later, Melissa got a call from HR. A new trainee was being assigned to her. The trainee, a twenty-six-year-old MBA grad named Christian, was to shadow Melissa until her FMLA leave began. Christian would handle Melissa's duties until she returned. That was the "official" plan, but things were about to take a dark turn.

---

*These ignorant attitudes toward pregnancy are not unusual, but that doesn't make them okay!

Christian was a good person. He was respectful to Melissa, even serving as her de facto assistant while she trained him to cover for her.

On the last day before her maternity leave, Melissa was called into the HR office. There, she was instructed to completely clear out her desk. And she was logged out of all company systems.

"I'm not going to be gone that long," Melissa said.

"This is all standard," HR said. "We'll get you logged back in when you return."

Melissa's leave began that weekend. I am happy to say she had a straightforward pregnancy, with no complications, and she gave birth to a beautiful, healthy baby boy.

But that's when the trouble really started.

About three weeks into her leave, Melissa got a direct deposit from the company. Strange, since her leave was unpaid. She looked at her pay stub and noticed it was all her accrued PTO.

A little odd, since she hadn't asked for her PTO to get cashed out, but every dollar mattered, so she didn't complain.

Still, it was a good reminder to check in with the office. How was Christian doing? Did he have any questions?

She emailed Christian and copied her boss. "Hi Christian! I hope you're doing well flying solo. I am just checking in to see how things are going. Do you have any questions? I am happy to offer any advice while I am gone."

No response.

Melissa thought the radio silence was unusual, since Christian had always been so responsive when she was training him. So a few days later she followed up.

"Hi Christian! Just circling back on this. My leave is going well, and I am looking forward to returning to work in a few weeks. If you have any questions at all, I am here to help."

Again, silence.

A week later, Melissa got a letter from a law firm representing Baby Haterz, Inc. titled *Notice of Termination; Order to Cease and Desist Unlawful Conduct.*

"What the fuck?" she gasped.

In short, the letter explained that she was being let go for violating company policy. Specifically, the letter threatened to sue her for violating the nonsolicitation and nondisclosure provisions in her employment contract.

"It has come to our attention that you have unlawfully attempted to solicit members of Baby Haterz staff for the purpose of disclosing systems, processes, and other confidential information. This unlawful solicitation campaign must cease and desist, and you are required to respond to this letter with a statement that you have ceased your unlawful activities. If you fail to comply, we shall initiate litigation and seek monetary damages against you . . ."*

Again, *what the fuck?*

Melissa scrambled for answers. She called one of her coworkers at the office, who sent her a screenshot of a Slack message that broke her heart: "Melissa is no longer with the company. We wish her well in her future endeavors. We are excited to welcome Christian as our new full-time account manager. Please direct account inquiries to him."

Melissa was devastated. They tricked her! They never planned on honoring her FMLA leave. They would have fired her the day they found out she was pregnant if they'd had a replacement ready to go. Instead of being honest, they tricked her into training her own replacement. To rub salt in the wound, they falsely accused her of breaking company policy. They even hired a law firm to send her a nasty letter.

Fortunately, she found my office.

We went on the attack right away. The letter from Baby Haterz's lawyers was bullshit, so we replied that (1) she had not broken any laws or company policies, and (2) she would be pursuing damages for wrongful termination.

Once Baby Haterz realized Melissa wasn't an easy target anymore, everything changed. You have to understand that bosses like Gordon

*In legal terms, this letter was horseshit. In my practice, I see a lot of companies try to bully employees with boilerplate cease and desist letters like this. Melissa did *not* violate any nonsolicitation or nondisclosure agreements by emailing Christian. Fortunately, these losers backed off once they got a *very spicy* letter from my office.

are cowards. They'll beat up on you until they realize you know your rights.

They initially offered a lowball settlement to make the case go away. It was something around $10,000. We pressed on. We sued for wrongful termination, FMLA retaliation, pregnancy discrimination, gender discrimination, and a few other state labor law violations.*

We deposed Veronica, the HR rep who was at the initial meeting with Gordon, the CEO. Unfortunately, she danced around the questions. She even claimed that the meeting between her, Gordon, and Melissa never occurred!

Her dishonesty was not surprising, since she was afraid of retaliation from Gordon. But with some effort (and about eight hours of questioning) we at least got enough to show that Veronica was afraid of Gordon because of his hostility to pregnancy.

Gordon's deposition was even more interesting. He was aggressive, rude, and clearly untrustworthy. He claimed not to remember key events, pretended that he hadn't known Melissa was pregnant, and stated he had no idea she was on FMLA leave. Like Veronica, he also denied the meeting with Melissa ever occurred. When asked why the company had hired Christian to replace Melissa, Gordon alleged (without proof) that Melissa's performance was so unreliable that they needed a permanent replacement.

It was clear he was full of shit, which is why we videotape depositions like this.

The litigation went on for about two years. It was a tough case, particularly because Melissa made a few mistakes:

- She did not document her pregnancy announcement to the company.
- There was no record of the fateful meeting with Gordon and Veronica—which they both denied ever happened.†

---

*By definition, pregnancy discrimination is usually a form of gender discrimination as well.

†I believe they met up to get their story straight prior to the depositions. This is common—which is why documenting meetings with a recap email is so important.

- Coworkers were afraid to speak out against Gordon, and several witnesses who Melissa thought would help her turned out to be very unreliable in their depositions.
- Melissa did not request FMLA leave in writing.
- Melissa did not document her preparations for taking leave.

I am not blaming Melissa for the challenges in this case. I don't expect everyone to be a labor law expert, and this book did not exist at the time. Melissa did what she thought was best under the circumstances. Ultimately, though, with some hard work, we got her a substantial payout for this case.

For me, the best part was seeing that the check was personally signed by Gordon. I like to imagine him sulking in his office, gritting his teeth as he was forced to write out those zeroes.

You can't outrun bad karma forever, pal.

In this chapter, we will discuss how to protect one of the most important events that will happen in your life: welcoming a new child into your family. This is a beautiful moment, and in the following pages, you'll learn every tool to protect yourself so you don't have to go through what Melissa did.

WHAT IS FAMILY LEAVE?

Family leave is just another way to say FMLA leave. As we learned in the last chapter, FMLA leave can be used for your own serious health condition as well as to care for a family member with a serious health condition—which includes pregnancy and birth! As we learned with other serious health conditions, family leave for childbirth and baby bonding grants you up to twelve weeks of protected time off for the birth, adoption, or foster care placement of a child.

When someone says they are on family leave, maternity leave, or paternity leave, they are actually referring to FMLA leave (even if they don't realize it). The same goes for baby bonding: The time spent developing that initial bond with your new baby and caring for them in their very first months of life is a reference to FMLA leave.

WHO GETS FAMILY LEAVE UNDER FMLA?

You can get FMLA for the birth, adoption, or foster care placement of a child. You can also get it to bond with the child.

Birth of a Child

FMLA gives you up to twelve weeks of unpaid but job-protected leave for the birth of a child. Note: FMLA is *not* reserved just for mothers!

I once had a case where my client, a thirty-four-year-old welder named Ramon, got the news that his wife was pregnant. His father had been absent for much of his childhood, and Ramon swore never to repeat his father's mistake. He'd learned about FMLA leave through some Google research, and so he went to his manager's office to request the full twelve weeks of leave. His plan was to take two weeks off to prepare for his child's birth, two weeks after that to help his wife recover, and then use intermittent leave after that to bond with his baby.*

Unfortunately, the conversation did not go well. Ramon ended up being fired for "insubordination," despite the fact that he had recently gotten a raise to reflect his good performance. He was clearly being punished for requesting FMLA leave. Although we were able to get a fair settlement for him through mediation, as I've said over and over in this book, written requests are essential to making a case. But we'll talk more about how to give a written request for family leave later.

---

*Ramon was a super smart guy. I personally loved his plan, and I would recommend it for other fathers as well.

Adoption

The FMLA applies to families who are adopting a new child, whether from an agency, from friends or family, or by way of a surrogacy. You are entitled to the twelve weeks of FMLA for up to one year after the child has been placed in your home.

However, you may need time off for important events before the adoption is finalized. You are entitled to take FMLA for these. Examples of preadoption events that qualify include (but are not necessarily limited to):

- Attending counseling sessions
- Court appearances
- Consultations with lawyers, doctors, or birth-parent representatives about the adoption
- Medical examinations related to the adoption or placement
- Traveling outside the country to complete the adoption process

These rights apply equally to same-sex and unmarried couples, as well as to people adopting as single parents, as they do to heterosexual and married couples.*

Foster Placement

Foster parents are protected by the FMLA too. And thank goodness, because without foster care, some children would not have a safe place to call home.

Under FMLA rules, *foster care* means you are providing twenty-four-hour care for a child as a substitute for (and away from) their parents or other legal guardians. The FMLA does not require that the foster placement be permanent. However, foster care is done through a

*The Trump administration has repeatedly attacked these rights and the agencies that enforce them. So far, as of this writing, these FMLA rights are still intact. But they are in danger.

formal process between you and the state, so be sure you meet all other requirements before accepting placement of a child for foster care.

Baby Bonding

Within twelve months of your child being born, adopted, or placed into foster care with you, you can use your FMLA to bond with them. The limit is twelve weeks, and it comes from the same twelve weeks allotted for pregnancy or childcare issues, so it's best to plan how you want to use that time in advance. How you do this is up to you, but my personal recommendation is to use a couple consecutive weeks in the beginning to get settled, followed by intermittent leave. This gives you a predictable routine, and it keeps the money flowing while you take intermittent time off to bond with your child.

HOW SHOULD I ANNOUNCE I'M USING FMLA FOR FAMILY LEAVE?

As we saw in Melissa's case at the beginning of the chapter, there are some key elements to keep in mind when announcing to your employer that you're planning on taking family leave.

For starters, your manager will probably not be an expert in FMLA leave. They might even be hostile to it, like Gordon was. Human resources is supposed to guide you in this process. But as we saw with Veronica, HR might be caught between wanting to help you and wanting to protect their jobs.

And let's not pretend all HR reps are experts in FMLA rules either. Many are great at what they do, but unlike the legal profession, human resources is unregulated. There is no formal licensing process to work in that field. I once had a case where the HR rep, who totally botched my client's FMLA request, had *zero* training. In fact, she had only worked in HR for a few months, and her prior experience was in a totally different field.

The point is that *you* will have to take control of your FMLA leave.

Once you accept this, it is actually empowering. When you learn the rules, *you* will have the power to control the terms of your leave.

Get the Announcement Right

Arguably the most critical phase of taking FMLA leave is the announcement. Tell management first, in writing, and keep a copy for yourself. Personally, I see no reason to wait. Announcing your pregnancy sooner, rather than later, makes it harder for companies like Baby Haterz, Inc. to make up a pretextual reason to fire you.

Many employees are afraid to disclose their pregnancy. I understand the concern, but it's my opinion that disclosing early—in writing—is the right call.

Tell management first. I know you're probably closer to coworkers and likely want to break the news to them first. But remember, the company will have a harder time denying they knew of your impending FMLA request if you have a paper trail.

There is also the issue of vicarious liability. If HR or a manager with hiring and firing power is notified of the FMLA leave, then generally the company is responsible for how they behave toward you when you announce.

Melissa made the first, worst, and most common error in FMLA—she let her employer take control of the paper trail. You won't always have 100 percent control, but taking the initiative early makes sense. There is no downside to having a good paper trail.

Here's a template I recommend using:

Sample Email Template: Announcing Pregnancy and/or Need for Family Leave Under FMLA

Dear Management / Human Resources,

I am pleased to announce I am [having a baby/adopting a child/accepting foster care placement of a child].

I would like to take FMLA leave for this important event, beginning on [DATE] and ending on [DATE].

Please let me know when we can discuss plans to prepare for my leave and subsequent return.

Respectfully,
Employee

I know this template is short. That's the point. There isn't much else to discuss—and saying more than necessary can lead to complications. Keep your FMLA announcement short and always keep a copy for yourself. Melissa's case would have been much stronger if she'd had a letter like this in her evidence!

When to Announce

I know I'm repeating myself, but that's only because it's so important: There is *no LEGAL benefit* to waiting. It is better to announce early and adjust later (if needed) than to wait until the last moment. Under federal guidelines, employees are encouraged (though not strictly required) to announce the need for FMLA at least thirty days before the leave begins, if possible.

The more notice you give, the easier the whole process will be. And if you announce a need for FMLA but later determine you no longer need it, then there is no harm. You can still initiate a new request later without penalty. For example, suppose you took some FMLA leave and later decided not to use the remaining time. In that case, the time you took will be counted against your twelve-week total for the year. But you remain entitled to use the remainder of your time for any qualifying reason.

And remember, use my ten-step checklist from chapter 13 on how to take FMLA leave after you've announced your intentions!

COMPLICATIONS WITH FMLA

FMLA rules are complicated, and none of this is paid leave. I won't blame anyone for feeling like these rules are almost punishing you for having a baby. I get it, but to be quite candid, that mentality doesn't help you. The twelve weeks of FMLA is unpaid, and that sucks. There are limits to what qualifies for leave and how much you can use, and that sucks too.

But in my opinion, it's worth the extra effort. Protecting your job is valuable. You deserve the stability and predictability of knowing your job will be there when you return, especially while having a new baby.

What About Paid Leave?

Historically, the United States lags behind with its labor rights. In a 2019 study, UNICEF surveyed the paid family leave rights of citizens in the world's richest countries.* Of those surveyed, forty-one of the richest nations provided some form of paid family leave. The United States ranked dead last with a whopping *zero* weeks of paid family leave under federal law.

For reference, Estonia topped the list, with a generous 166 weeks of total paid leave available for new mothers. Of those weeks, 85 are paid at 100 percent of the mother's salary.

Estonia is an outlier. Most nations in the study provided a range of twelve to thirty weeks of paid family leave. But again, in every single category, the US ranked last. The federal FMLA provides up to twelve weeks of protected leave, which is better than nothing, but the time is not paid.

If you want paid leave, you will first need to look at your company. In a 2024 study by the Society for Human Resource Management (SHRM), about 40 percent of surveyed companies offered some form of paid leave.

If paid family leave is not available through your company, then using any accrued sick time or paid time off (PTO) is an option.

---

*Comprising mostly member states in the Organization for Economic Co-operation and Development (OECD), of which the United States is a founding member. See Yekaterina Chzhen, Anna Gromada, and Gwyther Rees, *Are the World's Richest Countries Family Friendly? Policy in the OECD and EU* (UNICEF, 2019), unicef.org/media/55696/file/Family-friendly%20policies%20research%202019.pdf.

Can They Force Me to Use My PTO? I Was Saving It!

I get this question a lot. If you use FMLA leave, your employer is legally allowed to apply your PTO during that time. The good news is you get paid while on leave via the PTO. The bad news is that if you were "saving" the PTO, you won't have that option.

Unpopular opinion: I'll catch some flak for this, but my honest take is that there is no point saving PTO. Use it. Use it often. And family leave is a great time to use it. I understand that having an employer disperse your PTO without consulting you is frustrating, but it's legal, and you have more urgent priorities to focus on while taking FMLA leave.

Regardless, having protected time off so your job is waiting for you at the end is crucial. So even though it is unpaid, and even if you are forced to use PTO, it is worth taking.

Some States Give You Enhanced Protections

Though they are the minority, some states allow for supplemental or enhanced leave options.

In part I, we learned that states are allowed to make their own laws *on top* of federal laws. When there is a difference between state and federal laws about family and medical leave, employers must follow the rule that is most beneficial to the employee. In my home state of California, I am legally required to provide up to twelve weeks of protected leave to my staff, even though we have fewer than fifty employees. Why? Because the California Family Rights Act covers employers who have at least five employees in the state. California is not alone. Several states have enacted more generous family and medical leave laws to protect employees. State-level FMLA equivalents usually enhance your protections by covering more conditions, providing more leave, or including more employers than the federal FMLA. Some states even provide *paid leave* under the right conditions. Check your local laws to see if you might have any enhanced protections.

Summary

- The Federal Family and Medical Leave Act (FMLA) provides up to twelve weeks of unpaid but job-protected leave for qualifying reasons.
- The birth, adoption, or foster placement of a child are qualifying reasons for FMLA leave.
- The twelve weeks can be taken all at once, broken into pieces, or spaced out into intermittent FMLA leave.
- Notify management of your need for FMLA *first*, before you tell your other coworkers, and do it as early as possible.
- Always announce your need for FMLA in writing and keep a copy for yourself.
- The United States ranks *last* among OECD nations in terms of family leave. All these complicated rules are a policy failure, not a personal failure. Don't beat yourself up.
- Some states offer paid leave options, but they are the minority.
- Years from now, your boss won't remember all the late nights and long hours at work. But bonding with a newborn or newly adopted child is priceless. Dealing with FMLA leave requests is not always easy, but it's worth it.

CHAPTER 13

Pregnant at Work

PERP WALK

I struggled with where to start this story . . . and how much of it to tell. It was one of the wackiest, wildest, most crazy cases I've seen.

It was a foggy morning in East Los Angeles. My client Araceli worked in a shoe store, which we will call the Pregnant Employee Retaliation Place, or PERP for short.

Araceli had recently been promoted to assistant manager. She was ten weeks pregnant, and with a new baby on the way, she needed to make as much money as possible. The promotion didn't come with much authority, though. Just like the other retail associates, Araceli was expected to run between the storeroom, the display area, and the registers. She was on her feet all day except for lunch and designated break times.

But being an assistant manager came with some perks. She got a one dollar per hour raise. And the real prize was that she got a key to the business and five hours of additional overtime each week. Because as one of the new assistant managers at PERP, her job was to open and close the store.

PERP was located in a strip mall. There was a parking lot out front and an alleyway in the back. Technically, a manager was supposed to be on duty during opening and closing. But Araceli's manager, Larry, usually rolled in about thirty or forty minutes late—leaving her to do most of the opening by herself.

Larry was, to put it kindly, a bum. He showed up late, left early, and spent most of his shifts scrolling TikTok in the break room. The regional managers had no idea. The reason was Larry had hiring and firing power at the store, so none of the employees were willing to risk their jobs to call him out.

Unfortunately for Araceli, a very aggressive man with a known drug abuse problem liked to hang out in the alley behind PERP.* He yelled at anyone who crossed his path. He threw garbage. He smashed bottles. The police called him Billy. And Billy was always looking for a fight.

On that foggy morning, Billy found one.

Part of Araceli's job was to open the back door and dispose of any trash. But when she did so that day, she heard Billy screaming outside. She quickly shut the door and locked it. Araceli was only five feet, three inches tall, and well into her first trimester of pregnancy. She was not risking a fight in this condition.

Right on cue, Larry finally rolled into the store. Late as usual. "Why are the empty boxes still here? They have to be taken out," he said.

"Billy's back there," Araceli said.

"Aw shit, not again," Larry groaned.

"Should I call the cops?"

Larry brushed past her. He whipped open a supply closet and started rummaging around.

"Larry?" Araceli said.

He pulled a broomstick out of the closet. "Watch this," he said. He threw open the back door, then charged outside like a maniac.

Araceli ran after him. "Larry, no!"

"Hey, Billy!" Larry roared, swinging the broomstick like a bat. "I'm gonna shove this up your ass! I'll fucking kill you!"

Surprisingly, this actually worked. Billy shouted a few curses but

*I recognize this is a person who needed help, but unfortunately, the system failed him. For Araceli, an aggressive man with a substance abuse problem was a high-risk situation.

quickly retreated out of the alley. Basking in his . . . um, glorious victory, Larry smiled at Araceli. "I just saved your life," he said.

"I literally hated all of that. Never do that again."

"You just can't admit you needed a man to save you."

Araceli shook her head.

ARACELI WAS STRUGGLING, especially in the mornings. Her morning sickness was debilitating. Her ankles swelled. Her back ached. Her doctor said this was normal, but that didn't make it any easier.

"Being on your feet all day isn't helping," the doctor said. "I'll write you a note for an accommodation at work."

The next day, Araceli presented her note to Larry.

Larry groaned. "What am I supposed to do with this?"

"I need a stool when I'm behind the counter," Araceli said. "My knees swell up when I'm on my feet all day. And I don't think I can open in the morning. I can close at night, but my morning sickness—"

"So, you just want to sleep in?" Larry interrupted.

Wow. Talk about the pot calling the kettle black, right?

Araceli shook her head. "I'm puking my brains out most mornings. I don't think you understand."

"We can't put a stool behind the counter, it's a tripping hazard," Larry said, ignoring her. He rubbed the patchy beard on his chin as he reread the note. "I don't think we can approve this."

Araceli was angry but not discouraged. Later that day, she sent a text message to Larry and the regional manager, Mike.

Hi Mike and Larry, the text said, *I need to talk about some accommodations for my pregnancy. I need to limit how much time I am on my feet, and I need a schedule change. Early mornings are not good for me right now.*

She followed this text with a screenshot of her doctor's note.

Larry was furious the next day at work. "You went behind my back!" he complained.

"No, I didn't. I included you in the text too."

"I already said we won't approve this."

"You don't know what it's like being pregnant," Araceli replied.

"Maybe you should quit," Larry said, returning to his TikTok videos.

Later that week, Araceli, Larry, and Mike met to discuss Araceli's request for pregnancy accommodations. It did not go well. Mike, the regional manager, was combative from the beginning. "You're asking for a lot of special treatment," he said.

"I don't want this to be a big deal," Araceli replied. "I just need some help because of my morning sickness and the pain in my ankles."

"Why'd you accept the assistant manager job if you knew this would be a problem?" Mike barked. Meanwhile, Larry nodded like the good little yes-man he was.

"It doesn't have to be a problem," Araceli answered. "I just don't think I should do mornings while I am having morning sickness this bad."

"What's the point of having you if you can't open?" Mike said.

Araceli sighed. "We shouldn't have just one person opening anyway. It's too dangerous with Billy back there."

Mike raised an eyebrow. "Alone? What are you talking about?"

Larry shot up in his seat. He glared at Araceli. "No one is ever here alone," he lied.

Araceli gulped. She sensed she was in dangerous waters here. "Sometimes . . . I mean. Sometimes I'm here first, and it's too dangerous with the aggressive guy that hangs out in the alley. So no one should be alone during opening anyway."

"What's your point?" Mike said, frustrated.

"I just want a schedule adjustment for my morning sickness. And I'd like a stool for when I'm behind the register."

Larry sensed an opportunity to appear useful to Mike, so he chimed in. "The stool is a tripping hazard, and if we give it to you, we have to give it to everyone."

Freeze-frame—Attorney Ryan enters the scene

Hi, everyone. So this meeting clearly isn't going well. I want to point out a few problems here, lest anyone be fooled by Mike and Larry's bullshit. First, it is not "special treatment" to grant a pregnancy accommodation. The point of the accommodation is to help the pregnant employee have equal access to employment as anyone else. Standing for long periods was harder for Araceli than others, so a stool is reasonable.

As for the schedule change, the US DOL specifically lists that as an example of reasonable accommodations. And if Larry could just step up and be a leader for a change, he could easily cover for Araceli.

Okay, got all that? Good. Let's get back to the meeting . . .

Araceli felt defeated.

"So, what can we do? I'm still pregnant."

Mike slapped his hands on his knees. With a heavy sigh, he stood up. "Unless you'd like to resign, and you should really think about that, then we'll have to come up with a way to deal with this."

Mike came up with a way to "deal" with it, and it wasn't pretty. What followed was a campaign of retaliation, discrimination, and harassment.

First, he slashed Araceli's hours by half. *Half!* Araceli complained to Larry about the loss of her hours.

"Problem solved." He smirked. "No early mornings, and you aren't on your feet so long."

"I'm making no money now," she said.

"Careful what you wish for." He grinned.

Araceli hung on as long as she could. As she proceeded into her second trimester, her morning sickness subsided. But she still had pain in her back and ankles when she was on her feet too long.

She sent a text to Mike. She requested to have her morning shifts back and her hours restored. But she also insisted that she needed a stool or some extra breaks to protect her back and ankles.

You are causing a LOT of drama over this, Mike texted. *We need to talk.*

Araceli didn't have to be a mind reader to know what that meant.

Within a day of their text exchange, she was fired. Larry wrote up a little letter for her and printed it out. Among other allegations, it said she was fired due to being "unreliable" and "not available for assigned shifts."

The audacity.

Araceli asked me to help with her case. We sued PERP for violation of the Pregnant Workers Fairness Act, which entitled her to reasonable accommodations. We also sued for pregnancy discrimination, gender discrimination, retaliation, failure to accommodate, and wrongful termination.

After a few months of litigation, we secured a settlement. It was more than Araceli earned in a year, so she was happy. A few months later, PERP was totally out of business. Gone.

I like to think our lawsuit helped expedite that crooked company's demise.*

PREGNANCY RIGHTS AND DISCRIMINATION

Pregnancy discrimination is one of the most common forms of workplace discrimination I deal with, which is particularly offensive. Pregnant employees are extremely vulnerable to abuse. And this abuse comes while they are doing the most important thing a human can do—creating a new life.

Many bosses, especially men, simply do not understand the hardship of working while pregnant. Other times, it's just selfishness or cruelty. Either way, while most people are respectful toward pregnant employees, you must be prepared for the possible worst case (like what we saw in Araceli's story).

Fortunately, there are federal laws that protect you; this chapter will cover the accommodations you are entitled to and the rights that protect you against discrimination.

WHAT IS THE PREGNANCY DISCRIMINATION ACT (PDA)?

In Araceli's story, we sued PERP for pregnancy discrimination. Pregnancy discrimination is illegal in all fifty states thanks to the Pregnancy Discrimination Act (PDA) and the Pregnant Workers Fairness Act (PWFA).

---

*As an entrepreneur myself, I never like to see a business fail. But the way PERP treated Araceli was so outrageous I lost zero sleep over them shutting down. In my opinion, a business that abuses its employees has no right to exist.

The PDA, passed in 1978, protects pregnant employees. It amended Title VII of the Civil Rights Act to prohibit sex-based discrimination on the basis of pregnancy, childbirth, or related medical conditions.

Like most rules under Title VII, the PDA applies to most private employers who have fifteen or more employees.* It also applies to the federal government, employment agencies, and labor organizations. If the employer has a fluctuating head count, then the law applies if they had fifteen or more employees for at least twenty weeks in either the current or prior calendar year.

WHAT IS THE PREGNANT WORKERS FAIRNESS ACT (PWFA)?

A friend once told me that pregnancy was like an athletic event—and that really struck me. Your body goes through huge transformations. The demands on your muscles, organs, and even your mental health are extraordinary. Like an athlete in a major competition, you will feel fatigued, and you may require some extra help, or accommodations, to continue working.

Enter the PWFA. In 2022 President Biden signed this legislation, which requires covered employers to provide reasonable accommodations to pregnant employees. It generally applies to most employers of fifteen or more workers and to virtually all government roles. The accommodations must be related to limitations caused by pregnancy, childbirth, or related medical conditions. Employers do not have to provide accommodations if the accommodations would cause an "undue hardship."

Prior to the PWFA, most pregnant workers were not entitled to accommodations for their pregnancy unless they could prove they were disabled by the pregnancy. Tell me a law was written by men without telling me, right?

---

*State laws may cover smaller employers as well.

Anyway, thanks to the PWFA, federal law *finally* recognizes the unique challenges faced by pregnant employees. However, like Title VII of the Civil Rights Act, it does not usually apply to bona fide religious organizations like churches or religious nonprofits.

Examples of Reasonable Accommodations Under the PWFA

Accommodating you for your pregnancy is usually very easy. As we saw in Araceli's case, all she needed was a modified schedule and a stool. Here are some other examples that might work for you:

- Moving your workstation closer to a bathroom
- Allowing you to keep water at your workstation
- Excusing you from lifting loads over thirty pounds by yourself
- Switching to light duty or modifying job duties to accommodate pregnancy-related limitations
- Taking more frequent or longer breaks to drink water, eat, or rest, or taking extra restroom breaks
- Providing a chair or stool to sit on while working or keeping a seat nearby when needed
- Allowing for reduced schedules (if requested)*
- Letting you work remotely on a full- or part-time basis†
- Changing food or drink policies to allow for liquids or nutrition breaks during shifts
- Time off to go to health care appointments

IMPORTANT CAVEAT: All these are examples of reasonable accommodations. But employers cannot force an accommodation on you if you do not request it.

---

*Cutting your hours without consulting you may be illegal retaliation.

†It is amazing how many problems are eliminated when you can work from home. This is easily one of the most flexible accommodations you can get, so if possible, I always recommend at least requesting it if your job can reasonably be done from home.

That is not to say the employer cannot grant an accommodation you do not like. They must *consider* your preferences, but compromises are allowed. Still, there should be a good faith discussion between you and your employer about what accommodations are possible. We call this the *interactive process*, and we will talk about it in much more detail in chapter 15. For now, just know that there has to at least be a conversation before an accommodation is denied or imposed on you.

How to Request an Accommodation for Pregnancy

I recommend disclosing the pregnancy first. Do this as early as possible to establish your protected class. Then get a doctor's note describing your limitations in *general* terms. A common error I see in doctors' notes is when they request detailed, specific accommodations for you.

This is generally a bad idea. Specific accommodation requests can give employers an excuse to say your request is too difficult or creates an undue hardship, and therefore must be denied.

A better approach is to simply state what limitations you have in general terms. For example, "Araceli cannot lift more than forty pounds" is better than "Please excuse Araceli from changing the water cooler." Similarly, "Araceli may require more flexible work schedules to accommodate her pregnancy" is better than "Araceli must be allowed to work remotely full time."

By describing your limitations in general terms, you make it easier to find reasonable accommodations that work for you and your employer. Because these are not overly specific, it is much harder for an employer to simply reject your request without at least attempting a compromise.

You can use the following template to request accommodations. Employers are allowed to request medical documentation confirming the need for accommodations and the limitations you have. Because of this rule, I recommend including a copy of the doctor's note along with this template.

Sample Email Template: Requesting PWFA Accommodations

Dear Manager / Human Resources,

I am happy to announce I am pregnant. During the pregnancy, I will need reasonable accommodations to help me work. I am still able to fulfill all my job duties; I just need some adjustments to protect my health and the health of my baby.

When can we arrange a time to discuss possible accommodations?

Respectfully,
Employee

Short and sweet, like most of the templates in this book. You do not need to say much to enforce your rights. You just need all the key information!

What If You Do Not Like the Accommodations They Offer?

This can be tricky. Your preferences must be considered, but ultimately, the employer has a business to run. Push too hard for a specific accommodation, and you may end up creating an undue hardship, which excuses them from helping you. Don't push enough, and you will be stuck working without the help you need.

Here is a tip to keep the conversation going until you find an accommodation that works: Always indicate that your communications are part of an effort to continue the interactive process.

Sample Email Template: Response to Denial of Your Accommodation Request

Dear Manager / Human Resources,

I am disappointed to learn my initial request for an accommodation for my pregnancy has been denied. This email is to continue the interactive process so we can find an accommodation that works for both sides.

If they claim undue hardship: You indicated my request causes an undue hardship. In order to help us find a solution, can you explain in more detail how or why my request causes an undue hardship?

If they deny without explanation: Federal law requires reasonable accommodations for pregnant employees. These accommodations are required so long as they do not cause an undue hardship, and I feel my request is reasonable.

Reasonable accommodations can be flexible. Examples that might be helpful in this situation include but are not limited to:

- Schedule modifications
- Time off for appointments
- Remote or hybrid work assignments
- Additional breaks for rest, water, medication, or sustenance
- Allowing extended or more frequent restroom breaks
- Seating at or near my workstation
- Modification of work duties, such as limits on lifting, frequent trips up stairs or ladders, or long walks

These are just ideas to get us started. I would love additional input from the company until we find a solution that works for everyone.

Respectfully,
Employee

Religious Exemptions

One final caveat: Like Title VII of the Civil Rights Act, the PWFA does not usually apply to bona fide religious organizations like churches or religious nonprofits. Religious groups are exempted for a simple reason. The Free Exercise Clause of the First Amendment of the US Constitution says, "Congress shall make no law respecting an establishment of religion, or prohibiting the free exercise thereof." In plain English, this means Congress cannot pass a law that intrudes upon the doctrines or practices of a religion.

Religious organizations can have legitimate reasons to discriminate, even if people outside the religion disagree. For example, a mosque may only wish to hire practicing Muslims.

Unfortunately, some employers try to abuse this. Morality clauses, "righteous living" policies, or practices with other religious undertones can seep into objectively secular workplaces. An auto shop cannot claim to be a bona fide religious organization. But a charity group, a church, or a religious school are more likely to be exempt. By the way, I once had a case where a company (unsuccessfully) tried to claim they were a religious organization for this purpose, so look out for employers who try to fudge the rules!

PLANNING AHEAD: THREE PHASES FOR PREGNANT EMPLOYEES

Accommodations during your pregnancy can be a lifesaver. But don't forget that your relationship with your work during pregnancy and child-rearing basically boils down to three phases:

PHASE 1: WORKING WHILE PREGNANT. During this phase, you will want to establish a paper trail showing you are pregnant. This can help protect you against discrimination and harassment. You should also request reasonable accommodations for your pregnancy. Doing so will make work safer and more enjoyable, and it will protect you from retaliation.

PHASE 2: GIVING BIRTH AND BABY BONDING. This phase will require some time off. I recommend putting in for FMLA leave *early* and, as usual, doing it in writing. How you use the leave is up to you. However, I personally recommend taking a chunk of time to prepare for and recover from the pregnancy (usually three to four weeks). Then finish your FMLA with several weeks of intermittent leave to get the most out of your baby bonding time.

PHASE 3: WORKING AS A NEW PARENT. You may need breaks to pump breast milk during this time. The Providing Urgent Maternal Protections for Nursing Mothers Act, or PUMP Act for short, protects you for up to one year after the baby is born. We will discuss the PUMP Act in more detail in the next chapter. And both parents can also consider using what's left of their FMLA for important events following the child's birth.

Make a plan. Make a paper trail. Make your family the priority.

WHAT IF YOUR EMPLOYER GIVES YOU A HARD TIME?

Not all employers are understanding of pregnancies. Some are even hostile to them. If that happens to you, *don't panic*! I've seen this before, and I have a few tips to help you get through it. Let's first start with some of the common objections employers will raise and how you can respond to them.

"IF I GIVE YOU SPECIAL TREATMENT, I HAVE TO DO IT FOR EVERYONE ELSE."

A reasonable accommodation is not "special treatment." It ensures that pregnant employees have a fair and equal opportunity to work. If another employee gets pregnant, we would hope (and the law requires) that they be afforded reasonable accommodations as well.

"NO ONE ASKED YOU TO GET PREGNANT."

This is just plain disrespectful. You are a grown-up and you do not need anyone's permission, much less your boss's permission, to have a baby. The law requires that employers refrain from discrimination against you for your pregnancy. Further, they need to provide reasonable accommodations. It doesn't matter who asked (or didn't ask) for what—this is the law.

"THIS IS A PERSONAL PROBLEM; YOU NEED TO FOCUS MORE ON WORK AND LESS ON YOUR PERSONAL ISSUES."

First of all, your pregnancy is a blessing, not a "problem." Second, the goal is to be able to focus on work just like everyone else. Reasonable accommodations for the pregnancy will help you do that.

"I SHOULDN'T HAVE TO PAY YOU FOR BEING KNOCKED UP."

This one borders on sexual harassment. You are not "knocked up." You are about to have a child. Also, we live in the United States. Employers generally do not have to pay a single penny in maternity or family leave compensation unless they want to. Employers who say this aren't just gross, they are wrong.

"WHAT IF I JUST FIRE YOU INSTEAD? HOW ABOUT THAT? AND IT'S AT-WILL EMPLOYMENT, SO I JUST WON'T SAY THE REASON."

The litigation gods demand a sacrifice, and this boss has volunteered himself as an offering . . .

First, that's wrongful termination, retaliation, and pregnancy discrimination. And if you asked for all this in writing, then refusing to say the reason (or making up a reason) won't save them.

Second, at-will employment is no excuse. At will means you can be fired for any *legal* reason. And this is not a legal reason to fire someone.

Third, and this is a personal note from me, I dare them to try it. Pregnancy discrimination cases famously lead to very high verdicts and settlements. Why? Because judges and juries generally don't like to see pregnant employees getting pushed around by some loser boss.

And if you've read this book, then you already know to have a paper trail establishing your protected class before a boss threatens you.

Against a threat like these, I would quote Clint Eastwood in *Dirty Harry*:

Dear Boss,
You've got to ask yourself one question:
"Do I feel lucky?"
Well, do ya, punk?

I hope no boss ever threatens to fire you for disclosing a pregnancy, requesting accommodations, or requesting leave for your childbirth. Remember, employers cannot punish you for requesting accommodations under the PWFA. Nor can they punish you for reporting pregnancy discrimination. Doing either of these things is retaliation and is expressly prohibited by federal law. State laws may impose even tougher penalties for retaliation. If you follow the tips in this book, then I would seriously question the sanity of any boss who threatens you like this.

They are setting themselves up for a very bad time. ☺

[Summary]

- Pregnancy discrimination is common, but it is illegal!
- Dads and nonbirthing family members should familiarize themselves with pregnant workers' rights. This helps them protect their pregnant partners and family members!
- The Pregnancy Discrimination Act (PDA) prohibits sex-based discrimination based on pregnancy. The Pregnant Workers Fairness Act (PWFA) requires employers to provide reasonable accommodations for pregnant employees.
- The PDA and PWFA apply to virtually all public employers. They generally apply to private employers with at least

fifteen employees. Some exceptions exist, like for bona fide religious organizations.

- Disclosing pregnancy early, in writing, can help protect you from discrimination.
- Requesting accommodations early, in writing, can help make work safer and more enjoyable while pregnant.
- Employers can request a doctor's note to confirm the need for accommodations and confirm your limitations. I recommend doctors keep these notes fairly broad to allow for flexible accommodation plans.
- Employers may raise several objections to your request for accommodations. It is *not* "special treatment." Instead, these accommodations give pregnant employees an equal opportunity to do their jobs.
- It's your life. It's your body. And this is *your* baby. Be courteous and cooperative with your employer, but don't be afraid to put them in their place.

CHAPTER 14

After Your Baby Is Born—Lactation Rights

THE MILK MAFIA

My client Ellie was a twenty-one-year-old single mom. Life hadn't been easy on her, but she was a tough cookie. Her baby daddy was a deadbeat; he'd dipped the moment he found out she was pregnant. As for Ellie, she had no college education, no family to lean on, just her maternal instincts and a new baby boy to raise all by herself. But the hardship didn't make her bitter. Ellie was a firecracker with a smart mouth and a sharp sense of humor.

She also had an incredible work ethic. Ellie had a full-time job at a restaurant supply company. We'll call it the Milk Mafia, LLC. The Milk Mafia had a large two-story warehouse. The first floor had a meeting room, supply closets, bathrooms, and a break area. The second floor had a sort of catwalk design that circled the warehouse floor. All the offices were on the second floor.

Ellie had recently returned from FMLA leave. She was ready to work normally again, with one very small exception. She needed a few breaks each day to express breast milk for her baby.

The warehouse was a loud, crowded place. The break room on the first floor was slightly quieter. It had seats, a sink, and a refrigerator. Late one morning, Ellie was pumping breast milk for her son. One of the foremen was eating his lunch at the table across from where Ellie sat. He was a burly man with bulging forearms covered in faded green tattoos.

The foreman glanced at Ellie as the machine pumped. She smiled awkwardly, then adjusted the blanket that covered her breasts. The machine continued humming.

He dropped his fork with a *clang*. "Is there somewhere else you can do that?" he complained.

Ellie was tiny compared to the angry foreman. But she wasn't easily intimidated. "This is how I feed my baby," she said matter-of-factly.

"I'm trying to eat," the foreman grumbled.

"Then eat," Ellie quipped.

The foreman pointed at her chest. "That's disgusting. Can't you do it in a bathroom or something?"

"I'm not pumping my baby's milk in a bathroom. *That's* disgusting."

The foreman shoved his seat away from his table. Like a child throwing a tantrum, he loudly dumped his food into the trash.

"I lost my appetite," he huffed. He stormed out of the break room.

"You need a diet, anyway," Ellie taunted.

An hour later, Ellie was sitting in the human resources office. The HR manager lectured Ellie for being disrespectful to the foreman. "He is your supervisor, and if he says you are being inappropriate, you need to listen."

Ellie's jaw dropped. "Do you think I *want* to pump here? With all these creepy dudes trying to peep one of my nipples? That's why I cover up."

"So you see the problem," the HR manager replied. "It's not appropriate to be exposing yourself at work."

Ellie was so angry she wanted to throw up. The foreman was wrong. The HR manager was wrong. All she wanted to do was pump her milk in peace.

"I have to be able to pump. I can't stop my breasts from making milk. It doesn't work like that."

The HR manager said, "All we are asking is that you be more considerate of your coworkers."

Ellie wanted to pop off on her but stopped herself. If she got fired, then she wouldn't be able to take care of her son. Restraining her anger, Ellie forced a smile. "Fine, I'll be more considerate. But I still need a place to pump."

"You need to use the bathroom," the HR manager replied. "It's a private place with a sink, and it won't disturb your coworkers."*

"The men," Ellie huffed, unable to restrain herself any longer.

"What?" the HR manager asked.

"You mean it won't disturb the men," Ellie said.

After her meeting with HR, Ellie pumped in the bathroom once. It was disgusting. The bathroom reeked of bleach and farts. It was a totally unsanitary place for her baby's milk. Ellie did some research of her own. She came upon the federal requirements for pumping at work. She noticed that the space provided had to meet a few criteria. It had to be:

- Shielded from view,
- Free from intrusion,
- Available as needed, and
- ***Not a bathroom!***

Ellie marched right to the HR office and showed them the page she found on the US DOL website.

"Not a bathroom!" she said. "Says so right there."

"Fine," the HR manager said, clearly annoyed by Ellie's resistance. "We will try something else."

The next day, the company picked a (mostly) empty supply closet on the first floor. It did not have a lock or a sink, but the Milk Mafia was nice enough to place a single stool in there for Ellie to sit on.

Ellie tried it for a day.

The supply closet had a lingering chemical odor. Ellie couldn't place it, but it was something between spray paint and ammonia. It made

*I have to point out that this HR rep had very little experience. How she got this job is beyond me. In the deposition later in this case, I learned she was basically just googling stuff to see what rules she had to follow, and much of her "independent research" led her to incorrect assumptions about the state of the law. The point is that while many HR professionals are fantastic, it is still an unregulated profession, and some HR people have no clue what they are doing.

her feel woozy, and she worried about whether it was contaminating her milk.

To make matters worse, coworkers kept throwing the door open while she tried to pump.

"Occupied!" Ellie barked.

"Shit, sorry, Ellie!" one of the coworkers replied. "I'm just looking for the hand truck."

"Next door down," Ellie sighed, for what felt like the tenth time that day. *This isn't working*, she thought.

So Ellie complained again. "I don't see what's so hard about this," she said, her patience wearing thin.

The HR manager threw up her hands. "Ellie, you are drawing a lot of attention to yourself over this. That's not a good thing."

"I just want to pump for a minute without someone hassling me. I don't feel like I'm asking for much."

The HR manager relented. "We will try one more thing, but this is a huge favor we are doing just for you."*

The Milk Mafia sent Ellie upstairs. One of the empty offices had a sink, some cupboards, and enough room for her to sit and pump. There was no refrigerator, as was required by California state law, but Ellie brought a cooler to store her milk in the cupboards until her shifts ended.

The small office worked for a while. But then something stupid happened. Ellie entered the room to pump one day. To her surprise, a stack of four or five banker's boxes had been placed in the room. The room wasn't unusable, but it had already been a tight space before the boxes arrived.

Ellie alerted HR. "Clearly, someone didn't get the memo that this is my pumping space," she said. "Can we move the boxes, please?"

The HR manager was fed up. "Access to that room is a courtesy, and we still need storage for business operations or else it is an undue hardship."

That was a classic gaslighting move.

---

*Following the law is not doing anyone a favor. It's basic compliance. I can't tell you how many employers I've seen who try to guilt employees for asking them to obey the law.

Compliance with federal laws is *not* a courtesy. Also, it became apparent later in the case that the HR manager had learned about undue hardship via one of her Google research sessions. What she did not know, and what Milk Mafia learned the hard way, is that just calling something an "undue hardship" doesn't automatically make it so. Regardless, the problems were just getting started.

A few days later, Ellie's cupboards were stuffed with office supplies.

The day after that, a large vacuum was placed beside the stack of banker's boxes.

Each day, more and more stuff piled up in Ellie's pumping room. Ellie complained again, but HR made it clear that if she "didn't appreciate" all the "effort" the Milk Mafia was making to accommodate her, then she should "consider other options."

Days later, the room was packed to the ceiling with random stuff from around the warehouse. Ellie had to squeeze and contort her body to move around the tight space. But the Milk Mafia had made it clear she'd probably be fired if she spoke up again.

Then, one fateful day, Ellie walked upstairs to pump. She tried to push the door open.

Thunk!

"What the hell?" Ellie whispered. She pushed again, harder this time. *THUNK!*

"You've got to be kidding me," Ellie hissed.

The door opened only about six inches before being blocked by some unseen obstruction. The Milk Mafia had stuffed so much crap in there that the door wouldn't even open!

It was the last straw. Ellie quit on the spot.

Soon after, Ellie retained my office to teach the Milk Mafia a lesson. We sued for a laundry list of violations, including gender discrimination, FMLA retaliation, violation of the PUMP Act, hostile work environment harassment, and constructive wrongful termination, plus a half dozen state law violations.

In essence, the theory of the case was that Ellie was being punished because she was a woman who needed to pump milk. She was wrongfully denied adequate pumping facilities under state and federal law, and she was entitled to money damages for all the hardship they put her through.

Everything had been verbal, and that was a challenge when it came to proving the case. Still, we worked with what we had, and things turned out pretty well. The biggest thing Ellie did *right* was learning her rights. Because she knew what kind of facilities she was entitled to, she was able to advocate for herself.

Oh, and on top of the settlement check, she now works someplace that treats her like a human. Her baby boy is thriving, and I'm sure one day his mother will tell him how she stood up to the Milk Mafia and won.

LACTATION RIGHTS AT WORK

In this chapter, we will discuss what accommodations you are entitled to, what rules protect you from discrimination, and how your employer must act when it's time to breastfeed your new baby. We will mostly focus on the Providing Urgent Maternal Protections for Nursing Mothers Act, or PUMP Act, which, like the PWFA discussed in the last chapter, is another fairly recent law. It too was signed by President Biden in December 2022 and took effect in July 2023. But the fact that these laws are fairly new is no excuse for employers not to comply with them.

I'd also like to note that this chapter is equally important for non-birthing family members. If that's you, then you should familiarize yourself with these rules. Being informed helps you be a great advocate for your partner.

WHAT IS THE PUMP ACT?

The Providing Urgent Maternal Protections for Nursing Mothers Act (PUMP Act) greatly expanded protections for nursing parents at work. It requires employers of *all* sizes to provide reasonable break time for employees to express breast milk for nursing children. The law also requires employers to provide a clean, private space (that is *not* a bathroom), shielded from view and available as needed for you to pump. Finally, the PUMP Act requires that the space be "functional" for the purpose of pumping milk.* A closet reeking of strong chemical odors or an office packed full of junk, like what the Milk Mafia offered in Ellie's case, probably do not meet this requirement. These protections apply for up to one year after your child is born.

State laws can have additional requirements. In California, where this case occurred, the space provided for pumping must have access to a sink with running water and a refrigerator.†

Compensation for Pump Time

Break time used to pump milk generally must be *paid* unless you are completely relieved of your duties while on the break. For example, if your boss tells you to "remain active and available" on the company chat, that can count as remaining on duty, and you may have to be paid for that time.

If your employer provides paid breaks to employees, then you must be paid the same as anyone else if you choose to use the time to pump.

Here are a few examples to help you spot when you must be paid for these breaks:

- Ellie's employer provides all employees with two paid fifteen-minute rest breaks per shift. Ellie uses both paid breaks to pump breast milk for her baby. She must be paid the same as any other employee on a break. If Ellie takes additional breaks to pump, those cannot be denied to her (within reasonable limits). However, the additional break time does *not* have to be

*29 U.S. Code § 218d.

†The California rule doesn't require that these things be inside the space used for pumping, but they must be in "reasonable proximity." In English, that means they can't be super far away.

paid, so long as Ellie is totally relieved of her duties during those times.

- Molly is a paralegal at a law firm. During a pumping break, Molly goes to a legally compliant private space provided by the firm for her to pump in. While there, Molly proofreads some documents before filing them with the court. Molly must be paid for the time spent pumping because she was still doing her job.

Flight Crews

Airline flight crews (including flight attendants and pilots) are not covered by the PUMP Act. This doesn't mean they can't get time to pump, but their options are more limited.* However, other airline employees who are not part of the flight crew are generally still covered.

Railway and Motor Coach Employees

If you work for a railroad, there are some special rules. If you are part of the train crew or help maintain the tracks, then the PUMP Act protections are effective for you as of December 29, 2025.

The same goes for people who work in the motor coach industry (buses). If you're part of the team that helps move the bus, then your rights under the PUMP Act also started on December 29, 2025.

These industries have slightly different rules for accommodating you. They are not required to make a pumping accommodation that causes a "significant expense." For example, removing seats or adding unscheduled stops would probably count as a "significant expense." In that case, they may not have to provide the accommodation—although other options should be explored. Installing a privacy curtain or giving you time to pump during a scheduled stop are both reasonable solutions.

---

*The Federal Aviation Administration has issued guidance on general practices airlines must observe for employees who need to express breast milk, but these guidelines do not have the same force and effect as the PUMP Act.

Because both the railway and motor coach industries involve significant risks and safety requirements, they are not required to make any changes that would create an unsafe condition.

REQUIREMENTS FOR LACTATION ROOMS

The PUMP Act requires employers to provide a private space that is "functional" for the purpose of pumping milk. But what makes a space "functional"? Every case will depend on its own facts, but here are some guidelines I look for whenever I assess a PUMP Act violation:

- Must be shielded from view.
- Must be free from intrusion of coworkers and the public (a lock or a sign can satisfy this rule).
- Must *not* be a bathroom.
- Must be available whenever the employee needs to pump.
- Must be able to safely store breast milk. Federal law does not require employers to provide a refrigerator.* However, employers cannot stop you from bringing your own cooler. And they must provide a space for you to store it while working.
- No surveillance is allowed! Even if your boss cites "security" concerns, federal law does *not* allow them to have any recording devices while you are using the space.
- The provided space must have a seat and a flat surface to place your pump. The floor doesn't count. It has to be something like a table or counter.
- The space should have access to electricity, but it's not strictly required under federal law. A sink is preferable too, but again, it's not strictly required unless your state law says so.

---

*California law requires a refrigerator and a sink. Other states may have additional requirements.

Outdoor Lactation Spaces

As a former wildland firefighter, I understand a lot of jobs don't have offices or even four walls and a roof to work with. Many readers may work in outdoor conditions, but you still need to pump! So, what happens in a situation like this?

Fortunately, there are easy ways an employer can accommodate these situations. Pop-up tents are cheap and perfectly acceptable. Some companies even rent out pods designed specifically for pumping. However, the pop-up tent must be tall enough for you to stand in. It also must have a chair for you to sit while pumping.

A porta-potty does *not* count, even if it is clean.

HOW TO REQUEST A PUMPING ACCOMMODATION

It's best to request pumping accommodations *in writing* and keep copies for yourself. As a reminder, *in writing* can mean email, text message, or even on real paper (just be sure to make copies!).

One issue that comes up quite a bit is when an employer complains that the request is creating an undue hardship. We will talk about undue hardships next. But first, let's create that paper trail.

Sample Email Template: Requesting a Pumping Accommodation

Dear Manager / Human Resources,

I am writing because I am currently breastfeeding, and I need a reasonable accommodation. I am happy to engage in an interactive process with you to find ways to do this.

Under federal law, I am entitled to adequate break time to pump. I must also have access to a private space, which is not a bathroom, where I will be free from intrusion while pumping. Finally, I need a secure space to store breast milk for my baby while I am working.

When can we discuss options to accommodate my need to pump at work?

Optional: As you can imagine, this is an intimate aspect of my life. I appreciate your anticipated discretion in this matter.

Respectfully,
Employee

WHAT IF THE EMPLOYER CLAIMS UNDUE HARDSHIP?

The PUMP Act applies to most employers.* Covered employers with at least fifty employes *must* provide you with adequate space to pump. However, something interesting happens if that employer has fewer than fifty employees. Covered employers with fewer than fifty employees can get out of providing a space to pump if they can show it would create an "undue hardship."

But just saying it's a hardship doesn't make it so! Trust me, this is one of the oldest tricks in the book. The employer gets a request for a pumping space, then *boom*, all of a sudden it's too expensive, too disruptive, too hard. Nine times out of ten, I call bullshit.

Legally, an "undue hardship" means the accommodation would be impossible, or so expensive, or so severely restrict business operations, that it is no longer "reasonable" under the law.

Accommodating lactation breaks is really easy.

If your employer complains about the cost of accommodating you, or claims the request creates an undue hardship, document the complaint. Then reiterate your request in writing. In that new request, you should ask for specifics about the hardship the employer is claiming. If you really want to control the conversation, you should offer some feedback on how to accommodate you. It's important to indicate that this is all part of an ongoing conversation, and you want to keep working with them to find a solution.

---

*It is not possible to cover all rules and their exceptions in a single book. You should always check to see if you are a covered employee under these rules. However, this book was written with the intent of covering the vast majority of situations for most people.

Here's a template I recommend starting with.

Sample Email Template: Response to Claim of Undue Hardship

Dear Manager / Human Resources,

I am writing to follow up on the company's claim that my request for an accommodation to pump would create an undue hardship. To help me better understand the concern, will you please explain the potential hardship in more detail?

Fortunately, there are several low-cost options to meet the requirements. I'd also like to point out that [ROOM] or [LOCATION] would suit my needs well. Several companies will rent a pod for this use—and they are reasonably priced so as not to create an undue hardship.

Further, the requirements are only that the space provided be private, shielded from view, and contain a place to sit as well as a place to store breast milk. I am sure we can find a way to meet these requirements.

Respectfully,
Employee

RETALIATION IS ILLEGAL!

Like with the PWFA, the PUMP Act specifically forbids retaliation for exercising your rights under this law. Cuts in pay, demotions, harassment, or termination because of your need to pump are prohibited.

You can file a claim for free with the US DOL to enforce your rights under this law. However, I personally recommend speaking to a lawyer first. Your chances of success are exponentially increased if you have an experienced professional taking the lead.*

*I know a guy who's pretty good. I heard he's got a pretty cool book too.

Summary

- Even if you will never pump breast milk, you should be familiar with these laws. This is your chance to be an advocate for your family members who are entitled to these protections.
- Breastfeeding is a natural and important part of life. If your boss or coworker is "grossed out" by it, then *they* are the problem. Not you. Only a huge freaking loser would criticize a mother for feeding her baby.
- The PUMP Act gives nursing employees the right to reasonable break times and adequate space to express breast milk.
- The breaks generally must be paid unless you are relieved of all duties.
- The space provided must be private, free from intrusion, and suitable for pumping milk, and it cannot be a bathroom.
- Railway, airline, and motor coach employees have some special rules.
- Employers in outdoor settings can provide a pop-up tent or rent a pod for breastfeeding employees. Porta-potties are not acceptable.
- All covered employers of any size must comply with these rules, but employers with fewer than fifty employees are excused if making such a space available creates an "undue hardship."

- Undue hardship is a high bar for the employer to prove. The accommodations outlined in this chapter are easy to provide. Consider engaging in an interactive process (in writing!) to nudge your employer in the right direction—especially if they try to claim "undue hardship."
- Retaliation for requesting time or space to pump is illegal.

CHAPTER 15

Disability Rights and Reasonable Accommodations

KEEP YOUR EYES ON THE ROAD!

Do *not* skip this chapter just because you are not currently disabled!

Like death and taxes, disability eventually comes for us all. If not from illness or injury, then from old age. Disability rights are for *all* of us.

And there's no other case I'd want to open this chapter with than *EEOC v. Drivers Management, LLC and Werner Enterprises, Inc.*, featuring a brave man named Victor Robinson.

Victor did everything right. It was his dream to become a commercial truck driver. It was a good career with good benefits. And, as many Americans understand, the US economy depends on hardworking truck drivers. Victor was also deaf, which meant he'd have to work harder than other candidates to get the same opportunity.

Victor wasn't willing to quit his dream without a fight. A better life with a good career was possible. So he got to work.

He completed his training at Roadmaster, a truck driving school owned by one of the largest carriers in the country, Werner Enterprises. There, he earned his commercial driver's license (CDL). However, regulations by the Federal Motor Carrier Safety Administration (FMCSA) required drivers to be medically certified. The FMCSA requirement was to ensure that drivers were physically qualified to do the job.

Federal regulations required drivers to meet certain hearing requirements. But there was an important exception. For drivers with disabilities, like Victor, the FMCSA allowed something called a medical variance. The medical variance was required to prove that disabled drivers like Victor could still safely perform all the essential functions of the job.

It was not easy, but Victor worked hard, got his license, and obtained a medical variance as required by the federal rules. That exemption legally cleared him to drive.

But then he ran into trouble.

In 2016 Werner rejected Victor's application to drive for them. The rejection wasn't about his driving skills, his record, or his training. According to trial testimony, Werner's vice president of safety told Robinson he was not hired because he was deaf. Even after Robinson secured every legal clearance required—including approval from the Federal Motor Carrier Safety Administration—Werner still refused to even consider him.

Victor was devastated. He'd done everything an employer could reasonably ask for, and still found the door slammed in his face simply because he was deaf.

He wasn't the first deaf applicant Werner had rejected. A year earlier, another deaf driver, Andrew Deuschle, had also been turned away. Even at trial, Werner's vice president of safety admitted—under oath—that the company policy was to not hire deaf drivers. The company's excuse was that deaf drivers could not complete mandatory training.

The training paired new drivers with experienced drivers who would instruct the trainee in real time. Werner claimed there was just no way, no way at all, for a trainer to communicate with a deaf driver without taking their eyes off the road. Werner argued that this made hiring deaf drivers unsafe, and therefore the company could legally discriminate by refusing to hire them.

Let's pause right there.

I've heard many legitimate reasons for refusing to accommodate people with disabilities. Usually safety is a valid concern. But Werner tried to argue that drivers like Victor could not look away from the road, for even a moment, under any circumstances. That didn't hold up to scrutiny.

Let's use some common sense here. Have you ever looked in your rearview mirror? Have you ever read your speedometer, or glanced at a map, or checked your side mirrors while driving?

You averted your eyes from the road, but only for a moment. And in some cases, like checking your speed and your mirrors, the act of looking away from the road is actually *promoting* safe driving.

The judge on the case agreed:

> *While . . . the familiar maxim, "Keep your eyes on the road," has obvious value, there are any number of common occurrences that necessarily divert a driver's eyes elsewhere. . . . Clearly, a driver isn't required to maintain a thousand-yard stare on the road ahead at every moment.**

In short, there's nothing inherently unsafe about a driver briefly looking away to communicate, especially if this is done in a controlled manner. A head-up display, for example, is a quick fix. Such displays are available on many modern vehicles.

Legally, Werner should have had a conversation with Victor to discuss possible accommodations before rejecting him.

But Werner didn't do that. They slammed the door in his face. And they violated the Americans with Disabilities Act (ADA) in the process.

The Equal Employment Opportunity Commission (EEOC) took Victor's case to trial. Over four days, the jury heard all the facts. They listened to Werner's side of the story, as well as Victor's. They heard from expert witnesses who described how the medical variance obtained by Victor legally cleared him to drive, and even discussed ways an accommodation could have been possible.

---

*Equal Employment Opportunity Commission v. Werner Enterprises, Inc., No. 8:2018cv00329, document 292 (D. Neb. 2023), law.justia.com/cases/federal/appellate-courts/ca8/24-2286/24-2286-2025-07-10.html.

Before the trial, Werner was so confident that they refused to negotiate a settlement with the EEOC. Their hubris came back to haunt them.

It took the jury less than two hours to reach their final decision. They found Werner liable for discrimination, failure to accommodate, and failure to engage in the interactive process. But that's not all. The jury was so angered by Werner's oppressive treatment of Victor that they also added $36 million in punitive damages.

Ouch.

The ADA requires a good faith effort by employers to find a way to work with you. It doesn't require them to do anything that would cause an undue hardship. And ultimately, they can legally deny accommodations if implementing the adjustment would be too dangerous. Werner didn't do that, which is why they lost the case.

In this chapter, we'll take the lessons from Victor's case and apply them to *your* life.

This case wasn't just about one disabled employee. It's about the denial of equal opportunity to people with disabilities who are ready and willing to work. The problem is that Werner did not even try, despite having a qualified candidate who had successfully passed their own driving school.

Here are some key takeaways from this case to remember as you read this chapter:

- Reasonable accommodations remove barriers to equal employment opportunities for qualified workers with disabilities. They are required unless they cause an undue hardship.
- Werner messed up when they shut Victor down without at least hearing what he had to say. As the judge pointed out, there were plenty of ways to work with Victor, if only Werner had made a good faith effort to do so (we call this the interactive process).
- Standing up for yourself matters. It makes a difference not just for you but for everyone else in your position. Together, we can shift the balance of power in workers' favor, like Victor did for deaf truck drivers.

As an advocate for people with disabilities, I want my disabled readers to know that I see and appreciate what you are going through at work.

This chapter is for you. It is your shield against discrimination and your sword to enforce the legal rights you are entitled to.

Let's quickly address some of the stigma around disabilities before we dive in:

"DISABLED WORKERS ARE A BURDEN."

We all have limitations. Some are visible, others are not so obvious. None of us are perfect, but we all have something to contribute.

You are an asset. You have unique talents to contribute. You are *not* a burden.

"YOU'RE JUST NOT A GOOD FIT."

Let's be realistic. Sure, if you are paralyzed from the waist down, then you probably won't be a professional ice skater any time soon. If you are blind, then maybe driving race cars isn't for you.

But the limits disabilities impose on us are more like pathways than barriers. With some understanding of your rights, you will see those pathways guiding you someplace where you can thrive.

And remember, with some reasonable accommodations, you can do almost anything.

WHAT IS THE AMERICANS WITH DISABILITIES ACT (ADA)?

The Americans with Disabilities Act (ADA) is a federal law that protects you from employment discrimination based on your disability. It also entitles you to reasonable accommodations. The ADA protects applicants (like in Victor's case), interns, probationary employees, and full- and part-time employees.

In other words, if you have a disability and are qualified for a job, the

ADA protects you. These protections cover virtually all government employers, regardless of size. They also cover most private employers with fifteen or more workers.

WHAT COUNTS AS A DISABILITY?

Disabilities come in many forms. Under the ADA, a disability is a physical or mental condition or impairment that seriously limits a major life activity. The impairment is considered a disability, whether it is temporary (like a sprained ankle) or permanent (like missing a leg). The ADA specifically states that *disability* should be construed in broad terms, without excessive scrutiny, so as to afford the most protection for employees.

Major life activity covers a lot of ground:

- Hearing
- Seeing
- Speaking
- Walking
- Breathing
- Learning
- Working
- Caring for yourself
- Doing manual tasks

The condition must be "substantial."* This means it must *seriously* limit your ability to do one or more of these activities. Minor problems are not covered. There is no black-and-white rule to this; it is a fact-specific assessment done on a case-by-case basis.

QUICK TIP: Don't worry about whether your condition is considered "substantial" or "seriously limits" your major life activities. If you feel it is limiting your ability to work, then you should ask for reasonable

*Americans with Disabilities Act, 42 U.S.C. § 12101 (1990), ada.gov/archive/adastat91.htm.

accommodations. Do not downplay your own health conditions; don't be too quick to accept alternatives offered by the employer if they are not what you need.

Case Study: Perceived Disabilities

You are protected by the ADA when your employer *thinks* you have a disability, even if you do not. Sounds weird, but it makes sense when you see it in practice.

I had a client with a speech impediment. He was a smart guy. But when he felt anxious, he sometimes stuttered over his words.

"I'm not stupid, I know what I want to say," he explained. "But when I'm anxious, it's like the words are a square peg and my mouth is a round hole. I just . . . I just can't get them to match up. I can't control it. But I'm not stupid."

My heart really broke for him. "Why do you keep saying you aren't stupid? I don't think that. I think you're really smart," I replied.

My client sighed. "Thank you. A lot of people think I'm stupid when I stutter. My boss called me r——ded, a lot. He said it every day."

Oof. My blood boiled when I heard that.

"Do you have any mental disabilities?" I asked.

"No, just the stutter," he answered.

"Well, for starters, the R-word is a slur and it's totally unacceptable," I explained. "Even though you do not have a mental disability, the fact that your boss *thought* you did, and discriminated against you because of it, is still an ADA violation."

If a boss *thinks* you are disabled, even if you are not, then you are protected from harassment, discrimination, and retaliation motivated by the perceived disability.

Mental Disabilities

Mental disabilities, mental health conditions, and instances of neurodivergence—which include but are not limited to learning disabilities, dyslexia, ADHD, autism, diagnosed anxiety disorders, and depression—are all considered disabilities under the ADA. They are protected against illegal discrimination, and qualified employees with these conditions are entitled to reasonable accommodations. Like my client with a stutter, you are generally protected if your employer *believes* you have such a condition, even if you don't.

And I'll just note here: Some of the smartest people who ever lived have been neurodivergent or had mental disabilities. For example, F. Scott Fitzgerald, author of *The Great Gatsby* and widely considered one of the most influential writers of all time, was a neurodivergent person with dyslexia.

The point is that neurodivergence, mental disabilities, and mental health conditions are common. And they are legally protected, so there is nothing wrong with asserting your disability rights at work.

WHAT ARE REASONABLE ACCOMMODATIONS?

The ADA entitles you to "reasonable accommodations" for your disabilities. Similar to what we discussed for pregnancy under the PWFA, a reasonable accommodation is any change or adjustment to a job or work environment that permits a qualified applicant or employee with a disability to participate in the job application process, perform the essential functions of a job, or enjoy benefits and privileges of employment equal to employees without disabilities. The purpose is to remove barriers that prevent equal opportunities due to your disability.

There is no precise test for what makes an accommodation "reasonable"; it is a case-by-case assessment, and it depends on many factors. The only bright-line rule here is that it cannot be an *undue hardship* or an *undue burden* on the business.*

Here are some examples of accommodations that are generally considered reasonable for most situations:

**Undue hardship* is the most accurate legal term, but *undue burden* sometimes gets used as well. For our purposes here, they mean the same thing.

- Providing or modifying equipment or devices
- Job restructuring
- Part-time or modified work schedules
- Reassignment to a vacant position
- Adjusting or modifying examinations, training materials, or policies
- Providing readers and interpreters
- Making the workplace readily accessible to and usable by people with disabilities*

Accommodations Are *Not* Special Treatment!

I've said it before, and I'll say it again. Accommodations for disabilities are not special treatment. Rather, they are the removal of barriers to equal treatment.

Anyone calling these rights "special treatment" is not just wrong; they are also begging to get sued. You can tell them Attorney Ryan said that.

How to Request Reasonable Accommodations

The interactive process is where you work with your employer to find accommodations that are suitable for your condition and your job. This does not have to be anything formal. A quick chat in your break room, for example, works just fine. And if the meeting occurs in person, I recommend taking notes. It can also be done over email. Whatever it takes to get the conversations in writing is great.

During the interactive process, you and your employer should evaluate different ideas to accommodate you. This inevitably involves some back-and-forth. Your preferences must be *considered*, but the employer

*These examples come straight from the EEOC as of the time of this writing. However, the Trump administration has implemented major changes to the structure and function of the agency. Always check for the latest guidance.

is not required to comply with all your wishes if doing so would be an undue hardship.

However, they cannot refuse to engage in the process, and they cannot unilaterally reject you without at least attempting to find a solution. Werner made that mistake in Victor Robinson's case.

The key to protecting yourself is to know *how* to request reasonable accommodations. Further, you have to be strategic. In all your communications, make it clear that you are attempting to continue the interactive process. Here's a template that I recommend for requesting reasonable accommodations—it makes your intent for the interactive process crystal clear.

Sample Email Template: Requesting Reasonable Accommodations

Dear Manager / Human Resources,

I am writing to request reasonable accommodations for my disability. I can do the essential functions of my job with reasonable accommodations.

Recommended: Please see the attached letter from my health care provider, which describes my limitations in more detail.

When can we engage in the interactive process to find accommodations that work?

Due to my disability, this is a time-sensitive request, and I would like to begin the interactive process as soon as possible.

Respectfully,
Employee

What If My Request for Reasonable Accommodations Is Rejected?

If your boss or HR department rejects your request or even refuses to engage in the interactive process with you, here is a template to help.

Sample Email Template: Response to Denial of Your Request for Accommodations

Dear Manager / Human Resources,

I am disappointed that my request for reasonable accommodations has been denied. I am writing to continue the interactive process with you so that we can find a solution.

If they claim it's an undue hardship: To help us find a solution that works for everyone, can you explain in more detail why this request would be an undue hardship?

If they indicate they are unwilling to cooperate with you: The interactive process is required by federal law. This is our opportunity to find reasonable accommodations that work for everyone.

I have some ideas for accommodations that should not present an undue hardship [list your ideas—feel free to copy the list of examples I provided on page 233].

I'd like to reiterate that this is a time-sensitive request, and unreasonable delays may cause me a personal hardship due to my disability. I'd like to continue the interactive process to find a reasonable accommodation.

Please note that I wish to remain employed and have no intentions of voluntarily resigning.

Respectfully,
Employee

The idea here is to continue the interactive process. So long as you show you want to keep talking, it is very hard for them to get away with slamming the door in your face. Emphasizing that the request is time-sensitive is a deterrent against delay tactics. Finally, indicating that you have no plans to resign makes it harder for them to force you out.

To protect your evidence, keep copies of all these communications in a place where they will be safe, such as a private inbox, cloud storage, a personal file box, or your own device.

Common Problems in Reasonable Accommodations Requests

I cannot possibly prepare you for every issue that may come up. However, here are three common scenarios in disability accommodation disputes I've seen over the years.

1. **REASSIGNMENT BY EMPLOYER**

   Some employers will reassign you. That's fine so long as the reassignment is not a demotion—a demotion could be a form of illegal retaliation.

   Reassignment should not involve making you resign and reapply. This is usually a trap to trick you into quitting so they can claim they didn't actually "fire" you.

   Reassignment also should not involve making you compete for the role. And the employer must be proactive by informing you of the possible reassignment. You are not expected to find it yourself, but if you do, please alert your employer that the reassignment is available and you are interested.

   Some employers have policies against reassignment or require that very specific rules be followed to do so. An employer might try to say that because other employees can't be reassigned, you can't either. This is not true. The ADA requires that reasonable accommodations such as reassignment be provided, even if nondisabled employees generally don't get them. Regardless of the employer's policies, reassignment is considered a reasonable accommodation unless they can show it causes an undue hardship.

2. **NEW HIRES, APPLICANTS, AND PROBATIONARY EMPLOYEES**

   Unlike the FMLA, which only protects employees who worked for at least a year, the ADA protects you even *before* you have the job. These rules apply to applicants, new hires, probationary workers, and full-time and part-time employees.

So if your new employer is saying they can't accommodate your request because you haven't worked there long enough, they're wrong!

3. WORKPLACE POLICY

Oh, the pearl clutching I see from some employers. "We can't let you have a stool at your workstation, it's against policy!"

Oh no, the precious policy! Whatever will we do??

News flash: Federal law beats policy every time. Federal law is rock; company policy is scissors. Under the ADA, a reasonable accommodation to modify a workplace policy for disability-related limitations is required by law, so long as it does not cause an undue hardship. And no, the fact that it's against normal policy is not a "hardship," but nice try!

Remember that reasonable accommodations are not special treatment; they are the removal of barriers that prevent equal access to employment. Employers who bend their policies a bit to accommodate you are not required to cease enforcement of the same policy for other, nondisabled employees.

Allowing an employee with a sprained ankle to have a seat at their station, even if other employees typically do not get a seat, is acceptable.

Can My Employer Force Me to Take an Accommodation I Do Not Want?

Sometimes, but generally not. The interactive process is a two-way street. They need to consider your preferences (though they aren't totally bound by them). Therefore, they cannot force you to accept an accommodation you do not want unless there are no other reasonable alternatives.

But there is an important exception! Under current federal law, if the accommodation is to help you perform an essential function or to eliminate an imminent safety hazard, then they can require you to accept it. If you do not, then the employer may successfully argue that you cannot do your essential job functions, or that your refusal is an undue hardship.

If you find yourself in this situation, you may need to consult a lawyer.

What If I'm Disabled but Don't Really Need an Accommodation?

For me, the choice here is easy. It is better to have an accommodation ready to go and not need it than to need it and not have it. If you suspect that your disability might interfere with your work, request the accommodation right away.

I had a client once who had excellent performance at his company for years. Tragically, his friend died by suicide. My client was devastated. He experienced all the pain, guilt, and grief that comes when a friend takes their own life.

He couldn't sleep. At night his mind raced.

How did I miss the signs?

I should have called him.

Why didn't he ask me for help?

The grief and sleepless nights caught up to him. One Tuesday night, after hours of tossing and turning, he finally fell asleep at around 4:00 a.m.

When he gasped awake, it was bright in his room, too bright. He checked his phone. It was 11:30 in the morning! He had dozens, literally dozens, of missed calls from work.

He rushed to the office without showering, eating, or even brushing his teeth. He did his best to have a normal day, but the whole office was talking about it.

"What's gotten into him?" they whispered. "He's been weird lately," they said.

Ultimately, this was just one of many instances of my client slipping up. He was eventually fired. We pursued a resolution based primarily on wage violations, which it just so happened there were several, but the disability discrimination claims didn't get very far. The reason was that my client didn't want attention, so he never told anyone about the suicide, or how it affected him, or that he was depressed and couldn't sleep. Had he requested a reasonable accommodation for his mental health disability *early*, the outcome could have been different.

I am pleased to report he is doing much better these days, but it was a tough lesson to learn.

WHAT IS UNDUE HARDSHIP FOR ADA ACCOMMODATIONS?

An undue hardship for an employer means the accommodation would be impossible, unsafe, or so difficult or expensive to do that it is no longer considered reasonable.

However, just calling an accommodation an *undue hardship* doesn't make it so. Employees must show that the requested accommodation is reasonable on its face. For example, requesting a schedule modification, at first look, does not seem like an undue hardship. From there, it is the *employer's* burden to demonstrate how it would be an undue hardship, if at all.

What If It Really Is an Undue Hardship?

There are situations where the employer is able to show that your requested accommodation would be an undue hardship. Here are some examples of true undue hardship:

- An accommodation that reduces workplace safety (this is the big one).
- An accommodation that is impossible or requires so much expertise that it is functionally impossible, or at the very least, impractical.
- An accommodation that is extremely expensive. But watch

out: An accommodation is not automatically an undue hardship just because it costs money.

- An accommodation that infringes on employee rights.
- An accommodation that hurts efficiency in other areas of the business.
- An accommodation that would violate a federal, state, or local law.

I once helped a disabled veteran who wanted his service dog with him at work. Unfortunately, the veteran worked in a dangerous factory where the dog could cause injury to itself or others. The employer was right that this was an undue hardship, and so the requested accommodation could not be granted. But what they did next broke the law.

Human resources sent my client a note saying, "We are unable to approve your request because it's an undue hardship. If you cannot continue working without the modification, then we will consider your employment voluntarily resigned."

Yes. That's what they said to the disabled vet.

The reason this was illegal was not because the requested accommodation was an undue hardship; it was. The problem was that they did not engage in the interactive process with my client to find alternative accommodations. Reassignment, for example, would have been easy in this situation. My client even suggested reassignment to a position where he could still be an asset to the company but also benefit from having his service dog.

They didn't even have a conversation with him. They just shut him down. That was a failure to engage in the interactive process, and it was illegal.

What About Safety Concerns?

Companies cannot just scream "Safety issues!" to avoid accommodating you. Yes, safety comes first. Yes, an accommodation that reduces workplace safety could be an undue hardship.

But the safety concern must be legitimate. And a legitimate safety concern does not grant the employer free rein to discriminate. If safety is a concern, then they must first consider alternate accommodations.

We saw this in the Werner trucking case. Yes, the ability to communicate with drivers was a legitimate safety issue. However, the company was wrong to dismiss Victor Robinson without at least having a conversation about ways to accommodate him. And as the judge in that case pointed out—there are many ways to safely accommodate someone.

THIRD-PARTY ADMINISTRATORS

Some employers, especially large employers, use outside companies to help them facilitate things like leave or disability accommodations. These are called third-party administrators, or TPAs. They work on behalf of your company, and even though they are the ones processing your accommodation or leave requests, they still must obey the law, and your employer may be liable if they violate your rights.

While the vast majority of accommodation or leave requests with TPAs will be totally fine, here are some best practices to protect yourself:

- **DOCUMENT EVERY STEP OF THE PROCESS.** TPAs typically use online portals. They require you to make an account and submit requests and documents via the website. This makes it harder to protect your paper trail! Use a journal to record when, where, and how you submit your requests. Use exact time stamps in your entries and include the URL (web address) where you submitted documents, requests, or other communications. Always copy or screengrab what you submit.
- **DOCUMENT PHONE CALLS.** You may be asked to make requests via phone. If you receive calls from the TPA, document the number that called you (or that you called) and the name and title of the person on the call. In short bullet points, describe what topics were discussed. If there are next steps, record those as well.

- **FOLLOW ALL INSTRUCTIONS, AND ASK FOR HELP IF YOU NEED IT.** Most TPAs are not literally out to get you. Their main job is to protect your employer from liability. So generally, most want to follow the law. If you are confused by the instructions on a TPA website, CALL THEM. Ask for help. Document that you asked for help and what help was offered, if any. Keep all this in a journal as well.

WATCH OUT FOR INTERFERENCE

Employers are forbidden from retaliating against you for requesting accommodations. But that doesn't stop some of them from trying to slow down, frustrate, or interrupt your reasonable accommodation requests.

We call this interference.

It's less severe than straight-up retaliation. But it can still be illegal. Sometimes employers know they can't retaliate, so they try to *interfere* with your requests. They think they are being sneaky, but the law is ready for games like this.

A Mountain of Paperwork

One of the common forms of interference I see is when employers dump *mountains* of paperwork on you for simple leave or accommodation requests. Make no mistake—this is intentional. There are no specific paperwork requirements to comply with the ADA. However, there are many template forms available, and some employers will make their own paperwork requirements.

It's important to indicate that your request is time sensitive. Employers who delay or deny your request solely because of incomplete paperwork may be breaking the law. That is not to say you can safely ignore their paperwork requirements—that is unwise. Rather, if you are making a good faith effort to comply with their requirements, and they continue imposing unreasonable paperwork requirements, it may be illegal.

HIPAA and Privacy Concerns

HR and your employer are *not* your doctors. They do not need your complete medical history. All they need is (1) confirmation that you have a disability (disclosing the diagnosis is not required), (2) a note from your doctor describing the limitations you have, and (3) the requested dates and length of your accommodation.

You are not required to disclose your specific diagnosis. You only have to disclose the limitations you have. Inevitably, some information will become obvious. If the note from your medical provider comes from a psychiatrist's office, then the person processing your leave might deduce you have a mental health disability. In any case, your employer must exercise discretion and protect your private information.

Another concern that comes up is when your employer calls your doctor to request information about your disability. Personally, I think this is a massive overreach. It is my opinion that no honest, respectable employer will call your doctor for further "proof" that you have a disability.

Some have asked me if this violates HIPAA. For those who do not know, HIPAA stands for the Health Insurance Portability and Accountability Act. It is a federal law that safeguards your protected health information from improper disclosure. An employer who calls your doctor to request protected health information is not violating HIPAA. However, a doctor who discloses that information without your consent *is* violating HIPAA. And they can face severe legal penalties for doing so.

Some employers will ask for an authorization form from you so they can speak with your doctor. Again, I find this excessive, but it is legal.

WATCH OUT: I've had a few cases where the employer's authorization form was *way too broad*! For example, one employer wanted access to "any and all records" over the past ten years.

Over my dead body.

Don't assume you must comply with excessive disclosures like this. They only need enough information to confirm your need for accommodations and what limitations you have. Read the form and make sure it only authorizes your employer to speak with your doctor about specific issues in a specific time frame.

Slow as Molasses

The most common form of interference is ignoring or delaying your requests. Remember that the legal obligation to engage in the interactive process with you is triggered by your initial request. Always indicate if your request is time sensitive (hint: it usually is!).

If the process is very slow, consider the following emergency template:

Sample Email Template: Unreasonable Delays in Your Accommodation Request

Dear Manager / Human Resources,

I am writing to express my concern regarding the unreasonably slow processing of my request for reasonable accommodations. This has not been a good faith engagement in the interactive process, and I would like to reiterate that my request is time sensitive.

Federal law requires good faith participation in the interactive process. The law also prohibits unreasonable interference or unlawful retaliation for making such a request.

The delays are causing me an undue burden. When can we get the interactive process going?

Respectfully,
Employee

RETALIATION IS ILLEGAL

Retaliation is when the employer hits you with an adverse employment action, like a demotion or termination, as punishment for something you had a legal right to do. For example, demoting you because you requested disability accommodations is retaliation.

But not all adverse employment actions are legally retaliation. If the actual, truthful motivation for the adverse action is legal, then it is not retaliation.

What can that look like? Here are a few examples:

- Actual poor performance (not just a BS write-up)
- Not being qualified for the position (such as a reassignment that you do not meet requirements for)
- Misconduct (obvious things like threats or theft, but also disrespectful conduct, insubordination, unexcused absences, or dishonesty)
- Legitimate reductions in force or other downsizing due to business needs

As a workers' rights lawyer, I *always* want to dig a little deeper if you are punished for one of these legitimate reasons shortly after requesting an accommodation.

This is because we want to watch out for *pretext*. If you recall, pretext is when an employer uses a seemingly innocent excuse to cover up illegal labor violations.

The trick in these situations is spotting whether an adverse employment action is legitimate or if it is a pretext for illegal motives.

I've had more disability discrimination cases than I can count. In that time, I have seen all the ways employers try to create pretexts to abuse disabled workers. One company hit my client with five write-ups, including a public scolding from a manager, after he requested accommodations. They did this to create the illusion that he was "incompetent" before they illegally fired him.

How do I know this was a pretext? Because my client didn't have a single negative mark on his record. Then he requested an accommodation, and *boom*! Suddenly he was the worst guy in the world. Seems a tad suspicious, doesn't it? Like a wild coincidence, right?

And that's really the essence of what you are looking for . . . a wild coincidence. Here are a few examples:

- You've never been written up, but *after* you request help, you are constantly criticized by management. Seems suspicious!
- Taking a long lunch was never a big deal, then suddenly the boss is guarding the entrance with a stopwatch in his hand? Odd, don't you think?
- Everyone else gets plenty of flexibility, but you're under a microscope for every little thing you do. Very weird.

Pay attention to gut feelings that you are getting iced out, like "coincidences" that seem to target you. All these are hints that the employer is using a pretext to punish you for requesting accommodations.

We are not looking to sue anyone, except as a last resort. The reason you need to spot pretexts *early* is so you can regain control of the situation. Make that paper trail. Get ahead of the narrative so they cannot paint you as a poor performer. The sooner you take these steps, the more likely you'll be able to protect your job without the need for a lawsuit.

LEAVE AS A FORM OF ACCOMMODATION

This is super important: Oftentimes, when an employee has a disability or health condition that requires time off, their first instinct is to apply for FMLA leave. This is usually a good idea, and I encourage you to explore FMLA as an option.

But what if you don't qualify for FMLA?

What if you need more leave than FMLA allows?

What if you need more flexible leave options?

Fortunately, the ADA is more flexible than FMLA. Leave is a valid form of reasonable accommodation, so long as your absence does not cause an undue hardship. There is no legal limit to how much time you can take, but I will warn readers that leave under the ADA has less protections than FMLA, especially if the leave lasts a long time. While FMLA guarantees up to twelve weeks, the ADA has no minimum guarantee.

That said, it is still a perfectly normal and acceptable way to accommodate your disability.

If the company has a policy against extended leave, or places limits on leave, then modifications to the leave policy are legally allowed. This is true even if your employer does not offer the same leave to other employees.

So how do we use FMLA and the ADA to your advantage?

Here is your game plan if you need leave as a form of accommodation.

IF YOU QUALIFY FOR FMLA:

1. Alert your employer of your need for protected FMLA leave. Note in your leave request that you also have a disability that may require accommodations.
2. Take your FMLA leave.
3. Shortly before you return, request additional leave options as a form of accommodation under the ADA. Alternatively, request other reasonable accommodations to help you with your return to work.

IF YOU DO NOT QUALIFY FOR FMLA:

1. Request leave as a form of reasonable accommodation under the ADA.
2. Provide a note from your doctor confirming the start and end dates of your requested leave.
3. If your employer has an existing leave policy such as PTO, you should *still* indicate the purpose of the leave is for your disability. This may protect you from illegal retaliation.

Automatic Termination / No-Fault Termination

Some employers have a policy where employees are automatically terminated if they are on leave for a certain amount of time. Even if this is a firm company policy, it should be modified to accommodate disability leave. They must allow you to continue your leave for longer than the policy normally allows unless they can show that either (1) your extended leave causes an undue hardship or (2) there is another accommodation that will allow you to perform your job without the leave.

Number 2 is more appealing than you might think. Paid disability leave programs are available to some, but they are rare. Some employers offer paid disability leave as well. But in both cases, the disability payments will be a fraction of what you typically earn. It is usually better to continue working with an accommodation, if possible, than to rely on reduced income (or no income) during leave, though every case is unique.

And that leads me to my final point. You will have to take the lead in your disability requests. You will have to advocate for what kind of accommodations you want (or don't want). You will likely have to take the initiative in conversations with your employer. You will need to document every step. And finally, you will have to watch out for illegal interference or retaliation.

It's a lot to put on a person dealing with a disability. It is not fair. But life isn't fair, and if you had the gumption to buy this book, I think you already knew that. Standing up for our rights at work is hard, but it's worth it.

With the knowledge and templates in this chapter, you are well equipped to fight for the leave or accommodations you deserve!

[Summary]

- The Americans with Disabilities Act (ADA) protects you from illegal discrimination on the basis of your disability. It also entitles qualified employees to reasonable accommodations.
- The ADA applies to virtually all government employers, plus most private employers with at least fifteen or more employees.

- A disability is a physical or mental limitation that substantially interferes with major life activities. The disability can be temporary or permanent.
- *Reasonable accommodations* are modifications to your work to help you fulfill your essential job functions. Employers are required to provide reasonable accommodations unless they cause an undue hardship.
- *Undue hardship* means the accommodation is impossible or unreasonably expensive or challenging, or that it would create a safety concern, violate another law, or interfere with the rights of other employees.
- The *interactive process* is a conversation between you and your employer to find reasonable accommodations that work for everyone. An employer's failure to engage in the interactive process in good faith may be illegal.
- If your accommodation request is rejected, you should make it clear that you have no intentions to resign and you wish to continue the interactive process.
- Leave as a form of accommodation is usually reasonable, and it is typically more flexible than FMLA. If you qualify for both, you should ask for both. If you do not qualify for FMLA, then leave as a form of accommodation under the ADA might be your best bet.
- Disabled workers bring a variety of unique skills and value to the workplace. Often, the disability they have in one aspect of life sharpens their abilities in other aspects. Disabled workers are not a burden—they are an asset.
- **Reasonable accommodations are *not* special treatment. They are the removal of barriers to *equal* treatment.**

CHAPTER 16

Hurt at Work—How to Get the Money and Care You Need

LOOK OUT BELOW!

Eastern San Diego County, 1:55 a.m., late summer of 2013.

My crew and I had been working since early the previous morning. As Cal Fire firefighters, we worked in twenty-four-hour shifts, which were supposed to be followed by twenty-four hours of rest. However, the mission always came first, and some shifts stretched longer than twenty-four hours, as this one promised to do.

We were dirty, tired, and sore. But this was what we had signed up for. To fight fire.

The fire had burned all day and all night. It scorched hundreds of acres, reducing dry, golden hills to ash. Smoke blanketed the night sky, which glowed an eerie red from the fires below.

Two long rows of firefighters hiked through the blackened hills. Dozens of white headlamps twinkled as we approached the flames. Radios crackled. Fire captains shouted orders over the buzz of chainsaws.

In the heat of the day, high winds fueled the blaze's furious spread. Nighttime brought cooler temperatures. This was our chance to hit the fire while it was most vulnerable.

Dirt doesn't burn, so our orders were to cut a clean firebreak ahead of the fire. The purpose was to slow the fire's advance long enough for fire engines behind us to douse the flames with hose lines.

But we had to move quickly.

The terrain was rough, with steep slopes on one side and rocky outcroppings on the other. Every step risked a long tumble down the leeward side of the hills.

I dug the heel of my boot into the ground, then swung my Pulaski axe at a dry shrub. Its trunk snapped. I took one step forward, then hacked down another shrub.

Below us, another crew worked on a backup firebreak.

"Break!" our captain ahead shouted. "Hydrate, have a snack, we'll take ten minutes to rest."

Captain Chris was a good man. We'd been fighting fire all day. The mission wasn't over, and we had much more work to do, but Captain Chris knew the importance of keeping us in good working shape.

We dropped our tools. Some of us gazed toward the advancing flames. Others closed their eyes for a micronap. Everyone's face was black with ash.

"Hey, Stygar," a friend said. "Got any more jerky?"

"One last beef stick," I said. "Want to split it with me?"

"Yeah, I'm starving."

I snapped the beef stick in half. Together, we sat among our crew, chewing in silence.

Ten minutes' rest felt like ten seconds.

"Tools up!" Captain Chris shouted. "We're all tired. But we gotta keep moving!"

"Tools up!" someone said, repeating the order.

"Let's go!" another voice called out.

Gear rattled. Chainsaws roared back to life. I resumed swinging my axe at my sworn enemy—the dry shrubs.

"Watch your footing!" someone yelled.

I looked down, my headlamp illuminating the rocky, uneven dirt. But it was too late. Something snagged my ankle—a root, a rock, I never saw it.

The world spun. No, it wasn't spinning—*I was falling.*

"Heads up!" someone yelled. With a *thud!* I landed in the middle of the fire crew below us.

"Where the hell did you come from?" one of the firefighters exclaimed.

Fixing my crooked helmet, I pointed up the hill.

"Jesus, dude," the firefighter said. He helped me back up to my feet. "You okay?"

"Back hurts," I coughed. "But I'll be all right."

"Hey, Stygar!" my friend called from above. "You dead?"

"Not yet!" I quipped. I rubbed my back, but the pain didn't go away. *Don't be a wuss,* I told myself. *Shake it off. Just shake it off.*

I climbed back to my crew. Captain Chris jogged down the fire line to meet me. "You okay, Stygar?"

"Yeah . . . I think I'm okay," I said, ignoring the throbbing in my back.

"If you're hurt, I need to know," he said, more seriously this time.

I was in my early twenties. I had dreamed of being a firefighter my whole life. It was my everything, my reason for living. I'd heard rumors of guys getting fired because they were hurt.

I didn't know my rights as an employee. All I knew was that hurt firefighters don't get to work.

"I'm fine," I said.

Captain Chris nodded. "Then watch your fucking step. Everyone goes home in one piece, you copy?"

"Yes, sir!" I replied. I returned to my place in the fire line.

Shortly after sunrise, the firebreak was complete. My back ached. I gritted my teeth during the long hike back to base camp. I reported to the medical team for some ice packs and ibuprofen—but I downplayed the injury as much as possible.

Under no circumstances did I want to be pulled off the fire line. I was terrified that if I was deemed medically unfit, I'd lose my dream job. In hindsight, this was a remarkably stupid thing to do.

For weeks, my back ached, and my neck felt stiff. Some days, it was merely uncomfortable. Other days, it totally took me off my feet. A friend recommended I file for workers' compensation. But I was too scared. The system was confusing, and I was convinced I'd lose my job if I filed.

By the time I'd left the fire service, I figured it was too late to file. The back pain continued through law school. Long lectures felt like torture sessions.

Today, as I write this book, I am happy to report I have had excellent improvement. That's the good news. The bad news is that maintaining the health of my back has taken time, money, and effort that could have been avoided if I had sought help sooner.

It was foolish not to report the injury. My recovery could have been far worse. And who knows, maybe I could have gotten some money and early treatment to help.

As a workers' rights lawyer, I cringe when I look back on this event.

Workers' compensation is not a trap. It is not a handout. It is a benefits system meant to protect *you* if you are hurt at work. And firing you for taking workers' compensation, in many cases, is illegal.

I cannot go back in time to represent myself in a workers' comp claim (though if that were possible, it'd be an infinite money glitch). However, I can still give *you* the tools to avoid repeating my mistake.

In this chapter, we will talk about what you can do if you are hurt at work, what your boss is required to do for you, and what they are forbidden from doing. Unlike many other subjects we've discussed, there are no federal laws regulating workers' compensation for most people.* Instead, regulations vary from state to state.

Every state (except Texas) requires employers to carry workers' compensation coverage. The purpose of this coverage is to give you income and medical care if you are injured in the course of your employment.

You deserve so much better than to lose your job, lose your pay-

---

*Exceptions like the Longshore and Harbor Workers' Compensation Act (LHWCA) exist. The LHWCA is a federal law providing workers' compensation benefits to maritime workers, specifically those on navigable waters or adjoining areas, who are injured in the line of duty. This chapter will focus on general principles of workers' compensation coverage without reference to the handful of federal statutes like the LHWCA, since they apply to a minority of readers.

check, and lose your medical coverage just because you got hurt. That's not fair, which is why workers' compensation exists—to balance the scales.

WHAT IS WORKERS' COMPENSATION?

Workers' compensation* is an insurance policy your employer purchases to provide benefits to employees injured on the job. It provides medical coverage, lost income replacement, and financial compensation for injuries arising from your employment.

Workers' comp coverage is required in forty-nine US states; Texas is the only exception. In the Lone Star State, your employer *may* have workers' comp coverage, though it is not legally required. If an employee gets hurt, the employer is gambling on how much they may have to pay by way of a personal injury lawsuit.

And this raises an interesting point. When you get workers' comp, you are not suing your employer for the injury. In fact, you will expressly waive the right to sue for your injuries in many cases. But if your employer does not carry workers' comp, then your remedy is to sue them for any negligence that may have caused your injury.†

Benefits of Workers' Compensation

There are several benefits to getting workers' comp that can make a huge difference for you:

- Weekly payments to replace lost wages
- Medical treatment for your injuries

*Also sometimes called *workmen's comp* or *workers' comp*.

†This chapter is about workers' comp, not suing employers for injuries caused by their negligence. If you are injured due to employer negligence, report the injury right away, seek medical care, then talk to a lawyer about your options. It is a terrible idea to file an injury lawsuit against an uninsured employer without getting some professional guidance first.

- Cash settlements
- Retraining and job placement services

Another benefit of workers' comp is that it is an insurance policy. This means that there will very likely be money to collect if and when you win a settlement or workers' compensation award.

Drawbacks of Workers' Compensation

Although workers' comp has many benefits, it isn't perfect, and there are some drawbacks.

The first is that workers' compensation benefits are sometimes capped. You have heard about big multimillion-dollar payouts for things like car accident lawsuits, sexual harassment cases, or other kinds of employment claims. This can create unrealistic expectations. A workers' comp case is not a lottery ticket. Instead, you should think of it as a *benefits delivery system*. The purpose of workers' comp is to provide income replacement, money for your injuries, and medical care.

The second drawback is that workers' compensation benefits are usually paid by the worst, most sinister, and most devious elements of society: *insurance companies*.

Fake-Ass Restrictions and Threats (FARTs)

When you make a workers' comp claim, you will often do so through a workers' compensation insurance carrier. Unfortunately, these companies exist to make a profit. By fighting injured workers at every step and pulling a few dirty tricks along the way (we'll talk about these later), the insurance company can protect their bottom line. Because ultimately, insurance companies only care about shareholder value, not your health.

Insurance companies will often try to bully you with lowball offers. I call these fake-ass restrictions and threats, or FARTs for short. They'll downplay your injuries. They will conjure up restrictions and limits and even make threats. They might even accuse you of *faking it* to get free money. Don't let those losers scare you. Lawyer up when you have a possible workers' comp claim.

No, I am not standing on a soapbox. Rather, I am preparing you for the fact that your workers' compensation claim might become an adversarial process.

But do *not* let this scare you from making a claim if you are hurt! While they have drawbacks, workers' comp benefits are valuable, and they are worth fighting for.

And never trust a FART.

FAULT IS IRRELEVANT (MOSTLY)

A workers' compensation claim may *look* like a lawsuit—you have a judge, you have lawyers, you have sworn testimony and evidence—but it is *not* the same thing as suing your employer. As I have said before, workers' comp is a benefits delivery system. It is an insurance policy your employer purchases to cover workplace injuries.

Even if you are at fault for your work-related injury, you are still entitled to benefits so long as your injury arose from the *course and scope* of your employment. In other words, if you got hurt at work, you get workers' comp, even if you are at fault for the injury.

But heed my warning—when we say the injury must arise from the course and scope of employment, we mean it.

For example, in 2024 a Delaware judge ruled that an intoxicated UPS driver was *not* entitled to workers' comp benefits following an on-the-job accident. In her ruling, the judge reasoned that drinking multiple beers on the clock was *not* within the ordinary scope and course of the UPS driver's employment.

Injuries caused by fighting are also not likely to be covered. Even if you are trying to help the employer, such as by stopping a shoplifter, fighting is not within the ordinary scope of duties for most jobs, and your claim for benefits will probably get denied.

While fault is generally not a factor, this remains true only so long as you remain within the scope and course of your regular duties. And for the love of God, please do *not* get intoxicated on the clock!

WHAT IF MY EMPLOYER DOESN'T HAVE WORKERS' COMP?

For starters, unless they are in Texas, the employer may be subject to penalties for failure to carry a workers' comp policy. But that's just the beginning of their problems.

If your employer does not have workers' comp, then you will need to sue them for any negligence that caused your injuries. Unlike a workers' comp claim, fault matters in a lawsuit like this.

If there is no workers' comp insurance, then there is at least *some* risk that the money you need will not be there when you need it, even if you win. Don't let that deter you—find a good lawyer and sue if you need to sue. But ideally, you will get the benefits you need via workers' comp instead.

What to expect: Insurance companies do not make billions in profit every year by politely paying out claims without a fight. Your lawyer will have to do some work to get you what's rightfully yours. Is it fair? Not at all. But that's the system we have, so we need to be prepared for it.

SCHEDULED VS. UNSCHEDULED INJURIES

Workers' compensation is highly regulated, and it's subject to caps and limits on what can be paid out (thank your local insurance lobbyist for that). Believe it or not, the law has a preset menu of the monetary value of injuries to certain body parts and functions. We call these *scheduled injuries*.

What Are Scheduled Injuries?

Despite what the name implies, a scheduled injury is not a preplanned beatdown (though I've met a few bad bosses I would have liked to schedule an injury for). Rather, a scheduled injury is an injury to a body part or body function that's listed in your state's workers' compensation laws. These laws include a chart (or *schedule*) that says exactly how much money you get if that body part or body function is totally disabled.

The payout schedule establishes two things:

- The maximum weekly compensation rate for that body part, and
- The maximum number of weeks you can receive that compensation for.

For example, let's say you lost an index finger and filed for workers' comp. Your state's scheduled injury rules might list a total loss of an index finger at fifty weeks, so you'd be eligible for 100 percent of the fifty weeks. The medical expenses associated with the lost finger won't count against the amount of money awarded. But if you got twenty weeks of temporary disability benefits while the case was pending, then those will be deducted from the fifty weeks available to you.

What Are Unscheduled Injuries?

Unscheduled injuries are injuries that aren't listed in the chart. These are usually more complicated. In most states these are things like injuries to your neck, back, internal organs, or mental health.

Because these injuries affect people differently, figuring out how much compensation you should get may take more time than scheduled injuries.

The total benefit amount is based on several factors, including but not limited to the following:

- Whether the injury limits your ability to work (and to what extent)
- Whether you can still do your job
- How long you'll need medical treatment
- Your loss of earning capacity resulting from the injury

Unscheduled injuries often involve a little bit more time to sort out, since we do not have a preplanned schedule of awards to reference. Despite the relative uncertainty, unscheduled injuries are a critical component of your total workers' compensation claim.

HOW MUCH MONEY CAN YOU GET FROM WORKERS' COMP?

The money and benefits you get from workers' compensation can vary widely. The amount of your workers' compensation award will depend on a few factors, such as:

- The extent of your work-related injuries
- The extent of your disability
- How much you were earning before the injury
- Your lost earning capacity
- The medical treatment you will require
- Your state laws around workers' compensation

All these factors influence how much money you can get. But they are not the only benefits that may be available to you.

Medical Care

Workers' compensation provides money for medical treatment. This is crucial, because we all know health care is expensive, and you will probably have significantly reduced earning capacity due to your injuries. Depending on the extent of your injuries, workers' comp can save you thousands, or even hundreds of thousands, of dollars by covering medical expenses. It can even protect you from bankruptcy caused by medical debt.

So while medical treatment does not equate to actual dollars in your pocket, it is an extremely valuable benefit which cannot be ignored.

Temporary Disability Benefits (TDBs)

Temporary disability benefits, or TDBs, are also sometimes called weekly income replacement. Personally, I like that name better because it describes what TDBs actually do. If you are too injured to work, or if your injuries reduce your earning capacity, then a TDB, or weekly income replacement, helps replace some of your lost income. These are benefits paid to you through workers' comp.

TDB money is a critical lifeline, and unlike in a lawsuit, you can start collecting this money almost immediately after making a valid claim.

But there are limits to weekly income replacement that you need to be aware of.

Weekly income replacement is a fraction of your preinjury income. While the rules vary by state, the limit is typically around two-thirds of your regular earnings. Sometimes it's less, sometimes it's more. It depends on a number of factors, and this is just a ballpark so you have a rough idea of what you are getting into.

But that's not all; the total weekly income replacement is capped at a particular dollar amount, and this amount may vary by state. So although your weekly benefit is a percentage of your income, it cannot be higher than the cap. That means even if Mark Zuckerberg or Jeff Bezos got hurt on the job, the most they could possibly receive is the statutory cap, no matter how many millions they make in a day.

How Much Is the Weekly Income Award?

The cap is set by state law, and it will vary widely depending on the average incomes and costs of living in your state. In states with high average incomes, like California, the weekly cap is higher. In states with lower average incomes, like Mississippi, it is lower. This is because the cap is usually calculated based on the average weekly earnings in your state.

SETTLEMENT

So now you know about the available benefits. But what about the actual money? Let's dive in.

Generally, workers' comp settlements come in two broad categories: a lump-sum award or regular payments. Both settlement structures come with pros and cons, and you will want to listen to your lawyer's advice before deciding which is best for you.

Lump-Sum Settlements

Lump-sum settlements are appealing for a number of reasons. You get a huge payment all at once, and that can be exciting. Anyone who sees a check for, say, $200,000, might be tempted to sign whatever paperwork it takes to get it.

But while this is sometimes the right move, there are drawbacks. Accepting the money will require you to sign a full final release of the claim. This will often include releasing the insurance company from any obligation to continue paying medical bills. If you have a serious long-term disability, then that means you need to be certain the lump-sum award is enough to sustain you for the long run.

But what if you run out of money? That's the bad news. The door closes the moment you sign the release. Again, this isn't something to be freaked out about; sometimes it's the right call. But you have to be aware that the money can go quickly, and once it's gone, it's gone. Be sure the lump sum is enough to cover living and medical expenses, and carefully budget the money you are awarded!

Regular Payments

Regular payments are weekly or biweekly checks you get for your workers' compensation claim. They're not as sexy as a big lump sum, but they come with an important benefit. The insurance company will usually agree to keep paying for medical care while you're on a regular payment award.

This arrangement does not come with a big cash windfall, but it does provide stability and predictability. It also protects you from large medical bills eating up all your cash.

One is not better than the other. It entirely depends on your circumstances. Just weigh your options carefully, and always listen to your lawyer's advice!

HOW TO GET THE MOST MONEY FROM WORKERS' COMP

Okay, on to the really exciting stuff. How can you make sure you get the most money possible? Here is my five-part checklist to make sure you are getting every penny.

1. Lawyer Up!

The insurance company will have lawyers, lots of them. And they will use every trick in the book to pay you as little as possible (more on that soon). Workers' compensation is a complex process, and as I mentioned earlier, it's often adversarial. This means that while you are trying to navigate your health care, the workers' comp rules, and your dwindling savings, there will be a group of suits on the other side trying to mess you up.

Don't play the game alone. Get a lawyer.

Worried you can't afford it? Well, I've got great news.

Workers' compensation attorneys work on contingency! We don't get paid until we win, and when we win, we are paid a small percentage of what we recovered for you. Rates may vary, but 15 percent of the total award is typical. Sometimes it will be less, sometimes more. But for a workers' comp case, anything above 20 percent will require substantial justification (in my opinion).*

It bears repeating that the insurance company will have lawyers, and they will not play fair, so you really should get a lawyer too.

2. Be a Good Patient

Good patients get good settlements. Follow your doctor's treatment plan. Not only is it essential for your health, but failure to follow it tells the judge that you aren't taking this seriously. Missing appointments, not filling prescriptions, not adhering to the medical routine—these are all things the insurance company will use against you.

You don't want to hear "If they're really hurt, why are they skipping doctor's appointments?" in your workers' comp hearing. Not good.

So be a good patient!

3. Report in Writing, Report Right Away!

Fault is generally not a factor in workers' compensation claims. However, there is *zero* workers' comp coverage if your injury did not arise from the course and scope of employment. That's a fancy way of saying workers' comp is for *work injuries only.*

Don't make the same stupid mistake I did when I was a young firefighter. If you get hurt at work, you need to report it right away, always in writing. Here's a template you can use if you are not sure what to say. This works via text message or email—just make sure it's written down and saved!

---

*It's worth googling your state's maximum workers' comp contingency fee rules.

Sample Email Template: Reporting a Work Injury

Dear Manager / Human Resources,

I need to report my work-related injury. On [DATE] at [TIME], I was working on [specific job-related task] at [LOCATION]. While doing so, I suffered an injury. [Describe what happened in one short sentence]. I need medical care right away.

I need to file a workers' compensation claim. Can you please help me with this urgently?

This is a time-sensitive request. Thank you for your prompt attention to my injury.

Respectfully,
Employee

This template works because it establishes a few things. It shows that you were hurt while performing a *specific* task related to your work. This is very strong evidence that your injury arose from the course and scope of your employment. As for the injury, this request does not go into too much detail that could later be used against you. Instead, it establishes when, where, and how your injury occurred.

I know this template has more blanks than the others, so here is a sample of a filled-out template for reference:

Sample Email Template: Reporting a Work Injury

Dear Laura (Manager) and Carl (HR),

I need to report my work-related injury. On April 5, 2025, at 10:37 a.m., I was working on replacing light bulbs in the company warehouse. While doing so, I suffered an injury. I fell off the ladder and landed hard on the ground. I need medical care right away.

I need to file a workers' compensation claim. Can you please help me with this urgently?

This is a time-sensitive request. Thank you for your prompt attention to my injury.

Respectfully,
Ryan Stygar

If your employer carries workers' comp—as they should—then your next step will be to file a workers' compensation claim. The employer, or perhaps their insurance carrier, will have some paperwork for you. All of that will become evidence. Talk to your lawyer if you are not sure how to fill it out. But as a guiding principle, just tell the truth and don't say more than necessary. You don't need to write a long story. Just document that you got hurt while working in the course of your duties.

4. Prepare for Your Hearings

At some point in your workers' compensation case, you will have to attend some hearings and proceedings. Don't be intimidated—this is all a normal part of the workers' compensation process, and you are not in trouble (unless there's a fraud allegation; we will talk about that later).

Many workers' compensation proceedings are held remotely via videoconference. You will be able to see everyone, including the judge, your lawyer, and the insurance company's lawyers, and they will be able to see you. So even though it is remote, take it seriously!

Find a quiet, private place to log in. If you don't have access to reliable internet and a quiet place, ask your lawyer if you can make the appearance from their office. I am *always* happy to host clients in my office for virtual hearings, and I am sure your lawyer will feel the same way. Personally, I find clients are much less nervous when I am sitting right beside them anyway.

Dress well. You don't need a full suit, but please make an effort. Imagine you are visiting your grandmother for dinner. Dress nice. I happily lend dress shirts and ties to my clients if they don't have any.

Again, choose your lawyer wisely and pick one who you know will take care of you.

Oh, and for the love of God, do not log in while *driving your car*! Yes, I have seen this happen. No, it did not end well. On that note, do not eat, smoke, play music, or have any conversations while in your hearings. These are important legal events, and if you do not treat them seriously, the judge might think you aren't really hurt, which can affect your final award.

5. Cooperate!

In addition to listening to your doctor's instructions, please be sure to cooperate with your lawyer! It doesn't happen often, but once in a while I get a client who is a bit *too* hands off. If I'm trying to argue that you're so hurt and so disabled that you deserve the maximum award, I need you to show you are invested in the process. Simple things like returning your lawyer's calls, updating us when you have a change, following our instructions, appearing on time for hearings, all these things help *us* help *you*!

TRICKS INSURANCE COMPANIES PULL

Insurance companies didn't get their unsavory reputation by accident. There are deliberate, sometimes sneaky tactics they will use to pay you less than you are owed. Here are a few tricks to watch out for.

Lowball Settlement Offers

Insurance companies know that you might be in a bad spot, and they are not above exploiting people in vulnerable positions. They know you are hurt, they know you are running out of money, and they know you might be scared. So they'll dangle a lowball settlement in front of you and hope you take the bait.

Don't fall for it. Lawyer up; get a professional in your corner. Once the insurance company knows you have backup, they will (hopefully) get more serious about their offers.

Recorded Statements

Insurance companies want to get you on the record talking as much about your injuries as possible. The more you say, the more they can sift through their notes to find something, anything, that looks inconsistent. They don't care if you're not actually lying, they just want to attack your credibility any way they can.

For example, you originally say, "I got hurt on Tuesday night," but then a few months later, at your workers' compensation board hearing, you say, "I got hurt on Wednesday night." You're not lying; it just got harder to keep track as time went on.

But it doesn't matter. The minute you slip up, *BOOM*. They will jump up and down and scream, "Inconsistent statement! You said you got hurt Tuesday, but then you said it was on Wednesday, so obviously you weren't that hurt, or you're lying, or your memory is so bad we can't trust you."

This sounds petty, and honestly it is, but do not underestimate the damage this will do to your credibility and your case. Judges do *not* like inconsistent statements.

Never give a statement to the insurance company without your lawyer present.

When asked a question, keep your response short and only answer what was asked of you. Do not try to argue your whole case (that's what your lawyer is for). Do not get defensive, do not blame anyone. ("I'd never have gotten hurt if not for my negligent boss!")

Remember that fault is typically not relevant. Be honest, always tell the truth, but don't ramble, because even the most innocent, minor slipup could lead to complications.

"Independent" Medical Examinations (IMEs)

Independent medical examinations (IMEs) are when the insurance company hires a doctor to confirm (or deny) the extent of your injuries.

They are used to evaluate how seriously you are hurt, the treatment you will need, and other medical aspects of the case. But there's a problem with "independent" medical examiners: They aren't really independent.

They work for the insurance company, not for you.

That's not to say all independent medical examiners are evil or that they are out to get you. Many are good people just trying to do their job. But that doesn't necessarily mean they are on your side.

As a workers' rights lawyer, I take everything the examiner says with a grain of salt. I put a whole lot more weight on what *your* doctor says. But independent medical examiners still give important testimony, and you will need to cooperate with them, your doctor, and your lawyer to get a fair outcome.

Offer Light Duty, Attack You If You Don't Accept

Light duty is when you return to work but for less pay and with less strenuous responsibilities. Your workers' comp case can still proceed while you are doing light duty.

I don't want to demonize light duty. Sometimes it's the best thing for your case. But here's the trick. The insurance company will get their own doctor to say that you are medically capable of doing light duty. This may or may not be true; you'll need to confirm it with your own doctor. But when the insurance company finds a doctor to say you are clear for light duty, they will offer you the opportunity to return to work, with reduced pay, but also with reduced duties.

Light duty necessarily means earning less than your full preinjury income, and that is normal. You'll still earn more than if you were not working. But there is no need to rush your return. The problem with light duty offers is that the insurance company doesn't give a shit if you're actually healed enough to work or not, so here is what you need to do (and not do).

- **DON'T KNEE-JERK AND REJECT RIGHT AWAY.** Sometimes light duty is a good outcome. Even if it's not what you want, you have to consider it.

- **CONFIRM YOUR MEDICAL STATUS WITH *YOUR* DOCTOR.** Sure, the insurance doctor said you're clear for light duty, but they have a bit of a conflict of interest, don't you think? Confirm with your doctor that it is safe for you to resume work.
- **BE COURTEOUS AND COOPERATIVE.** The offer of light duty may occur during a workers' comp hearing, in front of the judge. They *want* you to get angry. They *want* you to freak out and say, "I'm not going back!" They want you to lose your cool so they can say to the judge, "Look, this person isn't really hurt, they just want a free ride." Don't let them play that game! When they offer light duty, say, "Thank you for the offer. I'll definitely consider it, and I would like to speak with my doctor first." After that, you can have a private conversation with your doctor and your lawyer about whether light duty is right for you.

Surveillance

Denise suffered a back and knee injury on the job. As she began to heal, she tried to return to her normal life. Walking her dog, enjoying a day at the beach.

But there was a problem.

Denise didn't know this, but she had a shadow following her the whole time. Like the KGB, the insurance company hired a private investigator to spy on her during the case. And he snapped a ton of pictures of her walking her dog, splashing in the waves. The insurance company presented this evidence to the judge, claiming that Denise was not really hurt, or else she would not be able to do any of these things.

We call this a facepalm moment.

Now, my perspective was basically, "Hey, injured people have the right to fight for a normal life. Denise is hurt, and she's too hurt to work, but she has every right, even an obligation, to try to be there with her family."

Is that the best argument in the world? Not really. But when an insurance company busts you playing hopscotch while you're claiming to have an ankle injury, you are putting your lawyer in the hot seat (and jeopardizing your case). You will have good days and bad days while recovering. Do not overdo it on your good days. You not only risk exacerbating your injury, you also don't know who might be watching.

Don't get scared—these guys aren't assassins or anything like that. But they *are* a problem. Don't do anything against your doctor's orders (be a good patient). And don't do anything that could be manipulated to look like you aren't really hurt.

FRAUD!

This is serious, so pay attention. Getting slapped with a fraud claim is *bad news bears*. You do *not* want this in your workers' comp case. Fraud is when you, the claimant, withhold, conceal, manipulate, or straight-up fabricate information to obtain workers' comp benefits.

One of the worst ways a claimant can do this is by trying to hide a preexisting condition. For example, you already had a bad knee, then you banged it on a hard surface at work. You might be tempted to hide the preexisting condition so your injury appears work related. This is a terrible idea, and even if you successfully hid this, it would not help your case. Preexisting conditions do not automatically mean you do not get benefits. In some situations, the preexisting condition could actually help your case. So don't hide this information.

You do not want an insurance company coming after you for fraud. It not only destroys your case, but it could expose you to severe criminal and civil penalties too. So tell the truth, don't hide preexisting conditions, and, once again, *be a good patient*!

CAN I BE FIRED FOR TAKING WORKERS' COMP?

Some states expressly prohibit retaliation for taking workers' compensation. Others do not. Generally, it is legal to let you go if you cannot do the job, which is part of the reason why workers' comp exists in the first place—to help cover that lost income due to your work injury.

If you are fired while a workers' comp claim is pending, talk to your lawyer about it right away.

CAN I BE DEMOTED FOR TAKING WORKERS' COMP?

Generally, yes, with some guidelines. Technically, things like light duty are a demotion. If you have reduced duties due to reduced work capacity because of your injury, it's legal. Again, this is a case-by-case issue, so talk to your lawyer right away if you are unexpectedly demoted after filing for workers' comp.

CAN MY EMPLOYER REQUIRE 100 PERCENT RECOVERY BEFORE I RETURN?

This is another one of those "generally, yes" questions. Employers are within their rights to require full medical clearance before you return to work. This ultimately boils down to a safety issue in most cases. But if the return-to-work requirement is unreasonable, you should talk to your lawyer about your options.

[Summary]

- Workers' compensation is an insurance policy your employer buys to cover workplace injuries.
- Workers' comp provides several benefits, like covering your medical bills, income replacement, and cash settlements.
- Report work injuries right away, even if they don't seem serious at first. In the long term, conditions can develop and you will want a paper trail confirming the injury

arose from your employment. Fault is usually not relevant in workers' comp claims. Instead, the question is whether your injuries arose from the scope and course of your employment.

- Workers' comp is required in forty-nine states. Texas is the only exception. But smart employers get the insurance anyway, because without it, they are vulnerable to a lawsuit.
- Workers' compensation comes from insurance, and it will sometimes become an adversarial process. This means you have to be strategic.
- Insurance companies use fake-ass restrictions and threats to deny or reduce your claims. Never trust a FART.
- The best way to maximize your award is to be a good patient. Follow your doctor's orders.
- Do not go into a workers' comp claim alone. Lawyer up. It costs nothing up front, and it makes a huge difference.
- Independent medical examiners are doctors hired by the insurance company to evaluate your injuries and recovery. These examiners are not your doctor, and they don't work for you. Always defer to your own doctor's instructions.
- Tell the truth, and *never* hide facts from your doctor or lawyer. A preexisting condition does not automatically ruin your case, but hiding it might.
- Insurance companies will spy on you. They will delay the case. They will try to bully and intimidate. Sadly, this is normal, but your lawyer is there to help.

PART IV

Embrace Your Power

LIE: You can't stand up to your boss!

TRUTH: The age of fear is over.
We know our rights, and we're not afraid to use them.

CHIMPS, CHUMPS, AND BULLIES

You can be brave when faced with a bully at work, even if you are scared.

How can I be sure? Because the bullies we encounter at work are more vulnerable than they appear. And we have science to prove it.

First, the bad news: Bullies tend to gain success quickly at work. The cutthroat coworker, the tyrannical manager, all of them will score some wins for a while. But their success comes at a cost. That cost makes them vulnerable. With knowledge of your rights, you can exploit that vulnerability.*

Scientists who studied bullying patterns in chimpanzees (our closest animal relatives) discovered striking similarities to our human experiences. Researchers found that male chimps who displayed patterns of aggression and greed tended to attain higher social status, greater reproductive success, and more access to food.† The correlation between a willingness to bully other chimps and positive outcomes for the bully is undeniable.

But that raised a puzzling question. If bullying correlates with better food, status, and mating opportunities, then why haven't *all* chimps evolved to bully each other? We don't have an exact answer, but the prevailing theory exposes a critical weakness shared by all bullies.

---

*There is a *lot* of information in this book that can totally be used to destroy a manager. Let's all agree to use our new powers for good and not for evil.

†Alexander Weiss, Joseph T. Feldblum, Drew M. Altschul et al., "Personality Traits, Rank Attainment, and Siring Success Throughout the Lives of Male Chimpanzees of Gombe National Park," *PeerJ* (2023): e15083, doi.org/10.7717/peerj.15083.

Bullying is effective only to the extent that the bully can outmuscle their opponents. And once they succeed, they leave a trail of bitter rivals behind them. When they reach the top, they can only remain there by constantly bullying others.

But that's not sustainable. The chimp bully eventually grows old, and their strength fades. Or they become sick or injured. Or attacked by predators. Or backstabbed by a rival they've offended.

Bullies do what they do because they are afraid of being bullied. They may appear invincible. After all, most opponents seem invincible while they are winning. But those fast "wins" come at the cost of security. The bully is surrounded by rivals, not friends. The bully is infected with insecurity, not confidence. And therein lies their weakness.

DON'T JUST *LEARN* YOUR RIGHTS—*USE* THEM!

Knowing your rights at work is half the battle. *Using them* is the other half. In this part of the book, we will talk about the importance of standing up for yourself at work. We will talk about the right way and the wrong way to assert your rights. We will also discuss a few tricks your employer might pull and how to counter them.

Learning to stand up for ourselves is crucial. Every time we fail to defend ourselves, our inner self—our self-esteem—takes a hit. But the opposite is also true. Whenever we push back against a bully, we grow stronger. Speak up, even if your voice shakes. Stand up, even if your knees wobble. Because each act of defiance against a bully builds you up, while shrinking away tears you down.

It's natural to feel nervous about being the kind of person who asserts their boundaries at work. These people seem brave, maybe a little crazy, and certainly a bit confrontational.

I am not advocating that you immediately become hostile to your employer. Quite the contrary. There are *right* ways and *wrong* ways to push back. In this section, we will explore the results of both, and we will commit to doing things the right way.

EMBRACE YOUR POWER

In his iconic book *Atomic Habits*, James Clear wrote that every action, no matter how small, slowly shapes us. He explained that each small act we take is like a vote for the kind of person we want to become. Wake up early to hit the gym? That's a vote for being in shape. Swap the late-night TV for a book? That's a vote for being a reader. Stand up for yourself at work? That's a vote for knowing what you deserve and refusing to settle for less.

And do you know what the best part is? These votes accumulate over time, and you can always cast one for the kind of person you want to be, even if you've made mistakes.

You don't have to be perfect, just do your best to be consistent.

You are very close to finishing this book. Part IV is short, but it is important. This is where it all comes together. In a few pages, you will have finished the most comprehensive book available about your labor rights, and you'll be ready for a new chapter at work.

It's time to stand up.

It's time to fight.

It's time to embrace your power.

[CHAPTER 17]

HR Is Not Your Friend

THE SNAKE IN THE OFFICE

Carol had been bullied by her boss for months. His name was Cranky Craig, and he constantly insulted Carol, calling her a "stupid little girl" when she made the smallest mistake. After an especially bad meeting where Cranky Craig screamed and threw his papers at her, she'd finally had enough.

Carol complained to her HR rep, Vicky Viper. Carol had heard warnings about HR in the past, but Vicky Viper was so kind and warm. She patiently nodded as Carol told her what was happening.

"Thanks for coming to me. We take this very seriously," Vicky Viper said.

Carol trusted Vicky Viper, and she thought things would finally get better. She shared more personal details, including emails, documents, text messages, even her social media posts. A few days later, Carol confessed that her mental health was suffering because of how Cranky Craig treated her.

"Thank you for sharing this," Vicky Viper said. "Please do not discuss this matter with anyone else but me for now."

Carol felt relieved that someone was on her side.

But behind closed doors, Vicky Viper was sharing *everything* with Cranky Craig. Together, they made a plan to protect themselves from a possible lawsuit. They called Carol into the office. They wrote her up, citing "performance concerns."

A few days later, they fired Carol for "poor attitude" and "not being a team player."

Carol learned too late: HR wasn't there to help employees beat their own employer in a dispute. HR was there to protect the company.

HR does not work for you. Some reps are amazing people who will absolutely help you when you need them. And others, like Vicky Viper, will smile while they sharpen the knife.

I've been pretty hard on HR in this book. This is not because I hate them, but because they are typically my opponents when I sue for unlawful labor practices. This means my sample size of human resources reps is typically limited to those who did something illegal. This doesn't mean all HR people are evil. What I am trying to say here is that I have had extensive experience dealing with unethical and untrustworthy HR people. I don't want you to be paranoid, but I also don't want you to let your guard down.

In this chapter, we will talk about the roles of management and human resources, and what's really happening behind the scenes when you have a conflict with them. And although HR is not always your "enemy" per se, one thing remains true no matter what:

HR is not your friend.

WHAT IS HUMAN RESOURCES?

Human resources, also called HR, is a department that advises your employer on labor management, compliance, and managing complaints. HR is usually responsible for hiring, firing, and disciplining employees. They will process complaints from employees, administer leave requests, process accommodation requests, and hold trainings on matters of company policy and compliance.

HR may be very kind. But they are not on your side in a dispute.

In the hit comedy series *The Office,* regional manager Michael Scott (played by Steve Carell) is routinely in trouble for his oafish, offensive behavior. In several episodes, he declares his most hated enemy in the world is his human resources rep, Toby Flenderson (played by Paul Lieberstein): "Why are you the way that you are? Honestly, every time I try to do something fun or exciting, you make it not that way. I hate so much about the things that you choose to be."

Wow. Tell us how you really feel, Michael!

But as goofy as the show was, Michael might have been onto something. Many people have an innate distrust of HR simply because they are seen as the enforcers, the tattletales, the people who write you up and fire you even if they have no clue about the work you really do. It's no way to be popular.

And while Michael Scott might have said it differently, I have to agree on one thing: **HR is not your friend. Further, HR is not your therapist. And HR is not your career counselor.** They are hired by the company. Their job is to protect the company from liability against claims of unlawful employment practices. For example, if you put in for protected leave, HR is there to administer the leave in a way that shields the company from a retaliation claim. If you complain about sexual harassment, HR's job is to assess the risk and do whatever it takes to limit the risk of a lawsuit. Sometimes these goals lead to positive outcomes: The leave request is handled fairly. The sexual harasser is held accountable. And everyone continues working just fine.

Other times, they do something terrible instead. For example, you get bullied and accused of "making trouble" when you report a manager for harassment. This is not the majority of cases, but, sadly, it's not rare either.

If you find yourself in this situation, do not be confrontational or cruel. You do not need to be combative with HR. Instead, you need to craft your approach in such a way that you are protected.

In an ironic twist many readers will not suspect, my sister is an HR executive for a major corporation. We have a fantastic relationship, and I was blessed to officiate her wedding. I share this because I do not want anyone to get the impression that I hate HR. I don't.

That said, HR's role sets them up to be my opponent when a dispute arises at work. It's why I am frequently in conflict with them in my cases. And it's why so many people distrust the profession.

I recognize this is pretty rich coming from a *lawyer* of all people, but bear with me.

Because HR reps are your primary point of contact for most of issues related to your employment, you should carefully document every interaction with HR.

HR Is an Unregulated Profession

There are shitty lawyers out there. Just like there are shitty doctors, shitty accountants, and, most tragically, shitty barbers. Fortunately, these are regulated professions. Every professional in these fields undergoes formal training, obtains a license, and must meet certain requirements every year to keep that license. If a lawyer makes a mistake, then the public can seek redress through a state board that monitors our professional standards.

But HR is an *unregulated* profession.

What does that mean?

HR professionals can get degrees and certifications in their field, but generally the profession does not require a license. There is no state human resources board monitoring HR reps for malpractice. When your company has an HR rep, there's not really a way to ensure you have a legitimate professional over an amateur.

True story: I have sued a company whose "HR department" was literally just a guy using ChatGPT to make things up as he went. As you can imagine, that place was a mess.

HR reps will vary widely in skills, experience, and integrity.

HR Is Not Your Therapist

Oftentimes, I see companies where the HR department evolves into a sort of "work mom" role. Perhaps your rep is a sweet woman with a couch in her office for you to sit on. She plays soft music, wears pleasant perfume, hands you a box of tissues, and says, "You can be vulnerable here, it's a safe space."

Sorry to interrupt this touching moment, but I'm calling *BULLSHIT*!

No matter how kind or sweet your HR rep is, they are paid by the company. No matter what they say. No matter how much you *want* to get close with them. They. Are. Not. Your. Therapist.

Your therapist is your therapist. Your friends are your friends. HR is neither.

Asking them to take your side over the company's isn't reasonable, because that's their career on the line. Nine times out of ten, HR will side with the company.

Assume the Best, but Prepare for the Worst

Learn your rights *independently*. Never rely on HR alone to explain the law to you. Some may not know. Others might know but will lead you astray anyway. Some might just be a guy using AI.

It is also wise to make sure you keep HR at arm's length. As I mentioned before, document all interactions. And never assume an HR rep is your buddy just because they are nice.

HOW TO TALK TO HR

"But Ryan," I hear you say, "if HR is not our friend, why should we talk with them at all? Isn't it better to avoid them?"

This is a reasonable conclusion, but the answer is no, you should not avoid HR. Although they are on the company's side, they are still your first, best resource when you need help at work. For things like complaints of harassment, requests for accommodation, requests for FMLA, and reports of missing pay or unsafe conditions, you should almost always go through HR first. Remember that their role is to protect the company from liability. Helping you with your issue quickly and legally is the best way to do that.

Dos and Don'ts of Speaking with Human Resources

- **DO:** Communicate promptly and professionally when you have a problem. Assume everything you write may later become evidence of your situation.
- **DO:** Communicate in writing and keep copies for yourself.
- **DO:** Fact-check HR when they make a statement about the law or what your company policies are. All HR reps are people, and all people sometimes make mistakes. Other times, they might be deliberately lying. But never ascribe malice to that which can be explained by incompetence. (This advice will keep you sane, trust me.)
- **DO:** Keep communications with HR work related, focusing only on the information they need to help you.
- **DON'T:** Overshare. Oversharing your personal life with HR is career suicide. *Do not do it.* They don't need to know about who your work crush is, they don't need to know about your hobbies or interests, and they definitely don't need to know your political views, the parties you attend, or who you are dating.
- **DON'T:** Follow or accept follows on social media from HR. Blocking people doesn't hurt them, and doing so might protect your career.
- **DON'T:** Assume they will take care of your needs for you. Like I said in previous chapters, you should notify them when you have an issue, but most of the time, *you* will have to be in the driver's seat. This is true for everything from leave requests to harassment complaints.
- **DON'T:** Get confrontational, hostile, or defensive when HR writes you up or does something you don't like. It's rarely personal, but even if it were, getting defensive doesn't help. There's a smart way and a self-destructive way to fight for your rights. *Lashing out at HR is the self-destructive way.*

WHAT IF YOUR HR REP IS UNTRUSTWORTHY?

In a lawsuit, should one become necessary, the company often is not liable unless they *knew* or *reasonably should have known* that you had a problem. As the company's representatives, when HR knows about an issue, then the law will assume the company knows as well.

Therefore, speaking to HR has two possible outcomes:

POSSIBLE OUTCOME 1: They follow the law and help you, and you carry on with your job.

POSSIBLE OUTCOME 2: They retaliate or try to force you out. But at least now, after reading this book and implementing its strategies, you have a paper trail proving the company *knew* you had a problem, and *then* they broke the law.

However, an untrustworthy HR rep might try a dirty trick: avoiding a paper trail.

What If They Avoid a Paper Trail?

This is a sneaky trick I see all the time. You file a complaint about a boss making creepy sexual jokes at work. Suddenly, an HR rep appears at your desk like some kind of corporate genie. "Let's talk face-to-face," they say.

Or how about this: You send an email alerting them of an unsafe condition at work. Suddenly, the phone rings. "Let's talk this out," they say.

Oh, and another one I see: Having you submit complaints to an online portal that only *they* have access to. If you want a copy of your report, oops! Suddenly it's not available.

See a trend here?

No. Paper. Trail.

They are deliberately pushing the conversation into spaces where it will be harder for you to prove what was said. Or that it was said at all. HR cannot deny an email chain as easily as they can deny a phone call. And face-to-face conversations have no record at all. As for online portals they control . . . yeah, good luck getting access to that without a subpoena.

If your HR rep thoroughly documents everything and insists on keeping a record, then you have a good HR rep. Don't let your guard down, but don't be paranoid either.

If they freak out when you email them, or if they seem to be trying a bit too hard to keep stuff off the record, you've got a Vicky Viper on your hands, and you need to watch out!

But for your own job security, you will treat the good reps and the bad reps the same.

The Power of the Recap

Recaps are my favorite way to make a paper trail. They can be done in a text message, a paper memo, or my personal favorite, email. The goal of a recap is to memorialize any conversations that occurred "off the record."

If you have a phone call, videoconference, or personal meeting with HR, send a recap documenting the following things:

- When and where the conversation occurred
- Who was there
- The purpose of the conversation
- What was discussed
- Any action items planned during the conversation

Here's an example you can reference if you are not sure how to start:

Sample Email Template: Recapping a Harassment Complaint

Dear Vicky Viper,

This email is to summarize our phone conversation at 3:30 p.m. today. I made the call to report Cranky Craig for harassment.

Specifically, I reported that his severe and pervasive abuse, including calling me a "stupid little girl" and throwing things at me, is creating a hostile work environment for me.

You said that you take this report seriously and that you will conduct an investigation. You also said I can expect an update in a few days.

I appreciate your prompt attention to this matter.

Respectfully,
Carol

"YOUR COMPLAINT IS UNSUBSTANTIATED"

When you submit a complaint to HR, be it about an unsafe condition, harassment, or something else, it's very common for them to stonewall you. It might look something like this: "After a thorough investigation, we have closed this matter. We found there is no evidence to substantiate your complaint."

This doesn't happen every time. But it's not unusual. So what can you do in this situation?

Best-case scenario, HR came to this conclusion because they simply didn't have enough information. In that case, you should submit a new complaint, telling them you feel important information was missed and explaining that you'd like to share those facts with them.

But if they actually are just trying to obstruct you, then these are your options:

- Escalate to a higher-level manager. (This is your first step, but you can file the complaints listed below concurrently.)
- If the issue involves a safety concern, file a complaint to the Occupational Safety and Health Administration (OSHA) or your state equivalent. Keep copies of that complaint.
- If the issue involves a problem with your pay, such as missing hours, late payment, unpaid overtime, possible misclassification,

or a problem with FMLA, then submit a complaint to the US Department of Labor or your state equivalent (usually this is your state labor board or labor commissioner).

- If the issue involves discrimination or harassment (including sexual harassment) for a protected characteristic, file a complaint with the Equal Employment Opportunity Commission (EEOC) or your state equivalent. (Usually this will be your state civil rights division. You can also check your state attorney's general website for more resources.)
- If the issue involves union busting, retaliation for attempting to unionize, or for any "concerted activities"* like talking about pay or work conditions, then file a report with the National Labor Relations Board (NLRB) or, you guessed it, your state equivalent (usually it's your state labor board or labor commissioner).†
- At any time in this process, it is wise to talk to an experienced workers' rights lawyer. If you are asking for legal advice related to a work problem, most lawyers will expect to be paid for the time they spend advising you. However, if you just need an evaluation to see if you have a case for a lawsuit, many will do the assessment for free. It's a subtle difference, but it helps to know what you're asking for.

WHAT IF HR IS INVESTIGATING YOU?

One of HR's most unpleasant duties is investigating violations of workplace policy. If you are accused of misusing company property, time-clock fraud, or breaking something, you'll probably get a call from HR.

---

*National Labor Relations Act, 29 U.S. Code § 151-169 (1935).

†As of this writing, the NLRB still exists as an enforcement agency to protect your rights. However, the Trump administration has indicated a policy goal of eliminating the agency entirely. If that happens, then you will want to speak to a workers' rights lawyer about alternative ways to address your situation.

Other times, a coworker might report you for some behavioral violation, like gossiping or being inappropriately flirty.

If you really did the thing, then you have to be an adult and own it. Say you're sorry, promise to do better, and move on. If you are fired for the violation, then it's a hard lesson, but you will survive, and life will get better.

If you are accused of doing something you did *not* do, then the game changes. It's natural to feel outraged. *How dare they accuse me of this?* You might feel embarrassed. *When word gets out, everyone will think I'm a fool.* You might even get angry. *This is WAR!*

All these are natural emotions. But do *not* act on them. Acknowledge the angry emotions, let them pass, then *lock in*. Here's the game plan for when you are falsely accused at work:

1. Do not get defensive. Getting angry and lashing out will make the situation worse.
2. Communicate that you deny the allegation, but also that you will cooperate with any investigation. You want to clear your name, after all!

Once you are made aware of the accusations against you, send a recap email that follows these steps. If you look closely, you will see it follows the five-step formula we discussed in "The Power of the Recap."

Sample Email Template: Recapping After Investigation

Dear Vicky Viper,

This email is to summarize the conversation we had in your office at 9:45 a.m. You, Cranky Craig, and I were in attendance. You said the reason I was called into the office is because I am being investigated for violating workplace policies.

I asked which policies I was accused of violating, and you declined to say. Cranky Craig did not say either. However, I was told I would be placed on a performance improvement plan.

Our next meeting to discuss the PIP is scheduled for Tuesday, April 8, 2025, at 1:00 p.m.

I take this quite seriously. While I do not agree I broke policy, I will cooperate with the investigation.

Respectfully,
Carol

WHAT IF HR CONFRONTS YOU?

What if you are confronted in person with an accusation of violating the rules? What if HR says, "We are very disturbed to hear reports that you may have defrauded the company"? What if your boss calls you and immediately starts throwing accusations your way? "Why didn't you file this report on time?!" they scream, without even asking to hear your side.

It's easy to feel scared or lose our cool.

In the heat of the moment, don't panic, just **ACT:**

Acknowledge the accusation.

Calmly deny the accusation.

Tell them you will cooperate.

Here's how that might sound in real life, using two examples we already discussed:

"Okay, Vicky Viper, I understand the situation, and I am taking it seriously. I did not defraud the company. I will happily cooperate in this investigation to clear my name."

"Okay, Cranky Craig, I understand you're saying the report was not filed on time, and I agree this is serious. I did not file the report late. Let me help you figure out what's going on."

Boom. We didn't get upset, we didn't make excuses, and we definitely didn't make the situation worse. We can't control other people, and I cannot promise that everyone will react well to these statements. But responding calmly and cooperatively is the best move, and it will work more often than not.

Don't panic, ***ACT***!

WRITE-UPS AND PERFORMANCE IMPROVEMENT PLANS (PIPs)

A write-up is used by employers to document discipline issues or unsatisfactory performance. A write-up can be informal, like a text or email, or it can be formal, like a detailed performance improvement plan (PIP). PIPs are formal plans that tell an employee what they need to improve and a time frame in which to do it. A PIP usually is accompanied by check-in times where a manager reviews your progress. Like a write-up, a PIP typically means you are at higher risk of termination. Write-ups and PIPs are a bummer—there's no way around it. Your boss is basically saying you suck at your job, and that doesn't feel good. But like other issues we discussed, there is a right way and a wrong way to handle this.

The *wrong* way is to get super defensive, deny everything, and get really emotional. The *right* way is to stay calm, make a paper trail, and regain as much control of the narrative as you can.

Obviously, if your performance is genuinely suffering, take a moment to check in with yourself. Why is this happening? Are you feeling burned-out? Is there a personal or family issue distracting you? If so, I recommend referencing other sections of this book around protected leave and accommodations. Not only are these protected against retaliation, like getting fired, but they will also help you recover.

But what if the PIP is bullshit? What if accusations are so vague you can hardly make sense of them? Or what if you *did* make a mistake but the PIP just blows it way out of proportion?

Allow me to introduce my good friend **the rebuttal**.

How to Rebut a PIP

When you get placed on a PIP, it will probably start with a call or meeting with your boss and HR. The tone will feel pretty serious. Don't freak out; it's unpleasant but totally normal. And let's be real—a PIP is better than getting fired.

In the meeting, they will address your work performance: You aren't hitting deadlines, you're not billing enough hours, you are too slow, or maybe they got bad reviews from customers. Whatever the issue, they'll probably give you a piece of paper with lots of examples of your poor performance. This will be upsetting to read. Just remember, it's only their side of the story, and half of that letter is probably boilerplate from an HR manual somewhere, anyway.

Next, they will say that they need to see improvement. If they are good at their job, they will give you clear expectations with reasonable time frames to meet them. If they are *really* good, they will plan at least one check-in meeting to monitor your performance improvement.

But some people suck at their jobs, so it's possible you will get a bunch of vague accusations, unclear metrics, and zero clue what to do next.

In either case, if you want to rebut a PIP, here is what you do:

1. Acknowledge the PIP and that you take it seriously.
2. Calmly explain what you disagree with, if anything. But don't make excuses.
3. Suggest alternate metrics, if appropriate.
4. Tell them you will cooperate.

Remember these steps, because in the heat of the moment, a lot of people lose their cool.

Of all the ways to crash and burn at work, a long rambling email about how none of this is your fault is the crashiest and burniest. Getting defensive is self-destructive; you might as well have just said, "Please fire me."

There is a much smarter way to fight back! Imagine every email you write has a big red "Exhibit A" written at the top. Imagine it will be read aloud to a jury.

Here's an example email to send after getting put on a PIP:

Sample Email Template: Rebutting a PIP

Dear Vicky Viper and Cranky Craig,

I am writing to discuss the performance improvement plan I was placed on today. I want you to know I am taking this very seriously.

The PIP states that I am not reliable. I understand the complaint is that I missed a deadline last week. I respectfully disagree that my performance is subpar.

Last week, I had to pick up some extra work when Dan fell behind. My goal was to be a team player, and though one deadline was missed, I feel I made the right call under the circumstances.

While I disagree with aspects of the PIP, I will cooperate in the process.

Respectfully,
Carol

This is solid work! Carol looks reasonable. She calmly explained her side of the story without getting defensive. Equally important, she looked cooperative.

But I have some advice for Carol. **She needs to apply to other jobs immediately.** She doesn't have to take any new offers, but she needs offers and she needs them fast. A PIP is often a warning light that a termination is imminent, even if you are cooperative. Do not risk losing your income by being complacent.

Acknowledge. Rebut. Cooperate. Then apply to other jobs so you have a backup plan.

DO I HAVE TO SIGN A WRITE-UP OR PIP?

Most PIPs and write-ups will have a signature block somewhere. It's very common for employers to require you to sign a write-up or PIP.

This can really freak people out. I've seen some pretty concerning advice on the internet about this, so let's clear a few things up.

Acknowledged Only

Most of the time, a signature merely means you received and acknowledge the write-up, not that you agree with it. It might even say so on the signature block. Here is a quote, verbatim, that I saw in one of my cases:

> *My signature below confirms that I have received this performance improvement plan. I understand that my signature does not necessarily indicate agreement with the contents, only that the plan has been reviewed with me, and I have been given a copy.*

Because your signature merely *acknowledges* receipt, it's safe to sign. You are not admitting anything. You are just being cooperative. And remember that being cooperative is one of the key strategies you are using to get through this process.

But watch out! What if the write-up doesn't have such a disclaimer? In that case, you can still sign, but write "acknowledged only" under your signature. If it's an e-signature, you should be able to leave a comment. If not, then your rebuttal email should make it clear that your signature does not necessarily mean you agree.

Signed Under Duress?

Signing a write-up or PIP really isn't a big deal most of the time—it doesn't necessarily mean you agree, and refusing to sign will probably get you fired on the spot. Still, it's an upsetting situation, and I've seen a few people say you can "nullify" the write-up by writing "signed under duress" or its fancy cousin, "VC."*

*VC is an abbreviation for the Latin *vi coactus*, which translates to "having been forced." The exact origin is unknown, but some say this practice originated in the Middle Ages. When prisoners were forced to sign a confession to escape torture, they worried about later legal (or spiritual) consequences. The VC was a plea for God to have mercy—to spare their souls from punishment for

The idea is that you can say the threat of losing your job was "duress," and therefore you cannot be held responsible for anything you signed while under duress.

Sounds like a cool legal loophole—except it's not. This doesn't work. *Duress* is a legal term. To prove duress, you have to prove you were being literally threatened with some kind of unlawful action, like physical violence, death, loss of valuable property, or gross humiliation (like revenge porn).

As you can see, these things are a *serious* escalation above simply being fired. Getting fired sucks, and it's scary, but the threat of termination is almost never considered duress, even when it's unfair.

Don't try any fancy tricks. Just stick to the "acknowledged only" line, and you'll cover yourself for the majority of situations. Remember, signing generally does not mean you agree, it only means you saw the write-up.

WHAT IF HR IS THE BULLY? OR WHAT IF THERE'S NO HR DEPARTMENT?

Sometimes HR will be the bully. Sometimes *they* are the ones you need to report. What do you do? If it's a large HR department, you can just report to another HR rep or their supervisor. If you are in a smaller company, then report the HR rep to your manager. If your manager is part of the problem, then any supervisor who has hiring and firing power will do. Just document it like you would any other conversation.

If you truly have no one to turn to for help, then you may need to submit the complaint to the person who is causing the problem. Legally, they are still in a position to represent the company, so you just follow the steps as you would for anyone else, but directed *to* them.

If all else fails, then it's a good idea to speak with a workers' rights lawyer about the best way to handle the situation.

---

the crimes they confessed to, swearing that they only confessed under threat of torture. I have no idea if this is true, but it seems about right, and the story is pretty interesting.

Summary

- The human resources department is responsible for managing the daily administration of employees. They handle things like hiring, firing, write-ups, leave requests, disability accommodations, and processing complaints of harassment and other unlawful behavior.
- Some great people work in HR. But it is an unregulated profession, so the competence (and integrity) of HR representatives will not always be consistent.
- Your HR rep might be very kind. Just remember they are not your friend; they work for the company, not for you.
- Document every interaction with HR. Use recaps to keep a record of phone calls, video calls, and face-to-face meetings.
- When faced with a write-up at work, do not panic; *ACT*! Acknowledge, calmly deny, and tell them you will cooperate.
- If you disagree with a write-up, it is wise to sign it anyway. Just be sure it says "acknowledged only" or something similar.
- Attempting to "nullify" a write-up by claiming it was signed under duress is a bad bet.
- If an HR rep is bullying you, or if you do not have an HR department, then escalating complaints to any manager with hiring and firing power will work. Consider speaking to a lawyer or filing a complaint with the appropriate state or federal agency.

CHAPTER 18

Arbitration and Noncompetes and NDAs, Oh My!

"DON'T PISS ON MY LEG AND TELL ME IT'S RAINING!"

Judge Judith Sheindlin (a.k.a. Judge Judy) is famous for her no-nonsense, sometimes hilarious rulings in her TV courtroom. For anyone who has not seen the show, let me tell you it is top-tier TV. Judge Judy is a real retired judge. She served as a judge in New York before she became a reality TV icon.

On the show, Judge Judy rules on small-claims disputes in her courtroom. She has a bailiff, an audience, and podiums for the plaintiff and the defendant. The cases are real, and Judge Judy's rulings are legally binding as if they came from a real court, but the disputes can sometimes be a bit odd and . . . well, maybe you should see for yourself:

- **THE BROKEN TOILET SEAT:** A woman sued her friend for allegedly breaking her toilet during a visit.
- **THE BURNT COUCH BREAKUP:** A pair of bitter ex-lovers argued over burn marks on a couch, with one blaming the other due to their fire-dancing hobby.

- **THE EBAY SCAMMER:** The plaintiff purchased a phone from an eBay seller. Based on the pictures, the phone seemed perfect. But when the package arrived, it was just a picture of the phone. The defendant claimed the listing was just for the photo all along.
- **THE TUPPERWARE LADY:** In perhaps the most famous episode of the series, Karina Roy sued her landlord for some missing Tupperware. Yes, she booked a flight, went all the way to Judge Judy's court, and then told the wildest story ever on national TV . . . all for some dishes and Tupperware. And believe it or not, she actually won about $199. Check this episode out—you'll be *Glad* you did.*

But while the cases and rulings are real, Judge Judy's "courtroom" is not. What you are seeing on TV is not actually a bench trial—though it's been dressed up to look like one. Rather, Judge Judy presides over something called *arbitration*. The people on the show sign a contract to arbitrate their claim before Judge Judy, and the arbitration agreement makes her rulings legally binding.

In this chapter, we will talk about some of the most confusing legal situations, contracts, and documents you might come across at work, what they mean, and how to deal with them.

These are things you might find in your hiring paperwork. Or sometimes they are in a new policy that comes up later. Other times, you get a piece of paper thrown in your face, and you're told "Sign it!" with no idea what it is.

Some of the most common issues like this include arbitration agreements, noncompete agreements (NCAs), nondisclosure agreements (NDAs), and trade secret or confidentiality agreements.

These can all look and sound a bit scary, so let's talk about them in a way that makes it all make sense.

---

*If bad puns were illegal, I'd be doing twenty-five to life for this. But hey, that's showbiz, baby.

WHAT IS ARBITRATION?

Arbitration is an alternative way to resolve a legal dispute *outside of court,* and it is governed by the Federal Arbitration Act (FAA). Basically, when an arbitration agreement is signed, parties *waive their right* to a lawsuit, and instead agree to take their disputes to a neutral arbitrator instead. The arbitrator is usually a retired judge who works with a private company, called an arbitration provider. Both sides present their case, and the arbitrator makes a legally binding decision.

Unlike a lawsuit in court, arbitration filings are private. And unlike a trial, the public generally cannot access an arbitration hearing without the consent of all parties. Arbitration is sometimes faster than a regular lawsuit, and it will sometimes have limits on how much litigation can occur. (For example, limiting each side to only two depositions,* whereas in court, no such limit typically exists.)

Before we proceed, I need to make something very clear: There is a *lot* I do not like about arbitration, and I am not alone. Many lawyers feel arbitration is unfair for employees. I will explain why in a moment, but remember one thing: You can still win a dispute against your employer in arbitration. Is it my favorite thing? Hell no. Would I prefer arbitration agreements not be allowed in employment? Hell yes.

It's not the end of the world if your case goes to arbitration. That said, arbitration tends to favor employers over employees.

Why Arbitration Sucks

There are a few red flags when it comes to arbitration in employment. First, the arbitration provider is a business, and businesses like repeat customers. Employers pay the fees to bring you into arbitration. Usu-

*A deposition is a legal proceeding in which lawyers ask witnesses questions under oath. A court reporter is present to make a transcript. Depositions are extremely common in lawsuits because they're essential for obtaining sworn testimony.

ally, if they do not pay the fees, you can take the case to court. But since the *employer* pays the fees, and because the *employer* is more likely to need an arbitrator again in the future . . . there is a clear conflict of interest here.

How is this legal? Great question. All I can say is thank your local lobbyist.

What about efficiency? While arbitration can be faster, it's not always better. The arbitrator can rule on motions more quickly, and you can get to a final hearing sooner than at trial. But there are also limits on how the case can be pursued. Limits on your ability to get evidence, such as witness testimony, can make it harder to prove the case. And frankly, from my own experience, the "rules" of arbitration sometimes feel more like general guidelines. As a serious litigator, I do not like the loosey-goosey approach to rulemaking within an arbitration. I much prefer the strict, professional, predictable rules of a real court—with swift consequences for failure to abide by such rules.

Hopefully I've given you a good sense of why big companies love arbitration agreements. They get to control the venue, they get secrecy, they get to pay the person making the decision, and they don't have to worry about a jury of "normal people" slapping them with huge verdicts. But to really understand why big companies love arbitration, we need to take a quick trip down to Florida, where a terrible tragedy—followed by a nationwide scandal—occurred.

Case Study: Disney+ and the Nut Allergy

A couple sat down for dinner at a restaurant in Disney Springs, a community in Walt Disney World Resort. The wife had a severe nut allergy, and she warned staff about it multiple times. Despite several assurances from waiters and management, the wife received a dish tainted with traces of nut and dairy.

This triggered a fatal reaction. Within forty-five minutes, she had stopped breathing. She died shortly after. This was a tragic and totally preventable death, so the grieving husband filed suit against Disney for the negligent, wrongful death of his wife.

Rather than settle the dispute, Disney decided to become a global supervillain. In a motion to dismiss the case, Disney argued that the husband had waived his right to a lawsuit. The husband was puzzled—he didn't sign anything when he dined at Disney Springs.

But then Disney whipped out proof that the husband had subscribed to the streaming platform Disney+. When he did so, he signed an arbitration agreement buried deep in the user agreement.

Disney claimed that by agreeing to those streaming terms, the husband had signed away his right to sue them in court, even in a case of wrongful death. In my opinion, this was an insane and legally unsubstantiated argument. And I wasn't alone.

The public backlash was *furious*. Disney ultimately agreed to back down, allowing the case to move forward in court. But the fact that a company tried to use a streaming subscription to silence a grieving family says everything about how far corporations will go to avoid court.

Why Employers Want to Arbitrate

Disney was willing to endure a *lot* of bad press, bad karma, and bad legal arguments to weasel its way into arbitration. What did they hope to gain from all that? They tried to pursue arbitration because it:

- Stacks the deck in their favor (since they are paying the fees).
- Is more private than a court case.
- Avoids class action claims by forcing plaintiffs to arbitrate as individuals rather than a group. (It's not impossible to have a class action if there is an arbitration agreement, but it complicates things.)
- Has limited discovery rules (makes it harder to prove your case).
- Involves no jury! So, it's less likely you'll have decision-makers "personalizing" your claim. They don't want a jury of your peers seeing you as a human—they want an arbitrator to take as impersonal an approach as possible to your case.

So yeah, all these pages to say that arbitration kind of sucks.* Still, they can be a condition of employment. So what can you do?

Opt out if you can. Refuse to sign if you can. That's the simple answer.

If you truly have no choice, then it's good to be aware of the drawbacks, but don't panic. I've been able to nullify arbitration agreements, but in cases where that wasn't an option, I've seen arbitrations go well for employees too. The point is that you should avoid them if you can, but if there's really no way around it, then it's not the end of the world. And if you are not sure whether your arbitration agreement is valid or not, it is worth asking a lawyer for an opinion *before* you sue your employer.

WHAT ARE NONCOMPETE AGREEMENTS (NCAs)?

A noncompete agreement, or NCA, is a contract where a worker agrees not to start a competing business or work for a competitor after leaving their job. It's different from a nondisclosure agreement (NDA), which protects confidential information, or a nonsolicitation agreement, which stops you from poaching customers or coworkers. Noncompetes are all about limiting *where, when,* and *for whom* you can work next.

If that sounds unfair, it's because it is! But what's fair and what's legal are not always the same. Thus, we need to understand what we lose when we sign an NCA (and what legal limits help us out).

Most noncompetes are governed by state law. Some states—like California, North Dakota, and Oklahoma—have banned or restricted NCAs in employment. But in many states, they're still allowed if they meet certain legal requirements. There are four primary factors courts look at when deciding whether a noncompete is enforceable:

*If it is ever in my power to do so, I will outlaw arbitration agreements in employment cases. Arbitration has a rightful place in many disputes—but employment is not one of them.

1. **CONSIDERATION:** You have to get something in return—like a job offer, a raise, or a promotion—to make the agreement legally binding.
2. **REASONABLE TIME LIMITS:** The NCA can't last forever. Most valid noncompetes last between six and twenty-four months. Anything longer, or an indefinite time frame, is less likely to be enforceable.
3. **GEOGRAPHIC LIMITS:** It must be tied to a specific area—like within fifty miles, or within a state. A nationwide ban usually won't hold up.
4. **INDUSTRY OR JOB LIMITS:** It has to relate to actual competitors. But "competitor" can be vague. Could a former Burger King employee be blocked from working at Chipotle? Or at a company that delivers food supplies? These gray areas can lead to confusion. Often the result is fewer opportunities for the employee.

Some of the most absurd cases involve frontline workers, even entry-level employees, getting sued just for taking a job at another company. I've seen gyms sue personal trainers, claiming they're a threat because they switched gyms. In these cases, no matter what the corporate lawyers say, it's not about protecting business interests, it's about *control*.

How Noncompetes Hurt Workers

To be clear, I'm not 100 percent opposed to noncompetes. I'm more like . . . 90 percent opposed. For high-level executives who know a company's inner workings, a noncompete make senses. For example, KFC has every right to protect its famous "eleven herbs and spices" from falling into El Pollo Loco's hands.

But using noncompetes to trap low- or mid-level workers? That's not protecting your business—it's just abuse. If a company underpays, mistreats, or endangers its employees, then the employees should be free to leave. Noncompetes make that harder, which drives down wages, keeps abusive employers in power, and reduces competition in the job market.

The Federal Trade Commission estimated that one in five workers in the US is bound by a noncompete.*

Under the Biden administration, the FTC led an effort to ban noncompete agreements in employment for all fifty states. However, since the Trump administration took office, the FTC voluntarily dismissed its efforts to advance the ban on noncompetes in employment.

What Should You Do If Presented with a Noncompete?

As of the writing of this book, noncompetes are legal in the majority of states. If signing one is required, check to see if they are enforceable in your state. And if they are, make sure the NCA is reasonable. It should have narrowly tailored language about how long you will be restricted for, what industries are covered, and the geographical extent of the restrictions. If any of these are overly broad, then request a revision or consider talking to a lawyer.

WHAT ARE NONDISCLOSURE AGREEMENTS (NDAs)?

Nondisclosure agreements (NDAs) are contracts where you give up the right to discuss, post about, publish, or otherwise disclose certain information. NDAs have become something of a boogeyman in modern culture.

They became infamous during the Harvey Weinstein trials. Harvey Weinstein was a big-shot producer in Hollywood. If you wanted to land a starring role in the next blockbuster movie, you needed him on your side. If he was *not* on your side, if he didn't like you for any reason, your

*Research used by the FTC revealed that NCAs cost the American economy up to $300 billion a year in lost wages, lower job mobility, and reduced innovation. See United States Federal Trade Commission, "FTC Announces Rule Banning Noncompetes," press release, April 23, 2024, ftc.gov/news-events/news/press-releases/2024/04/ftc-announces-rule-banning-noncompetes.

career was effectively over. He had a lot of power, and he knew how to use it.

Because Harvey Weinstein was a sexual predator.

He used his influence in Hollywood to force models, actresses, singers, and anyone else he could corner to have sex with him. For years, there were rumors. But when the criminal and civil lawsuits started to fly, a shocking revelation came to light.

Harvey's victims had been too scared to speak up because many of them had signed NDAs. As a condition of working with Weinstein, women were forced to sign nondisclosure agreements. They were threatened with lawsuits, being banned from working in Hollywood, even straight up blackmail.

Fortunately, a few brave survivors spoke up. While technically this was a violation of their NDAs, there was a little detail that Harvey and his crooked lawyers forgot to think about: NDAs cannot be used to stop you from reporting unlawful activity. And they cannot be used to stop you from truthfully testifying before a court, a government agency, or any other legal proceeding.

Anyway, as I write this book, Harvey Weinstein is currently in prison, where he will likely spend the rest of his life because he has a twenty-three-year sentence in New York and a sixteen-year sentence in California.

What NDAs Can and Cannot Do

I once had an old friend call me about a legal problem.

"My girlfriend needs help, but she's too scared to ask," he said.

"What's the problem?" I asked.

My friend told me that his girlfriend, who we will call Amy, was being sexually harassed at work. It was bad. *Really* bad. The boss was at least twenty years older than her, and he was married, and he knew she had a boyfriend. Still, he constantly talked to her about sex, including his favorite toys to use on women. He offered, many times, to let Amy "try out" his toys . . . but only if he could watch.

Disgusting.

But it got worse. One day at work, he grabbed Amy's face and kissed her without consent. She was furious. She went straight to her boyfriend and blew up about the whole thing. After ranting about her boss's gross behavior, she sobbed uncontrollably.

"I signed an NDA!" Amy bawled. "He said he's sued employees in the past. He's got a lot of money, I can't break my NDA!"

Heart-wrenching. And it made me furious.

I explained to Amy and my friend that an NDA could not be used to silence victims of sexual harassment.

"Not just that," I said. "Any NDA that tries to stop you from truthfully reporting unlawful activity is probably invalid. They can't make you sign an NDA, for example, saying you won't report safety concerns to OSHA, or report a crime to the police."

Later that day, I got a copy of the NDA and reviewed it with my friend and Amy.

"This thing is bogus," I said. "NDAs can legally be used to stop you from revealing sensitive company information, and they can prevent you from disparaging or talking bad about them, but they can't stop you from reporting sexual harassment."

Amy looked like a weight was lifted off her shoulders. "So . . . he can't sue me?"

"He can try," I told her. "But frankly, he has much bigger problems. The sexual harassment you experienced is way worse than breaking a bogus NDA."

We signed her case that evening. I am pleased to report that we got her a big enough settlement that she took a year off work, got a new place, went to school, and now lives a very happy (and harassment-free) life in California.

Prohibitions Against Discussing Pay

As Amy's case showed, an NDA is valid for protecting company information like KFC's eleven herbs and spices. But an NDA cannot be used to prevent the reporting of illegal activity. Another example beyond sexual harassment would be an NDA telling you not to discuss pay with your coworkers. Such a prohibition would violate the National Labor Relations Act, which protects your right to engage in "concerted activities" for mutual protection and welfare. In English, that means federal law protects your right to talk about pay.

NDAs, Severance, and Settlements

I see a *lot* of NDAs. I have even drafted a few myself. The reason is that NDAs are a common and normal part of severance and settlement agreements. Companies cannot stop you from truthfully testifying, nor can they stop you from reporting illegal activity to proper authorities. However, they are within their rights to have you sign an NDA promising not to discuss how much you were paid for a severance or settlement. This is usually enforceable, and as a workers' rights lawyer, I don't think they are anything to get worked up about. If you are being offered a settlement, and they want you to sign an NDA to get the money, talk to your lawyer about whether it's safe to sign. Usually it's fine, but always double-check!

WHAT ARE TRADE SECRETS?

In Atlanta, Georgia, there is a vault. It is completely off-limits to everyone in the world—except for two people.

Their identities are a closely kept secret. The vault itself is guarded by armed security 24/7. If you are caught within one hundred feet of the vault and you aren't one of the two humans allowed to view its contents, you are going to have a very bad time.

What could be so important, so secret, that these measures are necessary? It's not a mountain of gold. It's not the nuclear weapons codes. And no, it's not aliens either.

It's the original Coca-Cola formula.

That's right, all this security is to protect the formula for the world's favorite soda. The vault is shrouded in mystery, but it is a real place with a real recipe locked inside. But supposedly, even the two people who have access are not permitted to know the full recipe—only half.

This way, if Pepsi were to kidnap one of these people and torture them for the formula, it would be futile. Even if the victim sang like a canary, Pepsi would only have *half* of the information needed to re-create the Coca-Cola flavor.

Okay, so the part about Pepsi kidnapping competitors for information is a bit unrealistic (I hope). But the point remains that Coca-Cola is willing to take extreme measures to protect its trade secrets. The formula is valuable because it's unique. There are many copies, but nothing in the world tastes quite like an authentic Coke. The company dominates the market with this secret formula specifically because it's not known to the public.

If an employee were to reveal even *part* of the formula to a competitor, you'd better believe they'd be sued into oblivion before you could say "Have a Coke and a smile."

When you work for a company, you may become aware of certain trade secrets like this. The company can make you sign documents promising not to reveal this information, and they can sue you if you violate that agreement. In addition to state and local laws, much of this comes from the federal Defend Trade Secrets Act of 2016. In a nutshell, your employer can prohibit you from disclosing systems, recipes, formulas, charts, graphics, data, strategic plans, customer lists, techniques, technology, designs, schematics, or really anything else that could be considered a trade secret.

Typically, something is a trade secret when:

1. It is proprietary, meaning the company developed it themselves or purchased some kind of exclusive license to use it.
2. It is valuable for competing in the market.
3. It is valuable because it is not known to the public.
4. The company has taken reasonable steps to protect the trade secret. A vault isn't necessary; the bar for reasonable steps is pretty low.

If a piece of confidential information meets these criteria, it is usually a protected trade secret, and you can get into serious legal trouble if you disclose it. As with NDAs, however, there are reasonable limits here, and it is safe to ask a lawyer for help understanding your options if you are not sure what to do about a trade secret problem.

What does a trade secret problem look like, you ask? Here's a really petty, messed-up thing a company did to one of my clients. My client, Lucy, was an office manager. Her boss, an ogre who constantly overloaded her with work, demanded she write a huge financial report and have it ready the next day. There was no way Lucy could finish during office hours. So she emailed a few spreadsheets to her and her husband's shared email account to continue working on them at home.

She worked all night and got the report in on time. But the ogre was not pleased.

"Who the fuck is Ricky?" he growled.

"What?" Lucy said, startled.

"Don't play dumb, I know what you did."

She was shocked. "I . . ."

"Oh come on!" the ogre snapped. "You emailed our financials to some asshole named Ricky last night. I can see your emails, don't deny it! Who the hell is he?"

"You mean my *husband*?" Lucy said, exasperated that her boss still didn't know her husband's name. "I sent those spreadsheets to our email address so I could finish working on our laptop at home."

"Oh, so you admit it!" the ogre hissed. "I don't know what game you're playing. You violated our trade secret contract; I could sue you *and* your husband for this. Now why the fuck did you send our financials to him?"

Okay, this is what we call an *overreaction*. But I am telling you, as outrageous as this guy was, he's not even the worst out there. I have seen companies try going after employees for violating trade secret agreements—even for totally innocent things like what Lucy did in this story.

My goal isn't to make you feel paranoid—most managers aren't this intense. But it's a heads-up to be smart about how you handle company information. Whenever you are in doubt, be sure to ask your boss or HR for clarification (and get their answer in writing so they can't change up the rules on you down the road).

By the way, this may surprise you, but the boss didn't actually fire Lucy after the email incident. What probably won't surprise you, however, is that he did wrongfully fire her eventually (shocker, right?). The ogre fired Lucy for requesting FMLA leave, but he later tried to say the *real* reason was because Lucy allegedly stole trade secrets when she emailed her shared address. Fortunately, we had enough evidence to beat back those baseless accusations, but I think you see the problem. Right or wrong, companies aren't shy about going after alleged trade secret violations, so be mindful of what you do!

WHAT ARE SHOP RIGHTS?

Okay, so company trade secrets are serious, and legally protecting them is enforceable in all fifty states.

But what about *your ideas*?

You are a brilliant, creative employee, and you just got a great idea. So great it could be the next big thing. So you take some time outside your normal work to build it. You work hard, sometimes on your lunch break, sometimes using your company laptop. You don't think much of it, but when you try to sell your new idea, something terrible happens.

You get a letter from a law firm. Your employer is suing you. They say *they* own the new idea, and you have to give them all your profits.

Outrageous, right?

This is a real thing that can happen, and it's because of a legal principle called the shop rights doctrine. Basically, if you are an employee and you use any company equipment (such as tools, software, or facilities) or even company time to develop a new idea, then they have an ownership interest in that idea—possibly all of it. You used their property as a "workshop" to build the new thing, so legally, they have a claim for any money, profits, or other valuable assets that come from that thing.

In other words, they own the stuff you made because you used some of *their* stuff to make it.

This is a trap I see a lot of employees fall into. If you are building something new, NEVER use company time or company equipment.

Case Study: *Hooli v. Pied Piper*

One of my all-time favorite shows is HBO's hit comedy *Silicon Valley*. It was coproduced by Mike Judge, who also created one of my all-time favorite movies, *Office Space*.

Silicon Valley follows a group of young programmers trying to survive the cutthroat tech start-up scene in Northern California. In one of the most dramatic episodes, the main character, Richard Hendricks, got dragged into a brutal legal battle with his former employer, Hooli.

Richard was the founder of Pied Piper, a new software company focused on data compression—and burning cash like it was an Olympic sport. Despite the company's financial issues, Pied Piper's algorithm actually worked. And Hooli wanted it.

When they discovered that Richard had developed the algorithm using a company-issued laptop, Hooli took him to binding arbitration. He had signed an arbitration agreement as part of his employment contract—a detail that would become very important later.

Under the shop rights doctrine, Hooli claimed it owned Richard's invention. According to their lawyers, that meant they also owned Pied Piper.

Then things got weird. Hooli's lawyers found emails where Richard referred to the laptop as his "girlfriend." Turns out, Richard was single—and had been for a while. Hooli used more of these awkward emails to prove Richard had a deep (and weirdly intimate) attachment to the company-issued laptop. That mattered, because every time Richard referred to spending time with his "girlfriend," he really meant he was using the Hooli laptop to work on his new company. Often on company time.

This was extremely bad for Richard's case.

In their closing argument Hooli said that because Richard used

Hooli's equipment to build Pied Piper, that meant they owned the company and Richard's intellectual property.

But in a wild twist, the arbitrator threw out the case. Why? Because Hooli's employment paperwork was riddled with illegal provisions. According to the arbitrator, that meant the whole contract was unenforceable. And just like that, Hooli lost all rights to Richard's ideas.

Richard, and Pied Piper, were saved.

Now, this *is* TV. In real life, Hooli probably would've included something called a severability clause in the contract. That would've protected their rights to the invention, even if some parts of the agreement were invalid. But the takeaway is still the same: Don't count on a dramatic win in court (or arbitration). Protect your ideas by never working on them during company time or using company equipment.

Because you deserve to own everything you make.

[Summary]

- Arbitration is an alternative to a trial. It is a private forum where a neutral arbitrator will hear both sides and make a ruling.
- Arbitration is legally binding as if the decision came from a court. Unfortunately, arbitration tends to favor the employer. You can still win, but if possible, it's best to avoid signing an arbitration agreement at work.
- Noncompete agreements (NCAs) restrict your ability to start a business or work for another company that competes with your employer.
- Noncompetes are generally legal, so long as they have reasonable limits. A handful of states have outlawed or restricted noncompetes in employment.

- Nondisclosure agreements (NDAs) are contracts that limit your ability to discuss certain things, like sensitive company information.
- NDAs can feel scary, but they have limits. NDAs cannot prohibit you from reporting illegal activity, nor can they stop you from testifying about something that happened at work.
- Trade secrets are confidential information your employer uses to compete in the marketplace. Trade secrets are protected from disclosure when they are not generally known to the public, and they are valuable *because* they aren't known to the public, and the company takes reasonable steps to protect them (e.g., the Coca-Cola formula; KFC's eleven herbs and spices).
- The shop rights doctrine is an American legal principle where if you use company time or company equipment to make something, your employer has a legal claim to the rights, profits, and assets of what you made. Fortunately, this is easily prevented by never working on your idea, business, or invention on company time or using company resources.

CHAPTER 19

Don't Get Burned While Getting Fired

IN CASE OF EMERGENCY, OPEN TO THIS PAGE

This is your emergency chapter. It's your parachute if things go sideways at work. But like all emergency plans, it's good to get familiar with it *before* you need it. This chapter can be a helpful reference if you lose your job, but I *strongly* recommend reading it even if you are *not* currently worried about being fired. Having this information now, before you need it, will save you stress, legal problems, and money.

There's no way around it. Getting fired sucks. It sucks even worse when it is unfair, unexpected, or illegal.

"But Ryan," I hear you say, "I've worked hard. I've never had a bad performance review. What do I have to worry about termination for? Isn't that just for low performers?"

It's a fair question! But the answer is no, termination is not just for low performers. Mind you, I am a *wrongful* termination lawyer, not a *you-totally-had-it-coming* termination lawyer.

MYTH: Only bad workers get fired.

FACT: Good employees get unfairly fired every day.

This is not meant to scare you. It is meant to prepare you. You should always have a game plan for what to do if you lose your job. That's what this chapter is for.

THE BIG TUNA

Marlon was a senior software engineer at a large tech company. He had worked there for almost eight years. In that time, he earned a reputation for being a tough but fair leader.

Marlon was a good guy. I liked him. But truthfully, I could see why some people would have an issue with him. For lack of a better word, Marlon was a bit uptight. Don't get me wrong—he was kind, polite, and friendly. But the man had standards. And he expected everyone on his team to meet those standards.

Naturally, being a manager with high standards meant Marlon got teased a bit. Some subordinates called him Big Tuna around the office. Because *Marlon* sounded like *marlin,* people referenced an episode of *The Office* in which a character got that nickname after eating a tuna sandwich at work one day.

And just like that, Marlon became Big Tuna.*

The whole thing was childish but ultimately harmless. People could call him Big Tuna all they wanted. At the end of the day, Marlon delivered the best results, with the fastest production times and the fewest bugs.

And despite the teasing, people respected Marlon. Because there's one more thing about Big Tuna you have to know...

No one messed with his team.

Marlon wasn't tough just for the fun of it. He really cared. And he was known as a fierce advocate for his subordinates. If you came for some-

---

*I'm sure Marlon would have preferred a cool nickname like Ace or Maverick, but we don't get to choose our nicknames, they choose us. As someone who bore a passing resemblance to Napoleon Dynamite in high school, I learned this the hard way.

one on his team—accused them of a mistake, talked down to them, interfered with their work—then you better believe Big Tuna would be all over you like ants on a fish head.

Anyway, the company had a big annual retreat at a resort in Hawai'i, and all the leadership, including a few star performers, were invited to participate. As a reward for good performance, many employees were allowed to bring a plus-one. Most mornings involved workshops, meetings, and presentations. But in the afternoons and evenings, everyone, including the plus-ones, went out to enjoy the islands.

One night, there was a lū'au. It was a private event just for the company and its guests. The lū'au had fire dancers, hula, and a pig roast. The tropical cocktails flowed. Everyone was having a great time. But as the night dragged on and the alcohol flowed, some people's true colors came out. And let me tell you, they were not pretty.

Marlon was at a table with Charlie, a senior executive; several higher-ranking executives; and one of his top performers, Saba. And Charlie was sloppy drunk.

"Look, I don't care who anyone wants to sleep with," Charlie declared. "I'm chill man, bang a dolphin if that makes you happy, just don't shove it in my face, you know?"

A few people laughed, but some fell awkwardly silent. Marlon fumed. Charlie didn't know it, but Saba was a gay man. And his husband was sitting at that table with him.

"It's not about not liking gay people or anything," Charlie went on, his mai tai sloshing around in his hand. "It's like, *Star Wars*, okay? *Star Wars* doesn't need to have space lesbians or whatever."

A few more chuckles around the table. Saba and his husband looked down at their food. Marlon clenched his fists.

"I think we should change the topic," he said, a bit more sternly than he probably intended.

"Easy, Big Tuna!" Charlie hollered. This drew a few scattered chuckles, but Marlon wasn't deterred.

"Don't Big Tuna me, Charlie," Marlon said. "It's a work event, and this is inappropriate."

Embarrassed, Charlie doubled down. "What are you, a gay fish!? HAHAHA."*

Marlon left the party. Saba and his husband followed shortly after. They thanked Marlon for speaking up.

"Charlie is an ass," Marlon said. "HR is gonna hear about this, believe me."

Marlon reported Charlie to HR as soon as he got back home from the trip. At first, nothing happened. But then Marlon got a call from HR: "We need to speak with you in our office, privately."

Marlon went to HR, where he was confronted by Charlie, the HR rep, and Marlon and Charlie's supervisor, Antonio, who outranked pretty much everyone in the building.

Needless to say, having Antonio at the meeting was concerning.

"I understand things got confrontational at the retreat," Antonio began. "Care to explain?"

Marlon tried to recount the "gay fish" incident. But Charlie immediately jumped on him. "You can't be openly insubordinate in front of the team, that kind of thing is completely uncalled for," Charlie said.

"You were saying some extremely offensive things," Marlon replied.

"You are so uptight, even the smallest thing offends you," Charlie complained.

"You went off about how much gay people bother you."

"That's not what I said—"

Antonio interrupted. "Stop it. Both of you cut it out right now."

Marlon and Charlie fell silent.

Antonio continued, "I don't care who said what or who started it. When you bicker like that, it makes everyone look bad. It makes *me* look bad."

"Antonio . . ." Charlie began.

"Save it, Charlie," Antonio said. "You're cut off. No more alcohol at company events. You're on thin ice, understood?"

Charlie nodded humbly.

---

*If you watch *South Park*, you may recognize this reference. As with all jokes, context matters, and this was not the time or place for it.

Then Antonio looked at Marlon. "Charlie is your superior. You don't have to like what he says, but don't even think about making a scene like that again. I'm more upset with you than anyone else."

Marlon almost said something but swallowed his pride instead. "Understood," he said.

By now you've read enough of this book to know what's coming next. Long story short, Charlie went on a retaliation campaign, docking Marlon for any infraction he could find. When Antonio saw Marlon's name on the low performer list, he'd had enough.

Less than two months after that fateful lūʻau, Marlon was fired for cause.

The cause? Insubordination, lack of professionalism, and documented low performance (evidenced by Charlie's bogus write-ups).

The company offered Marlon one month of severance in exchange for signing a waiver. Fortunately, he refused to sign it. Instead, Marlon came to my office for help.

"It's a slap in the face," he said. "After everything I've done, they sided with a total ass like Charlie over me."

I agreed it was unfair. Technically, Marlon had a claim for retaliation. He had confronted Charlie for his inappropriate conduct and reported him to HR, but there was a problem.

It was Marlon's word against Charlie, Antonio, HR, and anyone who wanted to stay on the company's good side. Unfortunately, Marlon never documented the incident. His complaint to HR was done over the phone. He had no paper trial, no evidence, and very few people he could count on as witnesses.

On the other hand, the company had covered its tracks pretty well. They documented performance issues, which we all knew were BS, but Marlon never rebutted them.

"I was in hot water already," Marlon explained, "so I didn't want to rock the boat anymore."

"I don't blame you," I said. "But to be honest, we have a problem here. You have a valid claim, but not much to prove it with. If any of this was documented, even just the initial complaint, we'd have more ammo."

"So what do we do?" Marlon asked.

"I think we can negotiate for a better severance. But to be very frank, I don't see how you win a lawsuit without any proof. Let me work on them a bit. I think we can get better than just one month of severance. You deserve more than that."

We shook hands, and I got to work. After I wrote a letter to the company, they sent their lawyers to negotiate with me. It took a few weeks, and the company really enjoyed throwing all the uncontested write-ups in my face. But at the end of the day, the effort paid off. We got the severance up to eight months. Since Marlon was a high earner, this came out to six figures. He was happy, I was happy, and he had enough cash to unwind a bit before jumping back into the workforce.

Oh, and no one calls him Big Tuna anymore.

Standing up for a coworker was absolutely the right thing to do in Marlon's situation. But where he messed up was by not documenting anything along the way. As Denzel Washington said in the movie *Training Day*, "It's not what you know, it's what you can prove."

Fortunately, the situation was not a total loss. Marlon was smart not to sign his severance agreement right away. He was wise to interview several attorneys, and I am honored that he chose me to handle the negotiation.

This chapter will be a lifesaver if you are suddenly, unfairly, or illegally fired. It will also help even if your termination was perfectly legal. In this chapter, we will learn to avoid some of the mistakes that make a termination worse than it has to be. As for severance, it is never guaranteed, but we will discuss ways to make sure you get the most money possible.

WHAT IS WRONGFUL TERMINATION?

We learned a lot about termination and wrongful termination in part I, but since this is your emergency chapter, let's recap. Termination is just another way of saying you got fired. In every state except Montana, the default rule is you are employed *at will*, which means you can be terminated at any time, for any legal reason (this technically includes "no reason"), with or without warning. Of course, this default rule is subject to *many* exceptions, some of which we covered in detail earlier in this book. If your termination violates one of those exceptions, then it is an unlawful, or wrongful, termination.

Wrongful termination is illegal in all fifty states.

REALITY CHECK: Although this book deals with many kinds of wrongful terminations, the fact is that most terminations are legal. As a general rule, employers are free to fire you for most reasons, and that includes stupid, petty, or unfair reasons (so long as they don't break the law).

But whether your termination is wrongful, lawful, or in the gray area in between, it is smart to understand the different kinds of *ways* you could be terminated. To avoid a serious professional and financial crisis, you also need to know your options if it happens to you.

For Whom the Bell Tolls

It's useful to know the early warning signs that you are about to be terminated.

Termination sometimes happens in the heat of the moment. Your boss is so pissed off that they fire you in a rage on the spot. (This may or may not be illegal. It really depends on why they fired you and why they were so upset.) But this kind of termination is rare.

More often, it will follow a predictable pattern, preceded by a few red flags:

- Your boss suddenly stops communicating with you as frequently, or at all.
- You are getting fewer new responsibilities or not being assigned to new projects.
- Existing job duties are being taken away or reassigned to someone else.
- You have been written up or placed on a performance improvement plan (PIP).

- Business seems to be slowing down or management is suddenly very concerned about costs.
- Coworkers start acting weird around you. For example, their tone when they speak to you sounds like they just found out your dog died: "How are ya holding up, pal?"
- You hear rumors that you might get fired or that layoffs are coming.*

Don't be paranoid, but don't be complacent either. If you can catch the signs that you might be terminated soon, or that layoffs are happening at your company, it's easier to keep a cool head because you are prepared.

LAYOFFS AND REDUCTIONS IN FORCE

A legitimate layoff is not done because the employee did anything wrong but due to business reasons like budget cuts, restructuring, or downsizing. A reduction in force (or RIF) is a more specific term for a layoff. It refers to when an employer is reducing its head count for business reasons.

The reasons for layoffs and RIFs vary. But effectively, these are all involuntary terminations of your employment, so your response plan, which we'll go over shortly, will be roughly the same.

"But Ryan!" I hear some say. "Aren't companies allowed to let go of people they don't need? How can layoffs ever be illegal?"

It's a fair question! Business is tough and it requires tough decisions sometimes. It's not that layoffs are illegal per se; rather, it is *how* the layoff occurs that sometimes breaks the law.

---

*This is controversial advice, but I think hiding from office gossip is a bad idea. Here is my strategy: *Subscribe, but don't post*. In other words, listen to the gossip for clues about what's really happening at work, but don't engage in gossip yourself. This gives you valuable information without embroiling you in stupid drama.

WARN Act

The Worker Adjustment Retraining and Notification Act, or WARN Act, requires employers to give their employees fair warning before a mass layoff. If they don't, then the employer will owe a penalty.

Signed into law in 1988, the WARN Act got its first real trial by fire in the wake of the dot-com bubble burst. For my younger readers, this was a major economic downturn in the United States in the late 1990s and early 2000s. Internet companies were the new, exciting innovation, and everyone wanted to get rich fast by buying stock in them. Investors dumped billions into almost any company with *.com* in the name.

But then the bubble burst. It turned out many of these dot-com companies were grossly overvalued. Some were nothing more than an internet domain address with no product to sell at all.

Investors panicked.

The market meltdown triggered a recession that spread far beyond the tech sector. In the year 2001 alone, there were over 21,000 layoff events, causing 2.5 million workers to lose their jobs. The US Government Accountability Office (GAO) estimated that about 2,000 of those mass layoffs, affecting approximately 660,000 workers, were subject to WARN notice requirements.*

You don't have to be an economist to know that 2.5 million people suddenly losing their paychecks is bad news for the economy. Which is why we have the WARN Act—to soften the blow when this happens.

The law requires most US employers with one hundred or more employees to provide at least sixty days' advance notice before implementing mass layoffs. Employers who do not give such notice must pay a penalty. This often includes severance payable to employees for the amount equal to the lack of notice, up to sixty days.

---

*U.S. Government Printing Office, The Worker Adjustment and Retraining Notification Act: Revising the Act and Educational Materials Could Clarify Employer Responsibilities and Employee Rights, GAO-03-1003 (2003).

For example, if you are part of a mass layoff with only twenty days' notice, then you would be owed forty days of severance for the lack of notice: *60 days required notice – 20 days actual notice = 40-day severance for lack of notice.*

There are exceptions, of course, and a discussion of the WARN Act could fill a whole book on its own. But let's break down the most basic components.

What Is a Mass Layoff?

There are several ways a large-scale reduction in force can qualify as a mass layoff under the WARN Act. A company with at least one hundred employees is obligated to follow WARN when:

- Laying off fifty or more employees at a single site, representing at least 33 percent of the workforce, or
- Laying off five hundred or more employees regardless of the percentage of the total workforce affected, or
- Shutting down a location with at least fifty employees, or moving that location more than fifty miles from its original location

There are other triggering events, and there are exceptions and caveats to the events listed here, but these give you a general idea of when WARN notices might be triggered.

WHAT TO DO (AND NOT DO) IN A TERMINATION MEETING

Whether you are laid off, fired, or part of an RIF, you want to have a plan for how to handle being let go. Unless you are fired suddenly, you will probably get an email or a calendar invite to a meeting. It will rarely have a meeting topic or agenda. That's because they don't want you to freak out. Unfortunately, the result is that the whole meeting might feel like an ambush.

It's okay to feel upset, but do not show it! Try your best to remain calm.

What *Not* to Do

DON'T PLEAD YOUR CASE. The decision to fire you has already been made—perhaps by someone in the meeting, or perhaps by someone above their pay grade. Either way, no amount of begging, pleading, or arguing will stop the termination. Attempting to argue your case by saying how unfair this is or promising to do better if they let you stay will only make things worse.

DON'T GET DEFENSIVE OR ANGRY. It's okay to feel angry, but do not express it. You may say something you later regret, or you could even make a careless remark that destroys your shot at a severance payment or possible wrongful termination claim. This is not the time to demand answers or attack anyone.

Instead, you should listen. Ask why you are being fired. Write down their answer for future reference. The explanation they give may or may not be true, but knowing their side of the story will be helpful later.

DON'T THREATEN TO SUE. Nothing is less scary to a seasoned HR rep than a "hysterical" employee threatening to sue them. You have to understand that threats like this are common, and they tend to make you look weak. At worst, threatening to sue gives them a chance to hide evidence or build a case against you. So don't make threats, even if you plan on suing.

DON'T MAKE A SOCIAL MEDIA POST ABOUT BEING FIRED. We've all seen those TikTok videos where the creator is crying in their car about how they got fired. Sometimes these posts get a lot of views, but anything you say could become a problem when trying to negotiate severance (or during a lawsuit). It's not worth the attention. Keep quiet about the situation until you consult a lawyer.

DO NOT SIGN ANYTHING.

DO NOT SIGN ANYTHING.

DO NOT SIGN ANYTHING.

This is not a typo. I said it three times because it's important. In the heat of the moment, your boss might suddenly turn into a time-share salesman, shoving papers in your face and demanding you sign before you leave. This is a trap. And it's a sign of weakness on their part. Why are they so desperate for your signature? Is there something else going on?

Probably. Which is why you need to take those documents to a lawyer so you understand what you are signing and what the consequences of signing will be. They want you to sign because they are scared. Don't do it for free. At a minimum, do not sign anything in the heat of the moment. You are already fired; what are they gonna do, fire you again?

Tell them, "I need to review these documents before I sign." If they get angry, just say, "I'm not signing anything until I can read it carefully."

If they ask if you plan to sue, just say, "I haven't made any decisions yet," and leave it at that.

Now *that* is a good way to scare them!

What If You're a Union Worker?

One of the biggest benefits of joining a union is job security. You can still be fired, but as a union member, you get certain due process rights that regular at-will employees do not.

That includes getting a fair hearing, with your union representative present, before any decision to terminate or discipline you is made.

Thanks to something called Weingarten rights, you can invoke these protections to ensure you get the due process you are entitled to.*

But some employers will try to skirt these rules, so you need to know the "cheat code" that prevents them from illegally firing you. When you are called into a meeting that may result in you being fired, say this:

Weingarten Script

If this meeting could result in me being disciplined or terminated, or impact my working conditions, I respectfully request that my union representative be present at this time. Until my representation arrives, I will not participate in this discussion.

Once this script is invoked, the meeting must be suspended until your union representative is available to assist you. If they terminate you anyway, then you can usually get the termination nullified (except for things like gross misconduct).

BUT WATCH OUT: Legally, the protection is not triggered until you say the script, and your employer is not obligated to inform you of these rights. So if you are in a meeting and it feels off, just say the script.

What If They Say It's a "Voluntary Resignation"?

Holy gaslighting, Batman.

Oftentimes, employers will use the threat of termination to force you to do something you don't want to do. For example, they may deny your reasonable accommodation, then say if you don't return to work without the accommodation, they will consider this a "voluntary resignation."

*Recently there has been public confusion about what due process is. It is not acquittal, amnesty, or a get-out-of-jail-free card as some pundits have falsely claimed. Due process simply means you have a fair opportunity to present your case before any decision affecting your life, freedom, or property is made. Due process protects the innocent and holds the guilty accountable. In the employment world, many union members get due process rights to protect them from unjust termination.

What a load of crap.

Just *saying* you voluntarily resigned, when really it was a termination, doesn't make it so. You'll need to fight back by establishing a paper trail. It should show that you have no intentions of resigning and you want to keep working on a solution that keeps you employed. Send a text, email, or letter with the following information. Remember, *get it in writing*!

1. State your intent to remain.
2. Summarize the dispute.
3. Explain that you want to keep working on a solution.
4. Reiterate that you are not voluntarily resigning.
5. Provide an action plan.

Here is a sample of this game plan in action. You can rework it for most circumstances.

Sample Email Template: Countering a "Voluntary Resignation" Threat

Dear Manager / Human Resources,

I am writing to express my intent to continue working. In your latest communication, you indicated that if I do not return to work without my requested accommodation, then you will consider that my voluntary resignation.

As you are aware, I am trying to engage in the interactive process to find an accommodation that is reasonable and not an undue hardship.

I have no intention of voluntarily resigning. I want to keep working.

Please consider this my effort to continue the interactive process. I would like to discuss alternate accommodations or understand why my requested accommodation is being rejected.

Respectfully,
Employee

HOW SHOULD YOU ACT AFTER GETTING FIRED?

So it happened. You got fired. You may feel embarrassed or scared. Just don't show it yet. Put on a brave face and march out of there with your chin up. Quiet defiance is badass. When you get home you can cry all you want. But in front of everyone else, keep it together. Staying composed when you leave will make a huge legal, personal, and financial difference.

And on the bright side, your schedule just cleared up. Use that time to plan your next steps. Apply for unemployment, apply for another job, take an offer quickly so you have money coming in, then keep applying to other jobs that pay better.

Getting fired is not the end. Much the opposite, it's a new beginning. A new chapter. A fresh page in the story of your life. And when you realize that *you* are the author of that story, then turning a new page feels less scary.

What If They Withhold Your Last Check?

This happens a lot, but it's not legal.

Even if you are fired for cause, you are still entitled to your full final paycheck. Even if you are fired for gross misconduct, you still get your last paycheck.

The money needs to be paid when your state or local laws require, or within a reasonable amount of time, whichever is soonest. For example, in California, a fired employee is entitled to their full final paycheck on the same day they are dismissed. In other states, a reasonable time frame is typically the next regularly scheduled pay period.

No matter where you are, if you don't get your final check by the next scheduled payday, then something is wrong. Don't wait. You *must* take action to protect your money.

If they do not issue your final paycheck within a reasonable amount of time, you need to file a complaint with the US Department of Labor or your state equivalent. But before you do any of that, talk to a workers' rights lawyer about your options. If a company is stupid and petty enough to try withholding your final paycheck, then I bet there have been other violations as well. Get a professional opinion so you know what you might be entitled to recover.

WHAT IS SEVERANCE?

Severance is money paid to you after you lose your job. In most situations, it is not legally required. However, it is usually offered when you are let go due to a layoff or when the employer is concerned about getting sued.

And that leads to an important point about severance. It is not a gift. The employer will probably require that you sign a waiver of your rights to sue them before they pay you.

This is nothing devious, and I wouldn't call it hush money. It is a valid contract where you promise not to sue, and in return, they pay you compensation for waiving that right.

Severance Is Negotiable

Severance is almost always negotiable. You can do this on your own, or you can retain a lawyer to assist with the negotiations (I do this for clients all the time). The first step in negotiating is knowing what the end goal is—a fair severance.

But what makes severance fair or unfair?

How Do You Know If the Severance Amount Is Fair?

For starters, do a quick gut check. Does the amount feel especially low, even insulting? What about the circumstances surrounding your termination—did something feel suspicious? For example, were you fired suddenly, without warning, and then did everyone get *really weird* when you asked for an explanation? That's a sign something else is going on, and it could lead to a higher severance offer if you know what to look for.

While there is generally no requirement that companies pay severance, in the United States, it's customary to pay two to four weeks of your regular salary for every year of service. However, if you have a potential claim against the company, or if you have special circumstances, then the amount should be higher.

FACTORS THAT LEAD TO HIGHER SEVERANCE OFFERS

- You have a potential claim against the company for discrimination, retaliation, harassment, unpaid wages, or other violations.
- You were recently on protected leave, workers' compensation, or a disability accommodation.
- You recently complained of harassment, unsafe conditions, or other violations of the law.
- You have a contract that guaranteed your employment for a specified term, or it guaranteed some sort of severance.
- You did not engage in any misconduct.
- You did not have excessive poor performance issues. This includes tardiness or unexplained absences.

In my opinion, the best way to maximize your severance payment is to get an experienced workers' rights lawyer to help. In my practice, I typically get paid a percentage of whatever additional money I can get for you. When retained, my job is to help you get the most money possible, but I also make sure the waiver you sign is fair and that other important rights are protected.

Which leads to my next point. Do not get so focused on the dollar amount that you lose sight of other important benefits.

COBRA

This is a rule with a long, word-salady name that doesn't explain what it does. (Say "Consolidated Omnibus Budget Reconciliation Act" three times fast.) So, let's just do everyone a favor and keep calling it COBRA. Just remember: COBRA means you get continued coverage under your employer's health plan after your employment ends.

Continued medical coverage after losing your job can literally save your life. In addition to protecting your health, continued COBRA coverage can be worth *thousands*. It's worth even more if you have a condition that needs treatment.

Under COBRA, the employer can legally have you pay up to 100 percent of the premiums to stay on your health care plan, plus up to a 2 percent administrative fee.

If you are fired, your company is required to disclose your COBRA coverage options. But even if they don't, you should ask about COBRA. In a severance negotiation, I always try to get the employer to pay as much of the monthly premium costs as possible, and keep that coverage going for as many months as possible.*

Weighing the health benefits against the premium payment costs, you should think very carefully about your individual needs when getting continued coverage under COBRA.

WHAT IS UNEMPLOYMENT?

First, let's be clear about what unemployment (a.k.a. unemployment benefits or unemployment insurance) is and is not. Unemployment is not welfare. It is not a handout. Rather, it is a temporary lifeline to help you pay bills when you lose your job. Unemployment is basically an insurance plan that you pay into throughout your employment. When you make a claim for unemployment, there will be a set amount you

*How much COBRA coverage you can get depends largely on your circumstances. Some situations can entitle you to extended coverage; others will shorten your coverage. This can get complicated, so your best move is to talk to an experienced lawyer about your options. As a broad target, six to twelve months of coverage is considered normal, eighteen months is the higher end, and twenty-nine to thirty-six months is generally available when you have special circumstances. Again, this stuff can get tricky, so I highly recommend getting a professional opinion about what you may be entitled to.

qualify for, which you will receive in weekly or biweekly installments until it is all paid out.

THE CATCH: To qualify, you must have lost your job ***through no fault of your own***. Be aware that "poor performance" *by itself* will not disqualify you in most situations. Constructive wrongful termination, which is when you quit due to intolerable conditions, may qualify. But constructive wrongful termination is a very high bar to meet. I would not count on it unless you consult a lawyer first.

What If Your Employer Fights Your Unemployment?

This is a petty move, but it happens. Employers pay regular premiums into the state unemployment fund. Those premiums get more expensive as more people make claims for unemployment. This motivates some employers to fight your unemployment claim, even if you qualify.

When you make a claim for unemployment, the employer will get a notice. On that notice, they will have the option to confirm or deny that you worked for them and that you were let go through no fault of your own.

Big surprise, sometimes employers lie. This is usually because they want to save money or because they are being a bunch of Petty Bettys. Either way, the next step is usually a hearing. This is typically done over the phone, and both parties will present their side. From there, the unemployment office will make a decision.

If you need help with an unemployment appeal, it is sometimes worth asking a workers' rights lawyer about your options. Appeals are not scary—just tell the truth.

Document Your Unemployment Activities

In most states, you will need to certify every week that you are looking for work or performing some other qualifying action. For example, some states count going back to school or attempting to start a business as a qualifying action. But the main thing is that you need to document all of this. The unemployment office will verify that you are actually trying to find new work. If for some reason you do not do this, or if you can't prove you did it, then there are financial consequences. Typically, the unemployment office will issue a notice that you have to pay back those benefits, often plus interest or even a penalty.

So be smart!

When you lose your job, it's smart to apply for unemployment right away. Be sure to document your job search and other qualifying activities while collecting those benefits.

TO SUE, OR NOT TO SUE?

I did not write this book just to tell people to sue their employers all the time. Much the opposite. It is my hope that after reading this book, and keeping it as a reference guide, you will avoid many of the bad situations that lead to lawsuits.

Used well, this book is a tool to *prevent* a lawsuit. Used very well, it also prepares you to fight for your rights if a lawsuit becomes necessary.

How Do You Know If You Should Sue?

The best way is to consult a lawyer. Most workers' rights lawyers will provide a quick case evaluation for free. But if you want detailed advice, expect to pay a fee for their time. And be sure to shop around! Your case is too important to give to the first lawyer you talk to. Talk to a few lawyers, see who you feel most comfortable with, and make an informed decision.

How Do You Know If It's Time to Talk to a Lawyer?

It's sometimes hard to tell if your termination was legal or not. As we have seen many times in this book, employers will sometimes try to conceal the reason they fired you. We call this pretext. They might *say* it's a layoff, even if it's not. They may *claim* it's poor work performance, or that it's "just not working out." Or they may use my favorite line: "It's at-will employment, so I don't need a reason."

True, they technically don't need a reason. But once the lawsuit is filed, they better find a reason that makes sense, and which they can prove fast, or else they're gonna have a bad time.

If you are not sure whether your termination was legal or not, it helps to ask yourself a few questions. None of these are proof positive of a wrongful termination, but a yes to any of these is a sign that you should at least consult a lawyer about your options.

- Did you see something that you thought was illegal, like unsafe conditions, lying to shareholders or government agencies, or intentionally evading labor rules?
- Did you recently engage in a protected activity, such as requesting FMLA or a reasonable accommodation, reporting safety issues, or reporting harassment?
- Are they withholding your pay, or have you noticed your pay was wrong?
- Did you suddenly get fired with no warning at all?
- Did you suddenly get slapped with lots of write-ups and PIPs, despite having been a good employee for years?
- Were you fired immediately after reporting an issue to a government agency, testifying in a legal proceeding, or cooperating in an investigation?
- Did you recently have a change in management, and the new management made it clear they did not like you?
- Did you recently have a change to your protected class, such as turning forty, becoming pregnant, taking leave for military service or medical needs, or becoming disabled?
- Does the termination feel unfair? Do you have a nagging gut feeling that something is wrong?

None of these are a guarantee that your termination was unlawful, but they provide important clues. And here is the ultimate tell—the reddest of red flags:

- **When you asked why you were fired, did they dodge the question, or did the answer not make sense?**

A company that is following the law doesn't need to hide their reason. If they have a reason, it should make sense.

As Judge Judy has said many times, "If it doesn't make sense, it's usually not true."

EMBRACE YOUR POWER

Getting fired can make you feel small, powerless, and embarrassed. Legal issues aside, part of handling an unfair termination is leaving with your dignity intact.

It's not easy, but it's not complicated either. Preserving your dignity (and more important, your personal self-esteem) just requires a little mindset adjustment.

Feeling embarrassed is optional. No one can make you feel shame without your consent. Good employees get fired. Smart people get fired. The best, brightest, most wonderful people in the world get fired. That's why wrongful termination lawyers like me exist.

Getting fired is not a reflection of your worth as a person. And it doesn't have to be the end of your career, though it may feel like it is in the moment.

Remember, we all walk with fear. It is a human emotion that follows us wherever we go.

Brave people walk with fear too.

But they never ask it for directions.

Summary

- At-will employment means you can be fired for any legal reason. However, there are many exceptions to this default presumption. If your termination violates one of those exceptions it is illegal or *wrongful* termination.
- Most terminations are lawful, even if they are unfair.
- Layoffs are when companies terminate one or more employees due to a reduction in force, a budget cut, restructuring, or another business reason.
- Layoffs and reductions in force are generally legal. A mass layoff must comply with the sixty-day notice requirements in the WARN Act; otherwise the laid-off employees are owed a penalty.
- Do not panic if you are being fired. Stay calm, take notes if needed, and don't sign anything in the heat of the moment. Take the time to talk to a lawyer if you can.
- Severance is money paid to you after you are fired. You will almost always be required to sign a waiver of your rights to get the money.
- Severance is negotiable, and you will have more leverage if you have a possible claim against the company.
- COBRA coverage is when your employer keeps you enrolled in the company's group health care plan after your employment ends. It is valuable; don't ignore it.

- Unemployment is a benefit you can apply for after losing your job through no fault of your own.
- Getting fired sucks. But it's not the end. It's a new page. And when you remember you are the author of your own story, then turning the page doesn't feel so scary.

Conclusion

I wrote this book because it's the book I needed but didn't have.

We are all expected to "play the game." In the US, when you meet a child, one of the most common things to ask them is "What do you want to be when you grow up?"

Not who. What.

We are taught to value our careers from a young age. We define ourselves by the professions we choose. Then, as grown-ups, the first thing people ask us is "What do you do for work?"

I'm not saying this is a good or bad thing, though that could be an interesting debate on its own. The point is that our careers are extremely important parts of our identities.

That's in addition to being the number one way we pay for food, shelter, and medical care.

Yet despite how central our jobs are to our lives, not once does anyone sit down with us and say, "These are your rights at work. This is how to take care of yourself at work. This is how you fight back if someone comes for your livelihood."

Seems kind of important, doesn't it? Yet somehow, this book didn't already exist. But writing it means nothing if no one reads it. That's where *you* come in. By purchasing this book and learning from it, you have helped advance the cause of workers' rights.

From the bottom of my heart, thank you.

I hope you found value in this book. If so, you can follow me on Instagram @AttorneyRyan or YouTube @RyanStygar for more. You can also subscribe to my Substack @AttorneyRyan for regular updates from the world of workers' rights.

You have now finished one of the most comprehensive resources available about your rights at work. Keep this book as a reference guide in case questions arise in your career. If you liked the book, please consider recommending it to a friend.

It's been a privilege to write this for you. I hope it makes you feel empowered.

And I hope you embrace your power.

ACKNOWLEDGMENTS

First and foremost, I want to thank my wonderful life partner, Gabi, for being my number one fan, my cheerleader, my joy, and my peace. Nothing I do is possible without you. I love you.

I also owe a tremendous debt of gratitude to my team at Centurion Trial Attorneys, APC, Danielle Rini, Brook Hayes, Sirena Ortega, Kimberly Ybarra, and Trish Bentley. We fight hard, we fight together, and we *win* together. I am so very proud of you.

I am blessed to know many fantastic lawyers, and I want to extend a special thank-you to my friends Michael Alder, David Lee, Matt Margolis, Claudia Salinas, Bob Simon, Jefferson Fisher, Tommy Kherker, Vincent Xu, and Paige Sparks for being excellent examples of what it means to be an advocate for justice. I admire each of you deeply.

Thank you to Robert Waller Jr., who helped me start my firm when I was a fresh law school grad. To Judge Kenneth Medel, who taught me the ins and outs of civil litigation as a law student. To my mother, Patti Bentley, who instilled in me a love of reading and writing at an early age, which made this book possible. To my father, Andrew Stygar, for sharing his love of classical philosophy with me, which also made this book possible. A huge thank-you to Mary and Carlos Aboujaoude, who not only gave me their beautiful daughter but who have supported me through thick and thin since law school. To my brother, Drew Bentley, for helping me spread my workers' rights message far and wide.

And of course, to my friends and family, who are too many to list here, but who make my life joyful by supporting me every step of the way. I love you all.

Thank you, De'Anna J. Nunez, for helping me navigate the roughest waters life throws at me.

I also want to thank the fine people at Penguin and Portfolio for helping make this book a reality, with special gratitude to Helen Healey-Cunningham, Megan McCormack, and Adrian Zackheim. None of this would be possible without your help.

To my agents, Steve Troha and Jamie Chambliss, who put up with my crazy ass while helping shape the vision for this book. I truly could not have done this without your help.

Finally, I want to thank my clients. Trusting me to fight for your rights is the highest honor. It is a privilege to serve you.

INDEX

Page numbers followed by "fn" refer to footnotes.